# ESSAYS ON MEDIÆVAL GERMAN POETRY

Der von kürenberg.

This illustration precedes the songs of *Der von Kürenberg* as contained in the Heidelberg manuscript *Codex palatinus Germanicus* 848, commonly denoted among the Middle High German song-codices as C. The heraldic device at the top represents the quern (MHG. kürn) embodied in the name of Kürenberg.

# ESSAYS ON MEDIÆVAL GERMAN POETRY

## WITH TRANSLATIONS IN ENGLISH VERSE

M. F. RICHEY

BASIL BLACKWELL
OXFORD · 1969

© Basil Blackwell 1969
631 11710 5

First printed 1943
Second edition 1969
including additional essays

Printed in Great Britain by
Alden & Mowbray Ltd
at the Alden Press, Oxford

# CONTENTS

00144

*To My Friend*
*J. C.*

# PREFACE

This volume contains in the first place a new edition of my *Essays on the Mediaeval German Love Lyric*, published originally in 1943 by Basil Blackwell, under the editorship of Professor H. C. Fiedler. This remains virtually unchanged, except for the addition of a brief impressionistic sketch of Heinrich von Veldeke. To this series thus reproduced have been added four independent essays, each of them dealing separately with some aspect of Mediaeval German chivalric romance. They originally appeared at fairly long intervals in *London Mediaeval Studies*, *Medium Ævum*, *Modern Language Review*, and in contribution to the volume presented on his retirement to Professor L. A. Willoughby.

My very warm thanks are due to Miss Marion Gibbs for her ready and competent management of the practical details involved in this new publication. I wish also to thank the publishers and express my appreciation of their goodwill.

Finally, with memories long past, yet dear as yesterday to the generation who knew him, now much diminished, I wish most gratefully to record my enduring debt to the inspired teaching and wise, scholarly guidance of Professor Robert Priebsch, in this country the real and true founder of Mediaeval German studies. I will only say here how vividly I recall his beautiful lectures on the *Minnesang* and our own intimate talks on the genius of Wolfram von Eschenbach.

September, 1968                                             M. F. RICHEY

# ACKNOWLEDGEMENTS

For permission to reprint essays included as Appendices, thanks are due to the Editor of *Medium Aevum* for 'The German Contribution to the Matter of Britain', first printed in Vol. XIX (1950); to the Modern Language Research Association for 'The *Titurel* of Wolfram von Eschenbach: Structure and Character', first printed in *Modern Language Review* LVI no. 2 (April 1961); and to the Editors of *London Mediaeval Studies* for 'Die edeln Armen: A Study of Hartmann von Aue', first printed in Vol. I, part 2 (1936) of that journal. The essay 'Wolfram von Eschenbach and the Paradox of the Chivalrous Life' was first printed in *German Studies Presented to L. A. Willoughby*, published by Basil Blackwell (1952).

# INTRODUCTION

APART from a few isolated and fugitive traces, the history of the mediæval German love-lyric—or Minnesang—begins with a disparaging reference by Heinrich von Melk, lay brother of the monastery of Melk on the Danube (*circa* 1150). The work in which this occurs is a gloomy though bracing sermon in verse on the theme *von des todes gehugede*—in remembrance of death—the main idea of which, the vanity of this world's life and the need of stern preparation for the life to come, is fortified by a satirical and hostile view of contemporary manners. Here sexual love and knightly prowess, two evident aspects of the new life of chivalry, get their share of damnation, and are crudely presented as forms of vainglory and violence. " Wherever knights are assembled, they compete in telling how many this one and that have seduced. So far from concealing their vice, they glory in it : all their boast is of women. He who fails to win praise in this way thinks himself lowered in repute among his fellows. And again, wherever some tribute is paid to a man's worth, no one mentions the strength he needs to resist the devil, but instead, the most lawless deeds are the oftenest named. They bring dishonour upon themselves, saying : 'Such and such a one is a fine brave fellow : he has killed so many'."

This forbidding picture certainly gives one pause. Standing where it does at the threshold of the brilliant Hohenstaufen age of German chivalry, it serves as a grim foil to the high ideals expressed in the poetry of courtly love and of knightly honour. The truth we are sure, as indeed certain poets of the age bear witness, none more so than Walther von der Vogelweide, was of many colours and embraced many diverse grades between high and low. That Heinrich von Melk was not wrong in his estimate of the grosser side may be gauged from a passage in the *Büchlein* of Hartmann von Aue,[1] in which the lady's aloofness—a traditional motive—is excused on the very good ground that men are too apt to abuse their privileges. Many a woman, it runs, fears to risk her honour on the uncertain hope of her lover being true to her. Experience has shown how often a man sets himself to entrap the woman, and, once he has had his reward and his will of her, changes his tune and becomes her foe. It was a vile motive which made him strive with such zeal to win her love,

---

[1] Hartmann von Aue : *I. Büchlein* 216 ff. Editions : M. Haupt, *Die Lieder u. Büchlein u. der arme Heinrich von Hartm. von Aue*, Berlin, 1842, second revised edition by E. Martin, *Der Arme Heinrich u. die Büchlein von H. von A.* 1881 ; F. Bech, *Hartm. von Aue*, Band 2, Deutsche Classiker des Mittelalters, Leipzig, 1867, 1872 and 1893.

this he did *ûf betrogen êre*—with an eye to false honour—that he might brag of his conquest. However little the rest might think so —*swie wênic man ez vunde*—that seemed to him good fortune and glory. The saving clause *swie wênic man ez vunde* shows one difference at least between the presumptuous boaster of Heinrich von Melk and the one envisaged a generation later by Hartmann. The latter does not enjoy the same social support as the former. A sign that public opinion had changed, or that Heinrich von Melk had insisted on seeing nothing but black. Or both.

The love-song of his biased experience is alluded to by Heinrich von Melk in a characteristically grim setting. He pictures a knight lying dead and exhorts his widow to gaze steadfastly on the husband's corpse and mark how death has disfigured him. The sight of him is grown ghastly, his eyes are glazed and his tongue is mute.

> Nu sich in wie getâner haite
> diu zunge lige in sînem munde
> dâ mite er die troutliet chunde
> behaglîchen singen.

Now see in what manner his tongue lies in his mouth, wherewith he was skilled to sing love-songs for pleasure.

The word *troutliet* or *trûtliet*, detached from this grisly context, has a pleasant appeal of its own. There is no sweeter term of affection in the language of the period than the intimate *mîn trût*, used in addressing those who are near and dear. Side by side with the more wide-spread *minneliet* or *minnesanc*, the term *trûtliet* can be fittingly used, as both Vogt and Ehrismann have used it, to represent the older and simpler kind of German love-lyric in contrast to the younger, more sophisticated and courtly type of Provençal origin. The term *minnesanc* is assigned to this younger kind.

Our knowledge of both dates from the same time. The more archaic *trûtliet* with its simple measures and its natural and direct treatment of sexual love is represented for us by a small group of poets from the Danubian region, whose songs may reasonably be placed between the years 1170 and 1185. Those of Kürenberg and the oldest ascribed to Dietmar von Aist may quite possibly be earlier still. For the songs of the Burgrave von Regensburg we can at least take as terminus ad quem the year 1185 in which his title lapsed. There are otherwise no definite clues. Documentary evidence can establish the family to which each poet may be said to belong, but leaves the identity uncertain. Only in the case of the Burgrave von Regensburg and the younger Burgrave von Rietenburg the choice is narrowed to two out of three brothers, Friedrich, Heinrich and Otto, last of the male line in the family of Rietenburg and Stevening—

*tres fratres purchgravii de Rietenburch vel Ratispona.* The documents in general point to Austria as the home of Kürenberg and of Dietmar von Aist, to Suabia as that of Meinloh von Sevelingen, to Bavaria as that of the two noble brothers of Regensburg and Rietenburg. And this gives a definite geographical region which we regard as more conservative of older tradition than the lands further west. Romance influence shows itself, indeed, in the songs of von Rietenburg, in one of which there is an echo of Foulques of Marseilles; but it is in the valleys of the Rhone and Rhine, in the areas nearest Provence, that the impetus derived from the Troubadour lyric first fosters a rapid development of the new courtly Minnesang.

In this, as in the Provencal *canzone*, love is conceived as an act of elaborate homage, the lover's rôle is that of his lady's servitor or *dienstman*, the situation lays stress on her aloofness and on his pure devotion. There is also a corresponding development of musical and metrical technique, characteristic of which is the tripartite division of the strophe into *Stollen* and *Abgesang* (*pedes et cauda*), together with new and various patterns of rhyme-arrangement and length of line.

The Rhinelander Friedrich von Hausen, mentioned in documents between the years 1170 and 1190, is the first to represent the new phase completely in its typical tendencies of style and theme. To the same local group belong Bernger von Horheim and Bligger von Steinach, both, like Friedrich von Hausen, *Reichsministerialen* or retainers of the Imperial household, and Ulrich von Gutenberg, whose songs, however, are less important than his *Minneleich*, a long and complicated tour de force, the nearest affinities to which must be sought, this time, not in the Provençal lyric but in the more studied and intricate forms cultivated in Latin by the *scolares vagantes.* Further south, the Swiss poet Graf Rudolf von Fenis shows in his songs an especially close adherence to Provençal models.

Heinrich von Veldeke, whose career runs parallel to that of Friedrich von Hausen, stands apart, geographically as well as in the character of his verse. A native of the province of Limburg, he is naturally closer to French than to Provençal influence. The effect of this is seen not only in his epic work the *Eneide*, which is based on the French *Roman d'Enéas*, but also to some appreciable extent in his lyrics. There are, at the same time, marked affinities with the light-hearted, lively *amatoria* of the *vagantes.* The courtly ideal of love is crossed by a healthy enjoyment of life and by gleams of ironic humour, and the feeling for Nature is more intimate and objective than in any other Minnesinger before Walther von der Vogelweide. The key-note to his philosophy of life is *blîdscap* : joy.

The tradition of the Troubadour lyric, with its predilection for

3

melancholy moods and introspective trains of thought, is continued by the Alsatian Reinmar, who as Viennese court poet enjoyed a prestige and exercised an influence beyond that of any earlier German singer. In his subtle and exquisite art a stage is reached after which there is little left for the singer of courtly love to discover. Actually, it is the Thuringian poet Heinrich von Morungen who by his inspired lyricism raises the courtly love-song to its highest power ; but Reinmar's mannered artistry gave more scope to the imitator, and while echoes of Morungen are frequent, the finer essences of his art are not transmitted.

It would seem (here Gottfried von Strassburg is our chief witness) that the last decade of the twelfth and the first of the thirteenth century must have revelled in a far greater output of song than we know of, though, happily, we can be satisfied with what is left. Suabia is represented for us by two poets in whom the Crusader's zeal transcends the appeal of earthly love, Heinrich von Rugge and, of greater distinction and fame, Hartmann von Aue. The Bavarians Albrecht von Johansdorf and Hartwig von Raute bring with them to the cultivation of the Minnesang their own fresh and individual points of view. Wolfram von Eschenbach opens up new vistas with his plastic realism and compelling dramatic power. And a new phase begins with Walther von der Vogelweide, like Reinmar an inmate of the Viennese court, though only for a limited length of time.

Walther's life falls into three main periods. He was bred, and he may have been born, on Austrian soil. " Ze Osterrîche lernte ich singen unde sagen,"—" In Austria I learned to sing and say." His youth was spent at the Viennese court, where under the ducal house of Babenberg a gay and cultivated social life had matured, which remained his ideal and touchstone in later years. " Der wünnecliche hof ze Wiene,"—" the delightful court of Vienna "—is how he speaks in retrospect of his earlier home. The circumstances which forced him to quit can be guessed at. It was, he says, the loss of his patron, Frederick of Austria, which sent him roaming over the land a homeless man : this implies some unexplained breach with the new duke Leopold, Frederick's brother. The break belongs to the spring or summer of 1198, a year marked by Walther's first entry into the political arena, as champion of the Hohenstaufen against the Welf candidate in that dynastic struggle involving the still greater conflict of Emperor and Pope. This stormy and significant opening ushers in twenty years of vicissitudes, with varied experience of courts and patrons, stirring participation in public events, intervals, long or short, of want and hardship. Then the Emperor Frederick II bestowed on him a fief of his own, a welcome resting-place for his

4

old age, though it cannot be said that his keen and vigilant spirit ever rested. His last datable poem, the majestic elegy in which he surveys his past life and the life of his time, was uttered against the sombre background of the year 1228, when the Emperor decided to lead the Crusading army in spite of the Pope's ban. It is a far cry from the poet's youthful prime, with its songs of May sunshine, of singing birds and fields in bloom.

Walther's poetry covers a wide range, and in this he stands head and shoulders above his fellows. The Minnesang forms but a part of his entire output, in which social, political, ethical and religious themes are treated, and patrons and donors are drawn with a sure hand. But the Minnesang is all that concerns us here. Into this he introduced a new combative note and a strain of live criticism. The Troubadour ideal is challenged. "Minne ist zweier herzen wunne,"—"Love is the joy of two hearts"—not melancholy longing but glad fulfilment of a relation in which man and woman share equally, and there is no need for the man's one-sided homage. Sincerity of affection is made the touchstone for both. Judged by this, the lady of high rank is too often found wanting. The poet turns from her to the girl of low degree in whom he discovers his own ideal of unspoiled womanly goodness and charm. His *Lieder der niederen Minne* are fresh and true : time cannot wither them. Walther's Minnesang has in it a core of personal honesty, harmoniously combined with a lively and intimate appreciation of Nature, a quick sense of humour, and a gift for apt and vivid personification which gives colour and force to his treatment of abstract themes.

Only rarely, as in that perfect gem *Under der linden*, can he be called, in the strict sense, a lyrical poet. His strength lies mainly in dramatic presentation and in the bracing quality of his didactic verse.

Walther's revolt against the exaggerated conventions of the *frouwendienst* or *amor cortois* in no way impairs his allegiance to all that is best in the traditions of courtly life. The depth of that allegiance can be gauged from his extreme aversion to the new school of poetry founded by Neidhart von Reuental, the so-called *höfische Dorfpoesie*. "Höfisch" because intended to amuse the court, and "Dorfpoesie," because based on the village dance and on the accompanying circumstances of village life. This poetry, while representing the pastoral genus already well known in Romance lyric poetry, especially that of the *langue d'oil*, and in the Latin songs of the *vagantes*, differs from both in the strength of its realistic approach to peasant life. Whatever the debt to its literary antecedents, the poetry of Neidhart is really a new creation, exuberant, racy and graphic, the product of a Bavarian native genius whose life had

5

struck deep root in Bavarian soil. The family of Neidhart is lost in the same obscurity as that of Walther. Both belonged, like most of the earlier Minnesingers, to the class of the *ministeriales* or "Dienstadel", but while Walther was during the greater part of his life a landless man, Neidhart had an estate of his own, an unidentified place of small resource in the neighbourhood of Landshut. As a countryman, he can be seen mingling freely in the life of the local peasantry, whose material conditions in fact excelled his own, while on the other hand his clear sense of class-distinction gave him a point of vantage. Amorous relations with village belles alternate in his pictures of rustic life with satiric jibes at the swaggering, overdressed but underbred village youths. One can well understand the extraordinary vogue of his vigorous and picturesque verse as an offset to the graceful unrealities of the *amor cortois*. There is marvellous vivacity and beauty in his descriptions of the May season and of the dance in the open field, good entertainment in the pungent and clever satire and strong realism enlivening the winter scene. Yet one can also understand the antagonism of Walther von der Vogelweide to Neidhart's school. For in this new type there appear from the first germs of barbarous coarseness which in the long run gain the upper hand. A progressive decline of good breeding is seen not only in Neidhart's successors but, increasingly so, in the later songs of Neidhart himself. Walther's own revolt had been on quite different lines. Akin to Neidhart in his open-air freshness and love of Nature, he stands apart from him in his own ideal of dignity and balance.

Neidhart is first mentioned by name in Wolfram's *Willehalm* (1212—1217), a proof that by that time his fame was well established. Most of his life was spent on his native soil, until finally he lost the favour of his overlord and with it his small estate, said good-bye to his old home and migrated to Austria, where he obtained a little fief near Melk. Here he continued to exercise his art, providing the same spiced entertainment for the Austrian nobles as for his fellow-countrymen before. His village pastorals fall into two groups, *Sommerlieder* and *Winterlieder*, the latter an entirely new genre, unparalleled, so far as is known, in the bucolic poetry of either French, Provençal, or Latin.

After this, the history of the Minnesang flows on without major change, only a gradual slowing down of spiritual force as it widens out into the shallows. The two main fashions continue : courtly love-song and village pastoral maintain their separate conventions side by side. And the same poets cultivate both. The two fashions do not make two divided schools. Reinmar's influence keeps its lead in the one, Neidhart's in the other. Walther's, less marked, may be seen in the growing taste for personification, a tendency in which he

6

had certainly led the way. The personifications are sometimes of abstract qualities, sometimes of inanimate things. Just as Walther had quickened a personal life in the flowers and clover competing with one another in growth, so Kristan von Hamle personifies the meadow over which his lady walks as *Her Anger*—Sir Meadow. The influence of Wolfram von Eschenbach is seen in later forms of the *tagelied* or dawn-song : characteristic words and phrases of his are imitated, and his daring and exuberant style provokes some florid passages in his successors.

An interesting and unique experiment is that of the Styrian poet Ulrich von Lichtenstein, whose lyrics are skillfully woven into the texture of an autobiographical verse-romance. The story is that of his own young love-affairs. Opinions vary as to how far this is an ingenuous display of fact, how far make-believe. Ingenuous it certainly is not. The style is that of a conscious humorist, one who, whether recalling past follies or dressing them up to a higher pitch of absurdity than ever was, has anyhow a shrewd eye for effect. This agrees with what is otherwise known of Ulrich's life. His career is well documented, showing him as an astute and hard-headed man of action.

From the generation succeeding Walther we may single out Burkart von Hohenfels as the most original and forceful, the Schenk von Limburg as the most spontaneous and charming, Gottfried von Neifen as the most accomplished poet.

Virtuosity of technique is, as one might expect, the mark of the later period. But Gottfried von Neifen excels in his mastery of the most ingenious rhyme-devices. These include what is called " übergehender Reim," the last word of one line rhyming with the first of the next; " grammatischer Reim," with different grammatical forms from the same root rhymed together, *e.g.*, *bekleidet kleiden kleit leidet leiden leit blüete bluot güete guot* ; successions of " rührende Reime," the same word-form being repeated in the rhyme with different meanings. It is all rather artificial, though gracefully done. But there is other variety in Gottfried von Neifen besides that of technique. His songs include a most charming pastoral : the lover meets a girl going to the spring to draw water. Two others, in contrast to the more elaborate ones, have the simplicity of the later folk-song ; and the gem of the collection is a little cradle-song in two strophes, a perfect lullaby.

The virtuosity of this later period shows itself also in the increased cultivation of the form known as *leich*, which is characterised by a complex and continually changing pattern, while in the *lied* or song the same strophic pattern repeats itself unchanged. The *leich* is of twofold origin. On the one hand it developed from the sequence which has its place in Church music. The sequence, like the *leich*, has a changing metrical pattern, only on a less ambitious scale, and is connected in its origin with the elaborate melody of the Alleluia, which is in its turn of Greek provenance. The religious leich is the development of the religious sequence ; but side by side with this is the same kind of structure as determined by the intricate measures of the dance, and this type is particularly light and fluent. The religious leich of Heinrich von Rugge, a Crusading sermon in verse, is the first of its kind ; the finest is one executed by Walther von der Vogelweide, a splendid and moving masterpiece of proud device. The *tanzleich* comes to the fore in the succeeding period, a good example being one by Tannhäuser in which, incidentally, scope is found for an exaggerated use of foreign words, an evident skit on what was just then the fashion. The words *prîs, dulz amis, fores, tschantieren, toubieren, parlieren, riviere, planiure, creatiure, faitiure,* occur in quick succession. The subject is a pastoral, and it ends with a direct reference to the dance in progress and a final personal touch : " Heia, nu hei, des fidelæres seite ist enzwei,"—" the fiddler's string is broken," *i.e.* my song is finished.

Then, too, the strophic form of the *lied* tends to become longer and more intricate, as for instance in most of the metres used by Konrad von Würzburg. The language, at the same time, grows more decorative and studied. In contrast to all this artifice, there is also, as result of the standard governing the *dorfpoesie*, a deliberate cultivation of an emphatic and often coarse realism, of a style strewn with colloquial terms which, if life-like, is too much like life in the raw.

We notice two new types in the *dorfpoesie*. First, the *herbstlied* or autumn song, cultivated particularly by the Swiss poets Steinmar and Hadlaub. This is frankly a coarse type of song all in praise of feasting and swilling : the beauty of the season is nowhere. Its character may be summed up in the following line from Steinmar :

wâfen ! ich wil singen daz wir alle werden vol !

Second, a rustic parody of the *tagelied*, in which country wench and country swain, " dirne " and " kneht " take the place of lady and knight, " frouwe " and " ritter ", while the watchman is replaced by a shepherd calling out : " wol ûf, laz ûz die hert ! "—" Up now, let out the herd ! "

Johannes Hadlaub, burgher of Zürich, whose life belongs to the turn of the thirteenth and fourteenth centuries, has left a quite interesting collection of poems, some of them very novel, the novelty being indeed so marked that one cannot doubt he is telling of his own experience. As, for instance, when, disguised as a pilgrim, he meets his lady on her way to Mass and presses a love-missive into her hand,

and she takes it home with her to read. Gottfried Keller has, in one of his *Züricher Novellen*, utilised the material of Hadlaub's poetry in such a way as to construct from it a vivid and charmingly told story.

There is little to gain in pursuing the course of the Minnesang until, at the end of the fourteenth century, it peters out. Instead, we will limit ourselves to a short episode, told by the author of the Limburg chronicle in connection with the year 1347. This sheds an amusing light on the tyranny of fashion, being the story of a song made by Reinhart von Westerburg, a noble and talented knight in the Emperor's service. The song, of which all three stanzas are quoted, simple quadrains plainly worded, quite candidly announced that, if he should break his neck for his lady, no kin would avenge him ; he must therefore look after himself. The more so, as she had never done much to help him. If she does not want him, then he will take his leave : her favour is nothing to *him*, he would have her know :

> Auf ihre Gnade acht' ich kleine,
> Sieh, das lass' ich sie verstahn.

When the Emperor (Charles IV) heard this ungallant song, it displeased him, and he rebuked the author, saying that he must do the lady justice. The Herr von Westerburg bethought himself, and after a while produced a song in the right convention, saying how a lovely woman had driven him to despair, etc. And the Emperor said : Westerburg, that will do very well.

.        .        .        .        .        .        .

Something remains to be said on the social status of the Minnesingers, as well as on the relation of poet and patron. In Walther's time and before him, most of the Minnesingers were ministeriales, gentlemen of good birth but inferior rank. The only exceptions we know of (there may have been others) are the Emperor Henry VI —*Keiser Heinrich*—and Graf Rudolf von Fenis. Most of them were probably amateurs. Reinmar and Walther were quite definitely professional poets. But while Reinmar was attached to the Viennese court, Walther led a more precarious life, staying first at one court, then at another, possibly less from necessity than from choice. There were times, too, when he appears to have suffered the needy and hand-to-mouth state of the wandering gleeman, though he did not consort with that class. Walther's patrons were all men of the highest rank, a privilege due to his great prestige as a poet. Among them were three kings, the two Hohenstaufen, Philip of Suabia and Frederick II, and the Welf Emperor Otto who reigned between them. Other patrons include Duke Leopold VI of Austria, with whom his

9

relations were sometimes friendly, sometimes tinged with displeasure, Landgrave Hermann of Thuringia, extolled by him as a generous and mindful giver, Margrave Dietrich von Meissen, Bishop Wolfger of Passau, the Duke of Carinthia, and, of lower rank than these, the little-esteemed Graf von Katzenellenbogen. After Walther's time, we find the great lords taking part in the cultivation of the Minnesang, besides continuing to act as patrons. So, for instance, King Wenceslaus II of Bohemia, Henry Duke of Breslau (Herzog Heinrich von Pressela), John Duke of Brabant, the Margrave of Meissen (son of Walther's patron), Margrave Otto von Brandenburg, Graf Otto von Botenlauben. At the other end of the scale come poets of burgher rank, e.g., Konrad von Würzburg who, however, is thoroughly imbued with the courtly spirit, and the more typical burgher of Zürich, Johannes Hadlaub. The patrons of this period include rich merchants, but the majority are as before of aristocratic rank. Famous among them are the young king Henry VII, to whose circle belong Gottfried von Neifen, Burkart von Hohenfels, Schenk Ulrich von Winterstetten and others ; Duke Frederick of Austria, patron of both Neidhart and Tannhäuser, of Ulrich von Lichtenstein and of Bruder Wernher ; Wenceslaus I of Bohemia and his son Ottokar the Great. The patrons of the new burgher class culminate in Rüdiger Manesse, town councillor of Zürich, of whom Hadlaub relates that both he and his son collected songs. Bodmer, the rediscoverer of the Minnesang, erroneously took the Paris (now Heidelberg) song-codex for Manesse's collection, whence the term " Manessischer Codex ", though recognised as a misnomer, still clings.

This brings us to the MSS. in which the assembled wealth of the old German lyrics has been preserved. The most important of these are three parchment MSS. of Alemannic origin, designated for convenience' sake as A, B and C, of which A, the oldest and least imposing, was written towards the end of the thirteenth, B in the early part of the fourteenth century, while C, the largest and most famous, was completed about 1340. A, like C, is now in Heidelberg. Both belonged to the library of the Counts Palatinate of the Rhine ; but the history of A can only be gauged indirectly, no mention of it being made before 1796. Signs of Alsatian dialect in the spelling suggest Strassburg as its original home. It contains songs of thirty-four poets and consists of a major part (A) written by a hand of the thirteenth century, and six additional pages (a) of later date. B, now in Stuttgart, came originally from Constance. Its history can be traced as far back as the sixteenth century when its owner, Marx, bailiff of Constance, presented it to the Benedictine abbey of Weingarten in South Württemberg. Thence, after the abbey had been dissolved, it passed into the library of the King of Württemberg. B, while larger than A, contains only thirty-one poets. The MS. consists of 312 pages with regular allotment of 28 lines to the page, and with 25 illustrations, identical for the most part with the corresponding illustrations in C.

C, the most comprehensive and the most sumptuously produced of all three, comprises 140 poets arranged, though without strict consistency, in order of rank. The Emperor Henry VI—Kaiser Heinrich—represented as sitting on his throne in royal state, comes first and is followed by King Konrad the Young, formerly identified with Konradin, the last of the Hohenstaufen, now thought to have been more probably Konrad IV, second son of the Emperor Frederick II. Dukes, margraves, counts and freiherren precede the ministeriales, who in their turn are succeeded by poets of burgher rank, but the order grows more confused towards the end. C is copiously provided with illustrations, 137 in all, pictorial representations of the poets with heraldic devices, including, as aforesaid, those of B. The close relation between B and C points to a common lost source BC, but C has in addition connections with A and with the later Würzburg MS. (E), from which one can also postulate the sources AC and EC. The collection C contains besides *lieder* and *sprüche* (short didactic poems) two poems of considerable length. First, the *Winsbeke*, a series of knightly precepts cast in the form of a father's advice to his son, with sequels following : (1) the son's reply, and (2), as female counterpart, the *Winsbekin*, a mother's advice to her daughter. Second, the *Wartburgkrieg*, the theme of which is the singers' contest made famous in modern times by Wagner's opera *Tannhäuser*. The orthography of C shows that it was written in Zürich. Bodmer's conjecture was therefore not without reason. The history of C, as of B, begins in the sixteenth century. It belonged then, presumably, to the library of the Elector Count Palatinate of the Rhine. It was well known in the early seventeenth century to the scholars of that time, so much so that excerpts from it were published, chosen, in accordance with the antiquarian trend of the age, with an eye to their historical value. No interest was taken in the Minnesang as such ; the political poems were singled out, and Walther von der Vogelweide was described, not unfittingly, as *optimus vitiorum censor ac morum castigator acerrimus*.

After the sack of Heidelberg in the Thirty Years' War, the Palatine library was dispersed, and C by some means or other passed into the hands of the French antiquarian Jaques Dupuy, on whose death in 1656 it was placed in the royal (later national) library of Paris, whence the old term *Pariser Codex*. This held good until the year 1888, when the Codex was restored to the German nation and was placed, with the rest of the Palatine collection of books, in the University library of Heidelberg.

Of the later compilations, that designated as J (in Jena) is interesting because it alone gives the melodies accompanying the texts. Unfortunately, all these are so late as to yield no clue to what we most sorely miss, the musical side of the Minnesang at its prime.

Smaller song-books must without doubt have preceded the compilations; indeed, their existence is not merely assumed but is proved by internal evidence drawn from comparative study of the MSS. that remain. Side by side with those song-books there may also have been songs written on single leaves, *fliegende blätter*, as in the case of the fifteenth and sixteenth century folk-songs.

One earlier MS. remains to be mentioned. This is the codex of the Latin *Carmina Burana*, written in the thirteenth century in Bavaria, and eventually transferred from its home in the monastery of Benediktbeuren to the Munich State Library. The collection includes, interspersed with the Latin songs of *scolares vagantes*, a number of German stanzas, several being of known authorship, others unidentified. Most of the anonyma are pastoral ditties, some of them mere snatches of verse which, in their simplicity of tone and form, suggest a closer link with genuine native folk-song than the songs of Neidhart.

. . . . . . .

The rediscovery of the mediaeval German love-lyric in modern times, due first of all to the interest of the Swiss poet Bodmer, was part of that orientation towards things of the past which marks the Romantic movement. Simrock and Uhland, Grimm, Lachmann and Haupt are the names which stand out from this pioneer period. Uhland's warm and, despite the progress since made, fundamentally sound life of Walther von der Vogelweide signalises the close of the first, romantically inspired phase of research on the subject of the Minnesang. From the succeeding period of patient, systematic and seasoned labour, no less enthusiastic but more discreet than the one before, we may single out in this particular field the names of Wilmanns and Schönbach, Vogt and Burdach. The foundations have been widened and the difficulties of the subject are envisaged more critically and with a more careful discrimination than in the first flush of discovery. All this is sheer gain, and the tradition continues to bear fruit. But a third new phase has developed in which, under the guise of minute enquiry, an over-intellectual subtlety of approach threatens to obscure the promptings of common sense and experience. I am diffident of applying this stricture to Carl von Kraus, a veteran scholar whose high reputation is based on years of strict investigation and fine constructive thought; yet it cannot be denied that in his case the charge of over-intellectualism is particularly true. And the lead thus given has been too willingly followed. The latest extreme of this tendency can be seen in Max Ittenbach's *Frühzeit des Minnesangs*, a brilliant but distractingly wrong-headed attempt to interpret the older and simpler Minnesang (Kürenberg and his fellows) by the light of a youthfully clever, hypercritical cast of mind.

Personally I feel sure that, in spite of the occasional naïveté despised by the modernist, the " first fine careless rapture " of the Romantics strikes nearer to the heart of the matter than scholastically trained logic. Progress has been made since the pioneer age in definite knowledge, and, as complement, in the evolution of honest doubt. But the modern way of solving doubts and assuming positive results merely on the ground of skilled argument, and with the convenient hypothesis that what is potential and probable is therefore actually true : *this* is not progress in research but obstruction of knowledge.

The student of the Minnesang is faced with difficult problems. First, a problem which affects all periods of literature, but in this case especially arduous, that of distinguishing the poet's own personal note from the influence of tradition. Pure intuition alone cannot solve this, though it cannot be solved without. Knowledge of the poet's debt to tradition, increasing knowledge, must be leagued with but must not be suffered to overpower the intuitive apprehension of what he *is*. The second problem admits only of a very partial, often dubious solution. It is that of deciding how far one poet shows the influence of another. That is possible with a clear separation in time, it is, more often than not, impossible with poets of the same generation, because relatively few songs can be dated, and the evidence of the poets' lives is, with a few exceptions, extremely vague. So, for example, when Reinmar von Hagenau and Heinrich von Morungen, of the same generation, use the expression *ôsterlîcher tac*—Easter Day—in speaking of their lady, a term too recondite to have occurred independently twice over, how is one to say who coined it first ? To our imperfect knowledge of dates is added, for the time before Walther von der Vogelweide, an imperfect knowledge of the *liaison* between one court and another. Here every fresh detail which helps to fill the gap is a thankfully accepted gain ; but one must be content to go slowly. Substantial progress is due to the close investigations of Burdach and Kraus, so that we now see the relation of Reinmar and Walther as one, not of master and pupil, but of contemporary rivals. Reinmar's influence on Walther remains, but is no longer seen as an influence all on one side, there are signs of interaction between the two.

Both these problems are still further complicated by being interlocked with the third, which is the most crucial of all. It is that of deciding what part of the poet's work is authentic, what part spurious. There is sufficient conformity among the song-codices to prove, in the main, continuance of a reliable and firm tradition. At the same time, inconsistencies and palpable errors are there in sufficient strength to prove a host of exceptions. It could not be otherwise, considering the gap in time between the first generations of poets and the date at which the song-codices begin. The difficulty of course lies on the borderline of what is certainly authentic and what is quite certainly not. Here opinions differ ; and here, too, it is necessary to make a stand against criteria based on estimates of what is rational, probable or consistent.

It is a fallacy to overstate minor deviations from the poet's norm, to deny the authenticity of a poem attributed to him because it expresses a mood, or contains an idea, a word or metaphor which, from the rest of him, we did not expect. The tradition may have erred, but without real certainty of error, it is better to give it the benefit of the doubt. One must not say : This cannot be Reinmar's, if what we mean is only, This is not like Reinmar. One naturally expects a poet to think consistently, to express himself in characteristic forms and to follow up his own technique ; but it should not be held impossible for him to break away from his norm, whether from a sudden desire for change, or from the force of some particular circumstance, or the passing impact of another man's mode.

And here I must pay tribute to the late Eduard Sievers, unqualified though I am to appreciate the highly skilled methods with which he worked. For the principle underlying those methods is indubitably right : the recognition of rhythm and musical tone as the sole criteria by which the authenticity of a poet's work can be adequately judged. Here is something which lies beyond the poet's own power to control. His thoughts are free, he can direct them into new channels, he can consciously devise new metrical schemes, and use words he has not used before. But his rhythm and melody are pre-determined. Reinmar's delicate half-tones and dying falls are as impossible to Walther as Walther's firm, decisive notes are impossible within the scope of Reinmar. The veriest novice could never confuse those two.

.    .    .    .    .    .    .

The following essays are limited in their range. I have not wished to go beyond Neidhart, and have purposely omitted Hartmann von Aue because, though I am interested in him, my opinions are, to say the honest truth, unsettled.

# THE OLDER MINNESANG

In the mediæval German love-lyric, two main types are discernible, the primitive and the courtly. "Primitive", perhaps, is hardly the right term to use, but must serve for want of a better. The kind it covers is that in which sexual relation is direct and normal, the emotional quality free from intellectual implications and subtleties. Simplicity of content is matched by a corresponding simplicity of technique. The more primitive type of love-lyric need not, because it is direct and naïve, have sprung from the ranks of the people, at least not in its earlier stages. But it is not therefore any the less *volkstümlich*. Court and castle are not synonymous terms: the distance between the court and the small feudal castle was no doubt often greater than between this and the market place or village green, though of course with gradations which differed regionally and in regard to time. One may fittingly distinguish not two but three main grades of mediæval literary culture: either learned and courtly, as in the highest circles, or broadly aristocratic and in the best sense popular, or popular and plebeian. To the second belong most of the Old French *Chansons de Geste*, belong also the *Tristan* of Béroul, and those lovely ballad-like songs known as *chansons d'histoire*. Equally so, the Middle High German heroic epics or *Heldenepen* of Germanic ancestry, among which *der Nibelunge Nôt* stands out from the rest with its archaic nobleness of tone and bold simplicity of style and treatment.

That the old German love-songs distinct from those modelled on the Troubadour lyric belong to the same sphere as the *Heldenepen* follows from the sharing in both of similar strophic measures. Locally, also, they go well together, since the early Minnesingers belong to the same south-eastern, Danubian region as was the stronghold of the *Heldenepen*. It is certainly a loss that the older, twelfth-century forms of the latter, which would have been contemporary with the older love-songs, have utterly vanished; but the thirteenth-century forms are sufficiently archaic and traditional to show at least some of the connecting links.

The strophic measures are built on the same bases, either a short line with three accents and a feminine or with four and a masculine ending ($3+$ or $4$), or the long line divided by a cæsura as follows:

(*a*) $3 +_{,,} 2 +$
      den troum si dô sagete    ir muoter Uoten    (*Nib.* 14, ₁)

$3 +_{,,} 3$
      die herren wâren milte,    von arde hôch erborn (*Nib.* 5, ₁)

$4_{,,} 3$
      er was der künec Liudegast,    er huote sîner schar (*Nib.* 183, ₁)

It may be noticed that the second half is always slightly shorter than the first. The stronger pause at the end equalises the tempo.

(b) $3+_{\shortmid\shortmid}4$ or $4_{\shortmid\shortmid}4$

| | |
|---|---|
| ûf der linden obene | dâ sanc ein kleinez vogellîn |
| | (Dietmar von Aist, MF. 34, 3) |
| ez dunket mich wol tûsent jâr | daz ich an liebes arme lac |
| | (Dietmar von Aist, MF. 34, 11) |

Here both halves are equal.

The verse is accentual: there is no exact rule for the number of syllables, but a general dependence on tempo. The proportion of primary and secondary accents is variable, though there are as a general rule two primary accents in each half-line. The second syllable of the feminine ending has a very slight stress which may be conveniently indicated by

The rhymes are simply arranged in successive pairs. Alternating rhymes are a sign of younger technique. As, for instance in certain strophes of *der Nibelunge Nôt*, where rhyme is introduced in the cæsura as well as at the end of the line.

| | |
|---|---|
| Uns ist in alten mæren | wunders vil geseit |
| von heleden lobebæren, | von grôzer arebeit, |
| von fröuden, hôhgezîten, | von weinen und von klagen, |
| von küener recken strîten | muget ir nu wunder hœren sagen. |
| | (*Nib.* 1) |

There is a good deal of repetition of easily used rhyme-words like *lîp* : *wîp*, *guot* : *muot*, and in the older poetic forms assonances are frequent, e.g., *liep* : *niet*, *hemede* : *edele* in the songs of Kürenberg, *Hagene* : *gademe* and *Hagene* : *degene* in certain older strophes of *der Nibelunge Nôt*.

These are the general principles of the metre. The strongest similarity is between the songs of Kürenberg and *der Nibelunge Nôt*. The strophic form of the latter (hence called *Nibelungenstrophe*) shows this pattern:

$3+_{\shortmid\shortmid}3^a$
$3+_{\shortmid\shortmid}3^a$
$3+_{\shortmid\shortmid}3^b$
$3+_{\shortmid\shortmid}4^b$

| | |
|---|---|
| die herren wâren milte, | von arde hôch erborn, |
| mit kraft unmâzen küene, | die recken ûz erkorn. |
| dâ zen Buregonden, | sô was ir lant genant, |
| si frumten starkiu wunder | sît in Etzelen lant. |

The variation 4 for 3+ in the first half-line occurs, but not often. The favourite cadence in the last half-line is ×/×//×/ or /×//×/,

with suppression of the dip between the second and third accents,
e.g., sít in Étzèlen lánt.

The variation $3+_{„}2+$ (also infrequent) occurs only in the first two
lines of the strophe.

> den troum si dô sagete      ir muoter Uoten.
> si enkundes niht bescheiden      baz der guoten:
> "der valke den du ziuhest,      daz ist ein edel man.
> in welle got behüeten,      du muose in schiere vloren hân."

This in *der Nibelunge Nôt* is rare, and can be regarded as a trace
of an earlier technique which is fully carried out in the songs of
Kürenberg. Here is the same strophic form, but with a characteristic
difference between the songs put into the mouth of the woman and
those ascribed to the man. In the former the feminine endings
predominate, giving a heightened effect of suspense and longing, as in

> ich stuont mir nehtint spâte      an einer zinnen.
> dô hôrte ich einen ritter      vil wol singen
> in Kürenberges wîse      al ûz der menegîn.
> er muoz mir diu lant rûmen,      ald ich geniete mich sîn

where the proportion of feminine to masculine endings is 6 to 2.
The only exception to this is the first strophe of the "Falkenlied",
(MF. 8, $_{34}$—9, $_{12}$), in which all four rhymes are masculine.

In the strophes where the man is speaker, the final cadence in all
four lines is a masculine rhyme, and the prevailing note is one of
confidence and decision, as in his answer to what the lady says above:

> Nu brinc mir her vil balde      mîn ros, mîn îsengewant,
> wan ich muoz einer frouwen      rûmen diu lant.
> diu wil mich des betwingen      daz ich ir holt sî.
> si muoz der mîner minne      iemer darbende sîn.

It seems idle to renew the question, whether Kürenberg or the
unknown first maker of *der Nibelunge Nôt* created the strophic form
which has taken its name from the latter. The expression *Küren-
berges wîse* introduced in the song quoted above does not necessarily
give Kürenberg priority, since the word *wîse* might simply mean the
tune. One point is clear: the strophe can hardly have been used
for the first time in a poem of epic dimensions, but rather in the
lays on which the longer epic form was based. Its inconvenience
when used as an epic measure is seen, despite its general effectiveness,
in a frequent recourse to mere padding, particularly in the last line.

The two forms of the *Nibelungenstrophe*, used so expressively to
distinguish the woman's temperament from the man's, are found in
twelve out of the fourteen stanzas preserved in C under the name

of Kürenberg. The remaining first two show a slight variation, a single short rhymeless line being interposed between the second long line and the third.

> Vil lieber vriunde . . .    daz ist schedelîch.
> swer sînen vriunt behaltet,    daz ist lobelîch.
> die site wil ich minnen.
> bit in daz er mir holt sî    als er hie vor was,
> und man in wes wir redeten    dô ich in ze jungeste sach.

The songs attributed to Dietmar von Aist include among their simplest forms two in short lines with successive rhymes or assonances aabbcc . . . , and some four-line stanzas with the larger pattern $3 + {}_u4$ or $4_u4$.

> Ûf der linden obene    dâ sanc ein kleinez vogellîn.
> vor dem walde wart ez lût:    dô huop sich aber daz herze mîn.
> an eine stat dâ'z ê dâ was.    ich sach die rôsebluomen stân :
> die manent mich der gedanke vil    die ich hin zeiner frouwen hân.

Other four-line strophes are expanded by the insertion of an extra short line, and there is one especially happy form in which one pair of short lines (rhyming *bb*) is enclosed between two pairs of long lines (*aa . . . cc*). MF. 32, ₁₄ . . .

The larger pattern is the base of the strophic forms used by Meinloh von Sevelingen. These vary only in dimension. Nine of them have six long lines each, rhyming *aabbcc*, with a single short rhymeless line between the last two. Another two have six long lines without the odd short one. And, finally, one is made up of eight long lines, with a short rhymeless line in the favourite place, last but one.

The songs of the Burgrave von Regensburg, four altogether, are again four-line strophes, similar to those of Dietmar von Aist, but too irregular to yield a definite pattern.

Turning from all these to the metrical forms of the *Heldenepen*, we find, along with the close correspondence between Kürenberg and *der Nibelunge Nôt*, similar expansions and variations. The strophe of the *Hilde-Kûdrûn* epic is as follows :

> $3 + {}_u3^a$
> $3 + {}_u3^a$
> $3 + {}_u3 + ^b$
> $3 + {}_u5 + ^b$
> daz kom an einen âbent,    daz in sô gelanc,
> daz von Tenemarke Fruote    der küene degen sanc
> mit so hêrlîcher stimme,    daz ez wol gevallen
> muose al den liuten.    dâ von gesweic der vogellîne schallen.

The extra lengthening of the last half-line, though sometimes effective, is not a very happy invention, since it tends to make the verse drag, and gives frequent occasion for padding. And as the epic is inordinately long, this is all the worse.

The metre of the *Rabenschlacht* is exceedingly cumbrous. The last two lines of the *Nibelungenstrophe* are combined with the last two of the *Kudrunstrophe*, that is, the two heavier parts of both are put together !

An earlier and happier strophic form is that of *Salman und Morolf*, the work of a Rhenish gleeman whose naïve and spirited art has left us this bright example, not of a high heroic theme but of downright popular entertainment. The stanza consists of five short lines :

4a
4a
4b
3 + or 4c
4b

> Ze Jerusalem wart ein kint geborn,
> daz sît ze vougte wart erkorn
> uber alle cristen diet.
> daz was der kunic Salman
> der manic wîsheit geriet.

With this light, easy metre the narrative assuredly does not flag. There is evidence, too, of its use as a lyric measure. Two of the German songs which in the *Carmina Burana* have slipped in among the Latin have the same form. The first of these is a song of provocative content which, if we accept the correction of the MS. *kunegin* for *kunec* as the authentic reading can only refer to Eleanor of Aquitaine, queen of England from 1154. This would give an approximate early date.

> wære al diu werlt mîn
> von dem mere unz an den Rîn,
> des wolt ich mich darben
> daz diu kunegîn von Engellant
> læge an mînen armen.

As it happens, the *Carmina Burana*, preserved in a MS. from the monastery of Benediktbeuren in southern Bavaria, suggest the same region as the old German love-songs. But one cannot attach any value to this, in view of the international character of the collection. And, in fact, the German stanza just quoted points rather to the Rhineland.

One does not, of course, assume that the older German love-song or *trûtliet* flourished originally only in the south-east. But it is natural enough that it should have remained there longest, that the exotic fashion of courtly love, entering mainly by way of the Rhineland from its home in Provence, should have needed a little more time to penetrate inland. Not but that the new fashion was known long before it took root. There is mention of it in the *Kaiserchronik*, which we know to have been the work of a Bavarian cleric, with the year of the Second Crusade in 1147 as terminus ad quem. Then, too, there are signs of Provençal influence even in the songs of Kürenberg and the earliest of Dietmar von Aist, though one must add that this influence, which may well have reached the Danube via Lombardy and Friuli over the Alps,[2] is not one of ideas but of tangible concrete details. It shows itself in references to the *merkære*, the counterpart in the German lyric of the Provençal *lauzengier*, whose business is to thwart the lady's intercourse with her lover, and in the rise of the *tageliet*, where the situation is that of the Provençal *alba*, the parting of two lovers at break of day. Here there is no trace of *courtoisie*. Indeed, the *alba* itself differs essentially from the rest of the Troubadour lyric as an expression of the primitive passion of love, with the pure emotional quality of folk-song, stark and clear. The *merkære*, too, are actual live figures whose identity with the *lauzengier* does not rule out their independent place in the German scene. Both in *Rother*[3] (of about the same time as the songs of Kürenberg) and, later, in Wolfram's *Parzival*,[4] the word *merkære* is used with a wider connotation than *lauzengier*. The primary aim of the *merkære* is to keep a close watch on the stranger at court, lest he prove subversive : that is their general function, of which interference in clandestine love-affairs is but one aspect. Hence their association in *Rother* with the *kamerære* or chamberlains, who as guardians of household order are the natural foes of strangers —more especially of vagabond types as in *Salman und Morolf*— while in *Parzival* the word is used of the Seneschal Keye, whose task is similar.

Thus the first traces of foreign influence enter harmoniously into the native element of the old German love-song and are absorbed by it.

This older love-lyric is represented, first, by a small number of fugitive pieces, one, the oldest of all, marking the close of a Latin love-letter written by a nun (preserved among the epistles of Wernher of Tegernsee), some interspersed with the *amatoria* or Latin love-songs of the *Carmina Burana* ; secondly, by the five South German poets already mentioned and by two little songs ascribed to the

[2] A. Schönbach : Frühzeit des Minnesangs, 26—34.
[3] *Rother*, 2004—2010 and 2114–5. Edited by Jan de Vries, Heidelderg 1922.
[4] *Parzival*, 297, 5—15. Cf. also Walther von der Vogelweide 11, 26.

Emperor Henry VI, all of which has come down to us through the song-codices of later date. The five poets comprise, on the combined authority of those MSS. and of twelfth century local documents, two Austrians, Kürenberg and Dietmar von Aist; two Bavarians, the Burgrave von Regensburg and the Burgrave von Rietenburg, both of one family; and a Suabian, Meinloh von Sevelingen.

The songs of these fall again into two groups, those in which the courtly influence is completely absent, and those in which there are budding signs of it. To the first group belong the songs of Kürenberg, of the Burgrave von Regensburg, and of the older poet whose songs are among those placed under the ambiguous name of Dietmar von Aist. One might conveniently, if not correctly, speak of an older and a younger Dietmar : indeed, those terms are hardly less open to question than the now usual Pseudo-Dietmar and Dietmar.[5] To the second group belong, with one exception, the songs of Meinloh von Sevelingen, of the Burgrave von Rietenburg, and, let us say, of the younger Dietmar von Aist.

The word " primitive ", used with integrity, can only apply to the songs of the first group. Yet one would hardly designate the second group as " courtly ". For that, the spirit in which the new mode is approached is too ingenuous, the style too simple. And the verse-technique of Meinloh von Sevelingen and of the Burgrave von Regensburg is, as we have seen, built on conservative lines, the same being true, not of all, but of the greater number of the Dietmar-songs, old and new.

What distinguishes the small elder group is, quite briefly, its older and more universal conception of sexual love. As in the primitive love-song the whole world over—if one dare go so far—the relation between the sexes is either one of mutual passion, or, if the balance dips, it is the woman's devotion which, almost always, exceeds the man's. Patience, constancy, unaltered longing are sensed as qualities more natural to her sex than to his. The woman's lament for her lost mate is an ancient theme, filled with a poignancy of sorrow which is not of to-day or yesterday but goes back to the heroic age of the warrior caste and to the woman's keening for the man slain in battle. The lament, at a later stage, has other causes : not death alone, but fickleness and change of scene and the blandishments of other women draw the lover away from his own true love and leave her mourning. The poignancy then is as deep as though death had parted them : it will seem to her " a thousand years " since he went away. The German *trûtliet* include some most moving examples of this kind of lament. From Dietmar von Aist, or at least from the older poet

---

[5] The problem of authorship here is so complicated that I prefer to leave it undiscussed.

with a claim to that name, come two which it would be difficult to surpass for sheer plangency and simple beauty :

> Ez stuont ein frouwe alleine
> und warte uber heide
> und warte ir liebes.
> sus gesach si valken vliegen. . . .

and

> sô wol dir, sumerwunne ! . . .

The first opens with four lines of narrative, saying how a lady stood alone, looked out over the field and looked for her lover, and saw a falcon flying. And this brings into her mind the thought, how different her own lot is. For the falcon can fly where it will and choose a tree to perch on. So had she chosen herself a man, but he is hers no longer, other fair ladies, envying her, have enticed him from her. The same idea of the man lured away by other women from the one who loves him best is expressed in the next poem also, but the setting this time is that of the fading year : the joy of summer is gone and the woman's joy too. This symbolic association between the passing of summer and the transitoriness of the man's fleeting love is repeated in a song of unknown authorship which belongs to the same sphere :

> Diu linde ist an dem ende nu jârlanc lieht unde blôz.
> mich vêhet mîn geselle : nu engilte ich des ich nie genôz . . .

The lime-tree has throughout the year been both bright and bare. My comrade is estranged from me : now I pay dear for what I never did possess . . .

Meinloh von Sevelingen, whose songs, as arranged in C, give the continuous story of a lover's relation to his lady on courtly lines, has one which falls outside this scheme and fits in with the older lyric. Here, also, the woman makes lament for her lover's desertion and blames the rivals who have seduced him from her : he is so young, it is they who are at fault, not he. " Si enkunnen niht wan triegen manegen kindeschen man."—" They can do nothing but deceive many a young, untried man."

In the songs of Kürenberg the woman's plaint is heard but has in it a note of persistent courage. The situation implied gives no hint of the man's desertion. Either it is a case of unanswered love— " it grieves me to the heart that I have desired what I could not have nor can ever win "—or if the love is mutual, it is those hated foes the *merkære*, or, what comes to the same thing, the *lugenære*—liars— who have made a breach between the two.

The woman's lament is so distinctive a form of the primitive lyric that one is bound to dwell more particularly on it. In the courtly

Minnesang it either vanishes or is radically changed until in later folk-song it re-appears, the same in its primary motive, though with a loss of the original underlying sense of control and balance. Meanwhile, the elegiac note in the German *trûtliet*, real though it be, is not its determining key-note. There is also an exhilarating strain of fresh enjoyment, of proud blithe confidence which is often felt more in the lilt of the verse than in the actual words. And this spirit enters into the younger group as well. The new theme of courtly love is attacked with a frankness and force very different from the bitter-sweet melancholy of the more advanced phase, of which, however, there are also faint beginnings.

Thus in the songs of Meinloh von Sevelingen courtly love makes its appearance as a new and very definite conception, but is treated in a manner still far removed from the new courtly mode. The exposition of the lover's relation to his mistress : how he first heard her praised from afar, discovered as he came to know her that the truth outstripped report, contented himself for a while with unselfish service, grew bolder and sought her love and received it fully, and of how they both cursed their enemies the *merkære* who strove to part them—all this is presented with refreshing vigour, and gives the impression of a man going swiftly to work and of a women swift to answer him.

The rapid success of the lover as he passes from one stage to the next shows how purely outward the Troubadour influence still is. For here are stages which in the Provençal theory of love are intended as slow gradations in the lover's approach to his lady. The young man imagined by Meinloh von Sevelingen marches steadily on, accompanied at each stage by straightforward thoughts which reflect his good sense and candour.

Most of the younger Dietmar-songs show the same buoyant and simple attitude of mind towards courtly love. The position of the woman has changed, so that she no longer seeks the man but is sought by him and receives his service. But this service sits lightly on him ; indeed, he even welcomes it with gusto :

> Nu ist ez an ein ende komen, dar nâch mîn herze ie ranc,
> daz mich ein edeliu frouwe hât genomen in ir getwanc.

Now has the goal been reached whereto my heart had always striven, that a noble lady has taken me under her control.

For the very sound reason, that this will give him the discipline he needs.

> Si benimt mir manege wilde tât.

She takes from me many a wild deed.

The lover's note of despondency is also sounded, more out of regard for convention than from conviction, and belied by the cheerful lilt of " sô hôh ôwî ! " Nor does the lady's service require lifelong patience : the relation between the two becomes quickly mutual. And then we are on familiar ground, with the *merkære* plying their malicious task, and with sad partings and secret messages. For this typical situation there are two suitable poetic forms, the *wechsel* and the *botenlied*. The *wechsel* is a song of two strophes, in which the lovers' thoughts alternate : not a dialogue, but a thinking in unison. The *botenlied* is a song in which the lovers' messenger takes part. Of this there are variations. Where the presence of the messenger is but faintly implied, as in the first two strophes of Kürenberg, an exchange of thoughts with only this slight link has the same effect as a *wechsel*. In a song by Meinloh von Sevelingen, the messenger speaks for his master, not without skill in attuning the lady's mind to make speed and reward the knight's service because summer, the season of joy, is drawing nigh. With (the younger) Dietmar von Aist the *botenlied* is developed further. In a charming song of two strophes : " Seneder friundinne bote, nu sage dem schœnen wibe " . . . (MF. 32, ₁₄ . . .), the situation is expressed with a lively and instant sense of drama. The lovers are separated and cannot meet, and the knight sends his lady's messenger back to her with fresh assurance of his love and of his sorrow at being forced to stay away from her. The second strophe contains her answer, and begins with similar injunction : " Nu sage dem ritter edele " . . . What concerns her first is fear for his safety, in case he should not be sufficiently on his guard. *Wechsel* and *botenlied* are combined in another song (MF. 37, ₃₀ . . .) which reflects the same situation as that of Meinloh von Sevelingen, except that here there is evidence of the lady's love. And with a different season of the year : summer is past, the trees have faded, the birds have ceased to sing, but not as in the woman's lament of the older kind, in token of man's fickleness. For it is the man who speaks here, declaring that the love wherewith he has served his lady the summer through is immune from change. The lady, in *her* soliloquy, shows that she both appreciates this true affection and returns it ; and now comes the messenger, ready to clinch the matter and leaving the lady no choice but to declare her love plainly and to put an end to the knight's " long waiting ". Which, from what she has just said we may assume she forthwith does. Another song (a *wechsel*) tells of lovers' union and introduces a new thought (shared also by the Burgrave von Regensburg) that the joy of the winter-long night can vie with the joy of summer " swâ man bî liebe lange lît "— " wherever one lies long by his love." (MF. 39, ₃₀ . . .). The treatment of love in the songs of the younger Dietmar is pleasantly varied : different aspects are touched on, lightly and firmly and with a sense of drama which is not merely implicit, but shows itself also in the introduction of actual dialogue, on a small scale. As in " alsô redeten zwei geliebe, dô si von ein ander schieden"—"thus two lovers spoke as they parted " (MF. 32, ₅). Much is packed into this four-line strophe. *He* tries to comfort her with a wise saw; she denies its efficacy; both agree in a protest against love's unreason. But the clearest, most delicate picture of lovers' parting is that of the *tageliet* (MF. 39, ₁₈), which, from its elemental pathos, far deeper than in any of the poems we have just reviewed, one would place with the older love-songs, were it not for the finished form of the simple but pure technique. Finally, to make all complete, there is, in a more sophisticated tone and in a slightly more elaborate metre, a lovers' quarrel (MF. 40, ₁₉).

The *tageliet* deserves to be dwelt on a while longer ; and is short enough to be quoted in full.

> " Slâfest du, friedel ziere ?
> man wecket uns leider schiere.
> ein vogellîn so wol getân
> daz ist der linden an daz zwî gegân."

> " Ich was vil sanfte entslâfen.
> nu rüefestu, kint, wâfen !
> liep âne leit mac niht gesîn.
> swaz du gebiutest, daz leiste ich, friundin mîn."

> Diu frouwe begunde weinen.
> " Du rîtest und lâst mich einen.
> wenne wilt du wider her zuo mir ?
> ôwê du füerest mîn frôide sament dir."

" Sleepest thou, fair love ? soon we shall be wakened. A little bird so fine has gone to perch on the spray of a linden tree." " I had fallen softly asleep. Now, child, thou callest : Begone ! Bliss without bale cannot be. Whatever thou biddest, that will I do, my love." The lady fell a-weeping. " Thou ridest and leavest me alone. When wilt thou come back to me here ? Alas, thou takest my joy away with thee."

Provençal influence may be assumed to lie indirectly behind the *tageliet* of Dietmar von Aist, which, however, is unique in its brevity and concision. The theme is simplified by the absence of the watchman—the Provençal *gaita*—who plays so essential a part in the *alba*. Instead, the lady is roused by a little bird, hopping to its perch on a linden spray, and wakes her still sleeping lover. In the *alba*, the singing of birds in the trees forms a part of the general background. In Dietmar's song the effect of the first streak of dawn is evoked by the one isolated image of bird on bough. The style lacks the passionate emphasis of the refrain, which again is essential to the *alba*, and which is paralleled later by Heinrich von Morungen in his recurring melancholy phrase *do tagete ez*—then day broke—and by Wolfram von Eschenbach in the slightly varying, reiterated signal : " Ritter, wache, hüete din ! "—" Knight, awake, be on thy guard ! " . . . " Hüete dich, wache, süezer gast ! "—" Be on thy guard, awake, sweet guest ! "

The charm of Dietmar's small and perfect poem lies in its primal freshness : more than any other song of this genre (so far as I know) it creates an elemental sense of the still hour of dawn. The effect is delicately heightened by the vowel-melody of the first strophe with its preponderance of the high front vowel *i* : *friedel ziere . . . schiere . . . vogellîn . . . linden . . . zwî*, giving an impression of the faint silvery light of dawn stealing in on the lovers' rest, and of the tiny light rustle of the bird among the leaves. In contrast with this, the long broad *a* of the initial word *slâfest* and of the second pair of rhymes *getân* : *gegân* strikes a profounder note of grave pathos which is continued in the second strophe with the rhymes *entslâfen* : *wâfen*.

The lovers' dialogue, though brief, is wholly adequate, being made of direct, inevitable words which leave a haunting effect of restrained and tender feeling. The terms of endearment are very appealing, the rare and sweet word *friedel*, not heard again in the Minnesang before Walther von der Vogelweide in *Under der linden*, and *friundin mîn*. The scene, no doubt, is imagined against an out-of-door background, similar to that of the anonymous *alba*—the finest and simplest of the Provençal songs of this kind—where the lovers have spent the night together " en un vergier sotz folha d'albespine ".

Under the august name of Kaiser Heinrich three songs are preserved, of which the first is in the full courtly style of the Rhenish Minnesang, while the second and third belong, in technique and content, to the older tradition of the *trûtliet*. One is a *wechsel*, the other, composed, like this, of two simple four-line strophes, is a lady's address to her lover at the moment of parting. The first line : " Rîtest du von hinnen, der aller liebeste man ", recalls the *tageliet* of Dietmar von Aist with its similar phrase : " Du rîtest und lâst mich einen ", but the actual time of the parting is not defined.

The songs of the Burgrave von Regensburg express quite simply the relation between two lovers whom the *merkære* keep apart but have no power to estrange. The first two strophes are spoken by a woman, the other two form a *wechsel*, in which the knight's thoughts find an echo in his lady's. There is no sign of *courtoisie* : rather, it is the lady who proclaims submission : " Ich bin mit rehte stæteclîche eim guoten ritter undertân ".

The transition to the new courtly mode with its more studied form and its more intellectual trend of reflection is represented by the songs of the Burgrave von Rietenburg and by one among those ascribed to Dietmar von Aist, a lover's monologue in three long strophes, built on the Provençal tripartite pattern with division into *Stollen* and *Abgesang*. In its introspectiveness and in its preoccupation with abstract thoughts it comes nearer to the poetry of Friedrich von Hausen than to any other song associated with Dietmar. Entirely different, in its new modernity of thought and style, from everything else that name covers, it is placed, in C, quite unsuitably after the two most archaic of the Dietmar-songs : *ez stuont ein frouwe alleine* . . . and *sô wol dir, sumerwunne* . . .

It is not through oversight but with intention, that Kürenberg, the first of the early Minnesingers, is allowed to come last. For he is by far the most striking, and in many ways stands alone. First, with regard to metre. His long basic line is differently balanced from that of Dietmar and Meinloh. Instead of the two halves being equal, the second half is slightly less than the first, and this gives a stronger pause at the end ; whereas the full-length line is apt to run at a somewhat breath-taking speed. Even the eighth half-line of Kürenberg's strophe, which has four accents, not three, sounds very little longer than the others because of the suppression of the dip between the second accent and the third, *e.g., vil wól, des wǽr ích geméit* . . . *mir wárt nie wíp álso líep* . . . Then, as before mentioned, there is a characteristic distinction between the man's speech and the woman's in the first half of the strophe, the long line in one case ending with a masculine, in the other with a feminine rhyme. Not that the names signify, merely the fact that the single strong monosyllable conveys weight and decision, the disyllabic ending suspense and longing. There is an exception to this in the lines:

> Ich zôch mir einen valken      mêre danne ein jâr.
> dô ich in gezamete      als ich in wolte hân . . .

As this is a statement of fact without show of feeling, the strong ending is perfectly right. The tender mood is reserved for the second strophe :

> sît sach ich den valken      schône vliegen ;
> er fuorte an sînem fuoze      sîdîne riemen . . .

The songs of Kürenberg fall into two groups, according as the speaker is a man or a woman. Their chief point of interest is the clear-cut difference between the personalities of the man and of the woman, the former revealing himself as master of his fate, bold, resolute and self-assured, the latter entirely ruled by her heart's affection.

We can distinguish eleven songs, all brief. Three of these are

27

composed of two strophes each. One is a *wechsel*: the thoughts of the lovers here are in full accord. The second expresses, not harmony but a complete clash of views. The lady, standing on a battlement late at night, has heard a knight singing " in Kürenberges wîse ". She, not he, is the wooer. She gives him his choice : he must either quit her lands, or she will possess herself of him. His reply is evidently addressed to his squire, and it has a fine martial ring : " Nu brinc mir her vil balde mîn ros, mîn îsengewant ", " Now bring me hither quickly my horse, my armour ". For of the two alternatives offered him he prefers the second. Sooner will he quit this lady's lands than submit to her love for him. This knight is unquestionably heart-whole. Like the gay Gordon who, in a similar situation, made answer :

> " I thank ye, Lady Jeanie,
> But I'm promised awa'."

The third song is spoken by a woman. She tells of a falcon she had reared, and of how it flew away, and that later she saw it again flying in its beauty, its feathers decked as before with gold. The last line implies that all this has been spoken in parable. "God send them together, who would fain be joined in love", no more comment than that. It is the most arresting of Kürenberg's songs. The remaining eight are single strophes, each one complete in itself. Though they could be linked together, they stand best alone. Four, spoken by a woman, show her filled with love-longing. In two, it seems as though her love were unrequited or unknown; in two, as though spies and liars had come between her comrade and herself. The last four are spoken by a man, showing him as a lordly and an eager wooer. The concluding line is spoken by the poet in his own person : " When I think of this, my spirit rises high ".

The songs of Kürenberg are marvels of condensation: within the compass of the four-line strophe he instantaneously conjures up a self-contained picture. The meaning is given directly, with simple facts and simple expressions of feeling, and indirectly, by the use of symbols. The gold-adorned falcon soaring aloft and flying into other lands is an emblem of the truant lover. The dark star which hides itself prefigures a hidden subterfuge of love : the lady, when she sees her lover must appear as though she had not seen him. "Woman and falcon are easily made tame " : as the falcon comes to the man's lure, so does the woman. Fact and symbol unite where a woman, it may well be (as in the last song but one) a young girl, speaks of standing alone in her smock, and thinking to herself of a " noble knight ". The natural token of her privacy enhances the inward privacy of thoughts which cause her cheek to redden " als der rose an dorne tuot,"—as the rose does on the thorn.

The quality of Kürenberg is akin to that of the purest folk-song. Like this, his poetry is both tangibly immediate and hauntingly suggestive, and has a simple and compelling magic which it is folly to try and describe in words other than its own.

---

### DER VON KÜRENBERG

*Ich stuont mir nehint spâte     an einer zinnen . . .*

" I stood on a battlement     the late eve darkened.
To a knight sweetly singing     below I hearkened:
'Twas the tune of Kürenberg     rose amid the throng.
Either he must quit my lands     or else to me belong ! "

Now bring me hither quickly     my armour and my steed,
For I must quit the lands     of a lady with speed.
Fain would she compel me     her dear friend to be.
She must bear the loss for ever     of all love from me.

" When I am standing     in my smock alone,
And I think of thee,     noble man,
Then my colour flushes     as on thorn-spray the rose,
And many a sad longing,     deep within, my heart knows."

" I reared me a falcon     more than a year.
When I had tamed him,     and meant to have him near,
And had adorned his feathers     with gold bright and gay,
He soared aloft so proudly,     and flew far away.

" I saw the falcon later,     flying so rarely,
Silken cords he wore     became him fairly,
And his feathers were all     of a red-gold hue.
God send them together     who are dear friends and true ! "

" Tears come welling up     from my sad heart.
I and my comrade     were forced to part.
Liars the cause of that !     God give them bane !
O this were joy,     could we be reconciled again ! "

Beautiful woman, now come,    go with me !
Pleasure and pain,    I will share both with thee.
So long as I have life,    thou to me art full dear.
The ways of base lovers    thou hast no need to fear !

The star darkly gleaming    hides its dim light.
So do thou, fair lady,    when I stand in thy sight,
Then let thine eyes rest    upon some other man.
Then none shall guess easily    what we two there may plan.

She the charm of womankind    still goes a maid.
When to greet her from me    my messenger is sped,
Were it not to her peril,    I would after him go.
I know not how to please her,    I have never loved woman so.

Woman and falcon    are easily made tame.
Both will come flying    to a man's lure the same.—
Thus did a comely knight    woo a fair lady.
When I, too, think thereon,    my bold heart is ready.

---

## DIETMAR VON AIST

*Uf der linden obene    dâ sanc ein kleinez vogellîn . . .*

On the linden overhead    a bird was carolling its lay.
From the wood its music pealed,    whereat my heart was borne away
To seek a place where once it dwelled.    I saw the roses blooming where
They call into my mind the thoughts    that link me to a lady fair.

" Methinks a thousand years are fled    since in my lover's arms I lay.
Without or cause or fault of mine    he leaves me friendless many a day
Since the time when last I saw    the flowers and heard the sweet
                              birds' song,
Short, alas, my joy has been,    and my heart-sorrow all too long."

*Ez stuont ein frouwe alleine . . .*

A lady stood alone,
And looked out over the field,
And looked for her lover.
In the air above her
A falcon wheeled.

30

" Hail, falcon, it is well for thee !
Thou from a forest tree
Choosest what bough thou wilt
To be thy pleasure.
Thus have I also done :
I chose myself a man.
My eyes did measure
And single out his beauty.
Now fair ladies envy me that booty.
O why will they not leave my love to me ?
I never cared for love of theirs, but let them be."

" *Sô wol dir, sumerwunne* . . .

" Summer's joy, farewell !
Where the last leaf fell
From linden bough, the bird's song is mute.
Weeping has long subdued
My comely eyes.
My love, no other ties
Than mine should bind thee.
Other women, hero, shouldst thou flee.
When thou first sawest me,
Then didst thou find me,
In truth, fairest of all.
This, dear man, I pray thee to recall.

*Slâfest du, friedel ziere ?* . . .

" Sleepest thou, heart's dearest ?
Wake wilt thou when thou hearest
The little bird so dainty sweet
That on the linden bough has ta'en its seat."

" I slept, nor dreamed of waking.
Up, criest thou, Dawn is breaking !
Bliss without bale, this may not be.
Whatso thou biddest, that will I do, ladye."

She spake, and wept for sorrow.
" Thou goest : alas the morrow !
When wilt thou come to me again ?
My joy goes with thee ; I alone remain.

31

*Seneder friundinne bote, nu sage dem schœnen wîbe . . .*

" Messenger of my sorrowing friend, go to her now and say,
I am more grieved than words can tell for staying so long away.
Dearer to me her love's winning
Than when birds break forth a-singing !
Now she and I are torn apart :
Sadness thereof fills all my heart."

" Now tell the noble knight that he remain upon his guard,
And that I wish him to be gay, and not to grieve so hard.
I am much troubled for his sake :
Fear oft causes my heart to quake.
The cares I suffer are all too clear,
Which I would gladly pour into his ear."

---

## MEINLOH VON SEVELINGEN

*Ich sach boten des sumeres : daz wâren bluomen alsô rôt . . .*

I saw messengers of summer : they were blossoms red.
Knowest thou, fair lady, what for thee a knight said ?
Secretly, that he would serve thee : his desire is this.
Since last he parted from thee, a sorrowing heart is his.
Now raise and cheer his spirits as the summer draweth nigh.
He can feel no joy
Ere he is given leave within thy welcoming arms to lie.

# FRIEDRICH VON HAUSEN

THE courtly Minnesang begins in the Rhineland with Friedrich von Hausen (Friderich von Hûsen). Documentary evidence has in his case proved unusually fruitful. The salient facts about him have been set down, and when put together yield a slight but clear biographical sketch of one who, incidentally a poet, stands out in contemporary record as a capable and upright man of action. The son of a Rhenish nobleman, Walther von Hausen, whose name appears side by side with his own in a document of Archbishop Christian of Mayence dated 1171 (*Waltherus de Husa et Fredericus filius suus*), he occupied a position of some distinction as *Reichsministeriale* under the Hohenstaufen Emperor Frederick I, was in Italy during the regency of Archbishop Christian in 1175 and again during that of the young king Henry VI in 1186-7, and accompanied the Emperor on a diplomatic visit to Philip Augustus of France in December 1187. A year later we find him acting as escort to an embassy of the Count of Hennegau on its return home, then accompanying the Count to Worms to be invested with the marquisate of Namur. The Third Crusade, which he joined under the leadership of Barbarossa, occupying in fact a special place as one of *ipsius imperatoris familiares et secretarii* brought his life to a close. He was killed by a fall from his horse in a skirmish with the Turks near Philomelium in Syria on the 6th of May, 1190. The accounts of his death are filled with a sense of overwhelming loss : in one it is said how at the news of his fall the din of battle changed to a sound of weeping. *Miles strenuus et famosus . . . egregius miles . . . vir probus et nobilis* are the terms used in speaking of him after death.

The illustrated MSS. B and C represent him fitly in his character of Crusader, sailing in a boat with two masts over a billowy tract of sea.

Poetry was in his case a recreation. Both he and the other poets of the same local group are to be classed as knightly amateurs. Another kind of literary fame attaches itself to the person of his father, " von Hûsen Walther ", who is mentioned by the gleeman Herger among patrons remembered for their bounty towards the wandering professional folk or *varnde diet.*

The simple and homely art which the father enjoyed has no connection with the new and exotic art cultivated by the son. Provençal influence is dominant here both in technique and in the general outlook and ideas. The former shows a complete break with the looser and simpler measures of the older or at least more

33

conservative Minnesingers of the south-east. There is a greater variety of metrical pattern and rhyme-scheme ; the theme, instead of being confined to one or at most two stanzas, is continued for two stanzas or more ; the syllabic regularity of the verse shows a closer dependence on the music ; and the form of the strophe shows the Provençal model, with division into *stollen* and *abgesang*. The rhyme-technique, however, is still imperfect : there is a fair proportion of assonances together with pure rhymes.

The poetry of Friedrich von Hausen is, in conformity with its models, highly introspective, presenting the ideal type of melancholy lover loyally bound to the service of an ideally gracious and beautiful lady, whose affection he has small hope of winning. To this the record of his own fine, vigorous life serves mainly as a foil. Yet while his themes and the lines on which he treats them, together with his metrical patterns, are largely predetermined, there is character in his rhythm and tone. His poems, most of them at first sight abstract and formal, leave a deepening impression of clarity and concision, of austere and dignified reserve lit up by occasional flashes of manly spirit, which all seems perfectly in keeping with the type of the *vir probus et nobilis* who left a good name behind him.

There are, further, a few points of topical interest, not many,—even the Crusading songs show little of their actual background—but wherever they do occur, a sudden fresh tang of spontaneity invades the context with them. As, for instance, when he speaks of the distance between him and his mistress, an obvious thought, but in his case true to fact, or, in lines that sound vividly reminiscent of a fragment of real conversation, makes the lady remark that, if his be the part of Eneas, she will not for his sake copy Dido. More tangibly personal than this is the poet's reference to having left his native Rhineland when he crossed the mountains : that must have been when he was in Italy. This short song of experience is very attractive in the unadorned plainness of its clear-cut, matter-of-fact statements. Other slight traces of environment may be sensed in the declaration that " if he who is in all lands emperor kissed her sometime on her red mouth, he would say he had had good fortune ", or in the Crusader's assertion that if anyone could have the right to remain behind on grounds of love, *he* would still be about the Rhine, " al umbe den Rîn ".

Generally speaking, however, the ideals are too conventional to admit of personal interpretation, too lacking in concrete imagery to arrest one's fancy. Only two songs stand apart from the rest, and like those of the older Minnesingers call up definite pictures. One is a brief description of a lover's dream, metrically simple and vividly direct in style (MF. 48, $_{23}$). The other is a *wechsel*, and contains an energetic and spirited attack on the part of both lovers on their enemies the *merkære*. There is a touch of local colour here where the lady declares, that they might sooner turn the Rhine's course into the Po than that she would solace herself for the loss of him who served her so truly. This vehemence is a refreshing change from the more usual cold aloofness. The lady is generally pictured as utterly remote from her true lover, whose attitude is marked by unswerving constancy—*stæte*—whether he continues to hope for ultimate grace, or resigns himself to service without guerdon. Nor does he blame her for her indifference to him. Either he reproaches himself for having looked too high, or vents his feelings on personified Love.

> Wâfenâ wie hât mich Minne gelâzen !

Out and alas, how Love has forsaken me !

> Minne, got müeze mich an dir rechen !

Love, may God avenge me on thee !

The circumstances are such as to produce an entirely new point of view with regard to the *merkære*. These can have no part in a relationship so one-sided : here is a lover who would gladly change places with those they make suffer, sooner than feel that his lady's indifference is all his woe. " Envy of her love would please me better than to lack both love and envy."

The comparative bareness of the poet's style is redeemed by its intellectual clarity and by its freshness. Its most distinctive feature is a fondness for antitheses. Friedrich von Hausen loves to play with two opposite concepts, and has a gift for terse epigrammatic phrases which, if it does not entirely relieve the monotony of his austere statements, provides a number of arresting and memorable points.

The poem beginning

> Si darf mich des zîhen niet . . . (MF. 45, 37)

strikes a deeper note than any that have gone before, and is none the less structurally perfect because its first strophe is copied from a song by the Troubadour Foulques of Marseilles. Theme and metrical form are alike borrowed, but with a disarming grace which gives new reality to the rôle of the absent-minded lover, so distraught that he says Good-morning when it is night, so lost in thoughts of his mistress that when spoken to he returns no answer. The rendering is perfect in its effortless candour. What matters, however, is not this borrowed opening but that its light theme is prelude to one of greater weight. The four following stanzas, in which the same metre is used with an effect of grave reasoning, turns on the final

35

rejection of unsatisfied earthly love for the higher claim of God's service. The Crusader's problem, how to reconcile these conflicting claims, was already one of the themes of Provençal lyricists : it is none the less true that Friedrich von Hausen relived it. The authentic ring of personal feeling here does intimate the sacrifice of a real affection for a real person, however stylised this had been. " I was subject to a lady, who took my service and gave no reward. Of her I say nothing but good, save that her will towards me has been too ungenerous. I thought I should be free of all ill when my heart looked to her for favour, which alas I have never found. Now I will serve Him who can and does reward."

There is no deviation here from the correct standard of lover's courtesy. The change of will is effected without revulsion. If the tradition behind the MSS. is right, however, this was not the last word. A stronger, more individual note of revolt is heard in another song, so exceptionally frank that doubts are felt whether von Hausen were indeed the author. It consists of a single stanza of eight lines and begins :

> Niemen darf mir wenden daz zunstæte
> ob ich die hazze die ich minnete ê.

No one need blame me for inconstancy, if I hate her whom formerly I loved.

In the last two lines the lady is roundly accused of *tumpheit*, silliness ; a social defect more damaging to her good report than if he had called her selfish or fickle.

This is quite unlike Friedrich von Hausen, and the stanza may well be that of a later poet. If so, it could easily have slipped in among the authentic songs. The metre is that of the characteristic poem on the separation of heart and body (MF. 47 9) ; this has three stanzas, and the song of revolt comes just after the second, whence the editors have rightly transferred it to a place by itself. The criteria seem to me indecisive, and I prefer to leave it an open question whether Friedrich von Hausen did just once break free of the Amor Cortois, or maintained to the last his discreet rule concerning his lady : " Von der spriche ich niht wan allez guot "—" Of her I say nothing that is not good ".

His Crusading songs are the first we meet with in the German Minnesang. Here as elsewhere he followed Romance models. In particular, his song on the separation between heart and body—the body is eager to set forth and fight the Paynim, the heart is in a woman's keeping at home—is modelled on a similar song by the Canon de Béthune. All the same, it is very typical of von Hausen himself : the paradoxical subject is of the kind he loved to debate and analyse. Another song deals with the conflict between love for one's lady and love of God—*frouwen minne* and *gotes minne*—and resolves the debate by showing that it is to the woman's honour for the man to choose God's service. A third, actually in position the second of these three songs, deals with the purely religious aspect. " Si welnt dem tôde entrunnen sîn " . . . " They think they have escaped death who make lying excuses to God for shirking His summons " . . .

The Crusading songs of Friedrich von Hausen have a special interest, because we know definitely what part he took as a Crusader, and that he died a soldier's death.

*In mînem troume ich sach*
*ein harte schœne wîp* . . .

In my dream I saw a woman
Fair to gaze upon,
All night long till daybreak ;
When I woke, she was gone.
Where she is now, alas,
I have no means of knowing.
That joy came not to pass
Which she was showing.
My eyes did that to me :
'Twere best, if I could not see !

*Gelebt ich noch die lieben zît*
*daz ich daz lant solt aber schouwen* . . .

If I might live to see the day
When I could greet that land so fair,
Which harbours all I know of joy
Because my lady dwelleth there,
Then no tear should vex my eye,
No man or woman hear me sigh
Or utter words of care.
Many a thing my mind would please
That used to be my mind's disease.

I fancied we were far apart
Where I should now feel very near.
In a strange land, my constant heart
Knows grief that makes old hardships dear.

37

Were I somewhere near the Rhine,
I'd hear the news for which I pine
Since I am planted here,
Shut off beyond the mountain screen
That stretches ruthlessly between.

*Ich muoz von schulden sîn unfrô . . .*

To be displeased I have some cause,
Since she declared last time we were
Together, if I thought I was
Eneas, I must not infer
She would for me act Dido's woe.
Why tell me so ?
Though she be far removed from me,
All women else have not the power
To rob me of my heart, save she.

With thoughts I strive to while away
The time as well as I know how,
And learn, what in a happier day
I knew not, free of it till now,
How grief and care oppress the mind.
All womankind
Could not have driven me, I swear,
To such hard straits as she alone
Has forced me for her sake to bear.

My heart is hers, a secret cell,
Where while I live she fills the place.
All womankind, save she, might dwell
Unnoticed in that narrow space,
Though never a thought she gives to me.
Now let us see
If constancy may yet avail.
Her goodness is the reason why
My faithfulness can never fail.

# HEINRICH VON VELDEKE

THE songs which appear in the MSS. under the name of Heinrich von Veldeke have a unique place in the history of the Minnesang. Representing as they do the poetic tradition of a particular region, that of the Netherlands, they appear uninfluenced by the melancholy tone of the Provençal *Canzone*. The lover's homage, where present, is not excessive ; in contrast to the sophisticated mode of the Amor Cortois the relation between the sexes is seen from a refreshingly robust and cheerful point of view. The prevailing spirit is that of the mating season with Nature in full play.

Heinrich von Veldeke, a native of the province of Limburg, is chiefly famed for his *Eneide*, expressly recognised by Gottfried von Strassburg as starting-point for the chivalric romance in the German tongue. In this, as in its source and model, the French *Roman d'Eneas*, the subject-matter of the Virgillian epic is re-clothed in the fashions and trappings of the contemporary scene. The work was completed under the distinguished patronage of Landgrave Hermann of Thuringia, a circumstance which no doubt served to further the poet's fame.

There is much to be said for the view of Edvard Sievers that the songs grouped together under the name of Veldeke were in reality the combined product of poets belonging to the same Low German region, among whom Veldeke was one. Be that as it may, the songs thus represented certainly have a regional rather than a personal value. What they plainly reveal is a distinct and separate tradition of bracing quality. Their watchword is *blidscap* : joy. They are marked by good sense and gaiety and contain delightful descriptions of Nature in the spring of the year when the flowers are springing up, the trees, beeches and limes, bursting into leaf, the birds singing. It is noteworthy that in accordance with the milder clime of a seaboard region, the new season begins not, as with poets dwelling further inland, in the month of May, but earlier, in the month of April. So also with the English Chaucer. One may fitly compare the lines beginning

> In dem aberellen so die bloemen springen . . .

with the opening of the *Canterbury Tales:*

> Whan that Aprille with his shoures sote
> The droghte of Marche hath perced to the rote . . .

To the feeling so ardently expressed for the beauty and bliss of Nature are added occasional light touches of satirical humour. Thus she who prefers crude youth to mature old age is reprimanded for her folly in valuing new tin more highly than old gold.

Fresh and lively as they are, these songs are in no way naive, and their verse-technique is more advanced than that of Friedrich von Hausen. But the first and last to be said of these northern songs is that they give great pleasure.

# HEINRICH VON MORUNGEN

Turning to Heinrich von Morungen, in whose fiery lyricism the courtly Minnesang attains its apex, we feel, on comparing him with Friedrich von Hausen, the impact of a personality far more brilliant and vital. Few facts of his life are known ; but recent research has added sufficient new data to give the record, so far as we know it, coherence and character.

His early life still remains obscure. He probably came from Thuringia. In that case, some foreign travel must be assumed, to account for his excellent schooling in the art of the Troubadours. The documentary evidence belongs to his later years, not to his heyday as Minnesinger. What there is connects him with Margrave Dietrich von Meissen, of whose household he was a member, and with the church and convent of St. Thomas in Leipzig where, according to subsequent tradition, he died and was buried. A legend attached to his person has come down to us in the sixteenth century ballad of *Der Edel Möringer*, representing him as a votary of St. Thomas and as going on pilgrimage to " St. Thomas' land ". All this is established ground. To the scholarly research of H. Menhardt we now owe the addition that Heinrich von Morungen entered the convent of St. Thomas in 1217, died there in 1222, and, a point of prime interest, had at some time visited India. *Heynricus de Morungen obiit XIIcXXII anno qui visitavit Indiam.*[6] So the legend of his pilgrimage to the land of St. Thomas was founded on fact. The record, of which no earlier text is extant than the two sixteenth century copies which have been found, has by circumstantial evidence been proved reliable. The initial occasion, too, can be supplied. It is known that Dietrich von Meissen took part in the Crusade of 1197, but returned on hearing of the Emperor's death : the inference is that Heinrich von Morungen went with him, stayed out longer and pushed his experience further. He may not have travelled as far as what we call India : the region described by that name was of vague dimensions, and the land of St. Thomas might equally well have meant Persia. India or Persia, the journey in either case was beyond the common. Its interest is that of something unexpected which, after the first surprise, strikes one as singularly fitting. It is good to think of this high-spirited poet as a Crusader and as a traveller to distant lands.

The pilgrimage, as Menhardt has shown, gives a fresh value to

[6] H. Menhardt : *Zur Lebensbeschreibung Heinrichs von Morungen* (Zeitschrift für deutsches Altertum, 1933).

other recorded points. It may well be that Morungen brought back with him from the East relics of St. Thomas. That would explain the founding by Margrave Dietrich of a convent and church of St. Thomas in Leipzig some years later (in 1212) and the fact of Morungen's choosing to end his days there. Further, a sign of Oriental influence is seen in the poet's device, represented in C as four silver half-moons on a field of azure with two golden stars, in the *Wappenbuch* of Konrad Grunenberg as a golden half-moon on a field of azure surrounded by four golden stars, likewise in the simpler device worn by later generations of the family, a star and a half-moon.

The seat of the Herren von Morungen, mentioned in records from the fourteenth to the beginning of the eighteenth century when the family died out, lay south of the Harz Mountains, near Sangerhausen. Of the poet's twelfth century antecedents nothing is known.[7] Of his status all we can say is that he was a noble knight—in one document he is termed *miles emeritus*—and, on the evidence of his art, an accomplished courtier.

In his poetry are the usual ideal types, the faithful lover and his beautiful, proud mistress, but gloriously alive and seen through the medium of an enchanting variety of moods. A singer so passionate, so illuminating and thrilling must, we think, have been at some time of his life a passionate and desirous lover. Yet of personal experience his poetry shows no trace. All that has been transmuted : it has, without ceasing to exist as a hidden force, been completely subdued to the alchemy of a flaming and palpitating vision, expressed with all the resources of a marvellously fine technique.

In the treatment of the courtly love-lyric, it has, I think, been sometimes implied that the choice lies between a remote and artificial convention and the reflex of personal experience. There remains as third element that visionary conception of love which, whether it receives its main impulse from inherited tradition or new experience, is an inspirational force transcending both. It is the same with the love-song of all ages : experience, vision, convention all meet and join. From these three elements the intricate tripartite texture of love-poetry is invariably woven, with so magical a mingling of threads that the vision conceived in the poet's own mind is hardly to be distinguished from the stimulus of a potent and rich tradition. This is most obviously true of the courtly love-lyric, with its fascinating network of conventional ideas, of fashions in form and style. But it is also true of the more primitive love-song, the difference being that here the convention is simpler, the imagination is focussed on

[7] Menhardt's speculations on this are interesting, but require more support than the single fact on which he attempts to base them.

facts of elemental reality, and so the question of poetic artifice does not arise.

Mystery remains, in whatever order the elements occur. The vision, time-sanctified and strengthened by tradition, may precede the experience, transcend and survive it. That is probably so with Heinrich von Morungen, it is demonstrably true of Dante and Petrarch. Or the experience itself, mated with some peculiar tendency of the poet's mind, may generate a new kind of vision, a new convention, as, to take a quite modern instance, in the bitter-sweet fantasy of dream and disillusionment created by Heine. The proportions, too, vary. There may be an excess of convention and of convention-bred artifice : the result is a masquerade. Or the experience may be strong enough to show itself undisguised : then the love-poem becomes a confession. Or the vision, prevailing, with imaginative force works out a revelation.

The inspiration of Heinrich von Morungen's poetry is no less sincere because it expresses, with a strength and beauty in which he has no near rival, the ideal of the Amor Cortois. The technique of his verse is flexible and varied. No other Minnesinger equals him in his gift for so moulding the metrical form that it draws out the very heart of the song and expresses its mood with infallible rightness. From the rhythm and phrasing one can tell at a flash whether the mood is melancholy and earnest, or flown with ecstasy, lightly whimsical or boldly and sportively ironical or manfully defiant. Nor is there any other who reveals so many clear-cut moods and presents so many aspects of the Amor Cortois. What Reinmar der Videler said (mockingly) of his rival Liutolt von Sevene might, very nearly at least, be said of Morungen :

> Tageliet klageliet hügeliet zügeliet tanzliet leich er kan,
> er singet kriuzliet twingliet schimpfliet lobeliet rüegliet . . .

*Kriuzliet* (Crusading song) and *leich* are certainly missing. But the *hügeliet* or song of joy, so much rarer than the *klageliet* or lament, is represented with dazzling spontaneity in the lyrical effusion : " In so hôher swebender wunne Sô gestuont mîn herze an froiden nie " . . . (MF. 125, $_{19}$ . . .)—" My heart was never so lifted up in joy, in delight so high and buoyant ". The *lobeliet* or song of praise, for which his favourite choice is a flowing dactylic rhythm broken, to check its mellifluence, near the end of the strophe by one or two short iambic lines, this, represented by MF. 122, $_1$—123, $_8$, 133, $_{13}$ —134, $_5$, and 140, $_{32}$—141, $_{14}$, reaches its highest point in the melodious hyperbole of

> Diu mînes herzen ein minne und ein krône ist

vor allen frouwen die ich hân gesehen,
schône unde schône unde schône, aller schônist
ist sie mîn frouwe ; des muoz ich ir jehen.

She who is my heart's delight and crown beyond all ladies whom I have seen,
fair and fair and fair again, fairest of all is she, my lady : this must I say of her.

The *klageliet* shows gradations of light and shade which evoke a
far stronger pathos than the pale clear monotone of Friedrich von
Hausen. The *tanzliet* or dancing song is represented by a little poem
of three stanzas, each one a separate vignette : " Ich hôrte ûf der
heide Lûte stimme und süezen sanc " . . . (MF. 139, 19 . . .)—" I
heard in the field clear voice and sweet singing . . ." *Klageliet* and
*tageliet* are merged together in that singularly beautiful poem where
the lovers, looking back, recall the night they spent in each other's
arms and the dawn which parted them : " Owê sol aber mir iemer
mê " . . . (MF. 143, 21 . . .)—"Alas, shall I ever again . . ." This
is cast in the form of a *wechsel*: the lovers speak in alternate strophes,
always with the same opening word *owê*, and the same bleak-sounding
refrain *dô tagete ez*—then day broke—with its recurring effect of
sudden cold, changing the beauty of the night to a lost dream. Of
the *rüegliet* or taunting song there is one clear example, the swift-
spoken, angry and arrogant declaration of war : " Ich wil eine reise,
Wünschet daz ich wol gevar " . . . (MF. 145, 33 . . .)—" I am going
on a foray, wish me good luck ! . . ." where rhyme and phrasing sug-
gest, at the same time, the tone of the *zügeliet* or marching song.[8]

Of the poet's *flair* for the right kind of metre, which is something
far easier to feel than to describe, two examples may—and must—
suffice. First, the strophe in which he tells of his lady's power to
pass into his heart through his eyes.

Wiste ich ob ez mohte wol verswigen sîn,
ich lieze iuch sehen      mîne lieben frouwen.
der enzwei gebræche mir daz herze mîn,
der mohte sie      schône drinne schouwen.
si kam her      dur diu ganzen ougen      sunder tür gegangen.
owê solte ich von ir reinen minnen sîn      alsô werdeclîche
                                        enpfangen ! (MF. 127, 1 . . .).

If I knew whether it really could be kept secret, I would let you see my dear
lady. Whoever broke my heart in two might gaze on her within there in her beauty.
She came hither through the eyes which did not break, without a door. O if
only *I* could be as nobly welcomed by her pure love !

In the *stollen* a smooth-running, long-breathed line alternates
with one in which the sense is abruptly checked by an arbitrary pause;

[8] The terms *twingliet* and *schimpfliet* may be regarded as synonymous with *rüegliet*.

and this device is continued with heightened effect in the *abgesang*, where the first line is broken short at three points, and the second begins with a long continuous sweep which dominates the ensuing pause for breath and carries the sense to a triumphal close. The contrast between the two types of line, between the liberal sweep of the one and the springing gait of the other, gives the impression of a lively and impetuous mood in which exultation and humorous insight combine. The extent to which the mood is involved in the metre can be gauged by comparison with a song of Reinmar's, where the same theme is treated with all due seriousness, and with a stately-moving grace which befits its grave mood. As thus—

> Sie gie mir alse sanfte dur mîn ougen
> daz sie sich in der enge niene stiez.
> in mînem herzen si sich nider liez.
> dâ trage ich noch die werden inne tougen. (MF. 194, 22 . . .).

The difference between this deliberate grace and the exhilirating ring of

> si kam her      dur diu ganzen ougen      sunder tür gegangen.
> owê solte ich von ir reinen minnen sîn      alsô werdeclîche
>                                                                enpfangen

needs no further comment.

This song of Reinmar's—incidentally one of great beauty—has as it happens almost the same metre as a *klageliet* by Heinrich von Morungen: "Owê war umbe volge ich tumbem wâne" . . . (MF. 136, 1 . . .)—"Alas, why do I follow a foolish dream . . . Both songs are composed with the same regular iambic rhythm and in strophes of the same dimension. But while Reinmar's song is a plaint in a minor key, that of Heinrich von Morungen is charged with desperate yearning, and inasmuch as the mood is stronger and more passionate, he introduces into the regular strophic form (as shown by Reinmar) a single effortless yet wholly expressive variation which alters the effect. For while Reinmar's quatrain is perfectly regular with five accents in every line, Heinrich von Morungen in his lengthens the fifth line, the first of the *abgesang*, by just one bar, giving it six accents instead of five, and this prolongation draws out and intensifies the sound of yearning as in a long-flung wave :

> Doch wart ir varwe liljen wîz und rôsen rôt . . .
> alswîgende ie genôte und ein verholner wân . . .
> wie ich si minne und wie ich ir holdez herze trage . . .

The difference between the two metrical forms can be best judged if to illustrate it the opening strophes of both songs are compared directly :

45

*Reinmar:*

Mîn ougen wurden liebes alse vol
dô ich die minneclîchen êrst gesach
daz ez mir hiute und iemer mê tuot wol.
ein minneclîchez wunder dô geschach :
si gie mir alse sanfte dur mîn ougen
daz si sich in der enge niene stiez.
in mînem herzen si sich nider liez :
dâ trage ich noch die werden inne tougen.[9]

*Heinrich von Morungen:*

Owê war umbe volge ich tumbem wâne,
der mich so sêre leitet in die nôt ?
ich schiet von ir gar aller fröiden âne,
daz si mir trost noch helfe nie gebôt.
doch wart ir varwe liljen wîz und rôsen rôt,
und saz vor mir diu liebe wolgetâne
gebluhet rehte alsam ein voller mâne.
daz was der ougen wunne, des herzen tôt.[10]

Not, of course, that the metre alone makes the effect, rather, the combined strength of metre and phrasing.

It will be seen that the rhymes are arranged in the same way. But now it is Heinrich von Morungen who chooses the more uniform pattern *ababbaab*, in contrast to Reinmar's varying rhyme-sequence *ababcddc*. For it is a feature of Morungen's technique, a sign of Provençal influence not found with Reinmar, to make use throughout the strophe of the same pair of rhymes. What matters more is that, in this particular song, the rhymes bring out with increasing pathos the tone of the lament and by their fourfold occurrence haunt and enthrall the ear. Thus in the first strophe the feminine rhymes *wâne . . . âne . . . getâne . . . mâne*, with their long open vowel-sound and liquid ending, enhance the sense given of infinite longing, an effect continued by the corresponding rhymes of the other two strophes, *winde . . . kinde . . . underwinde . . . vinde, gesungen . . . betwungen . . . gelungen . . . gerungen*, with a lovely deepening of tone in the *rime riche* of *underwinde . . . wunder vinde*; while in the first

[9] My eyes were so filled with pleasure when I saw the lovely one for the first time, that it gladdens me to-day and always. A lovely marvel then befell. She passed so gently through my eyes that she received no knock in that narrow space. In my heart she settled down : there within I still harbour the noble one in secret.

[10] Alas, why do I follow a foolish dream which leads me into hard straits by a path so painful ? I parted from her quite deprived of joy, since she never offered me help or promise. Yet was her complexion lily-white and rose-red, and before me sat the dear and beauteous one radiant as a full moon. That was the eye's delight, death to the heart.

strophe the alternative masculine rhymes *nôt . . . gebôt . . . rôt . . . tôt,* heavy-weight syllables, convey the dead halt of frustrated hope.

This superb lament, the creation of one who could with equal power express the joy of requited, the sorrow of unrequited love, is, I cannot but think, the highest point reached in the development of that much cultivated, much abused genre of the courtly Minnesang, the lover's complaint.

Hyperbole is as native to the style of Heinrich von Morungen as antithesis is to that of Friedrich von Hausen. Hence his delight in radiant imagery, in all that suggests brightness and swift movement and height. Again and again he sees his lady as the sun and in the light of all seasons, sunrise and sunset, the glorious hour of noon and the clear-shining month of May. Or he compares her with the full moon for brightness, or, again, calls her his " ôsterlîcher tac," his Easter Day. Finally she appears to him as " ein wunnebernder süezer meie, ein wolkenlôser sunnen schîn,"—" a sweet, joy-bringing month of May, a cloudless sunshine ". His feelings of ecstasy towards her find vent in daring and fantastic statements which are yet fired through with a white-heat of reality. He would not take a kingdom if he had to choose between that and her love ! When she looked at him so kindly with her sparkling eyes, and sent him a secret smile from her red mouth, then his spirit rose high as the sun. When he is alone, she appears before his eyes as clearly as though she had come right through the walls to him ; when she will, she can with her white hand lead him high above the battlements. And when, as he relates, she actually sent for him to meet her alone, on a battlement, his eyes were so dazzled by the glory of that moment that he thought all the lands had burst into sudden flame.

The same wild vein of extravagant fancy comes into play when the lady is envisaged as hostile. Then she is a robberess, *eine rouberin,* who by the invincible power of her beauty and excellence will in the end lay waste all lands. No one can look on her but he becomes her captive and must live in grief for evermore. As for *him,* without declaration of war she has never ceased to do him injury. Though he was her bondman and her servant, this did not save him from being attacked and wounded to the heart. Her bright eyes robbed him, and her rose-red mouth. Another song contains a piquant variation of that last image. " I am sick, my heart is wounded. Lady, my eyes did that to me, and your red mouth." The *rüegliet* already mentioned is a song of the lover's vengeance, in which he pays the lady back in her own coin. " I am going on a foray, wish me good luck ! That will make many an orphan. I will burn up the lands. Wherever I cross my lady's realm, all that must be lost, unless she turn away my anger. Help me to sing, all of you, my

47

friends, and go to meet her with loud noise, so that she be forced to do me grace. Cry so that my pain break my lady's heart and pass into her ear. She tortures me too long."

All this is conceived in an atmosphere of high-wrought fantasy. But there are also touches of a more objective reality, little sketches from life, as when the lady is pictured standing at her casement,— true, fantasy here supervenes, the glory of her appearance is like the sun !—or in simpler actuality, as caring for her pet bird and training it to speak. "She has a little bird she loves, that can sing, and speak a little after her." And her lover envies the bird that familiar place : if it were his, then would he sing to her as not even the nightingale had sung before. Most concrete of all is the little pastoral of three stanzas depicting three small but vivid and near situations. " I heard out in the field," says the lover, " clear voice and sweet singing." And he found his beloved dancing as she sang, whereat he himself leaped for joy. Then he came on her alone, her cheek wet with tears, one morning when she had presumed to wish him dead ; and her anger and sorrow on his account gladden him more than when she had sat aloof. And once more he found her alone, when she sent for him to meet her on a battlement, and the joy of the moment which gave him leave at last to take a pledge of her dazzled and over-powered him ; and here the reality passes into sudden mad fantasy, as he sees all the lands on fire. The joy of requited love soars to its utmost height here and in the earlier *hügeliet* where all nature is seen rejoicing in unison with the lover's supreme hour of bliss.

> luft und erde, walt und ouwe
> suln die zît der fröide mîn enpfân.

Air and earth, wood and meadow shall welcome the season of my joy.

There is evidence in the songs of Heinrich von Morungen that, like Reinmar, he probably held the position of court poet, in contrast to knightly amateurs like Friedrich von Hausen. Like Reinmar and, after him, like Walther he sometimes addresses his audience by way of prelude to the song in his lady's honour. So, for instance, he once enters into a debate on whether to sing or to remain silent. If he is silent, he will be told he ought to sing. If he sings, he exposes himself to mockery and malice. He admits to having let that weigh with him, and regrets that he ever succumbed to his detractors, and because of them ceased singing. Now he will refrain no longer. And the song is one of lament, but unexpectedly, disarmingly, not for failure to win his lady's love, but for the bright delightful days he has wasted in fruitless mourning, for all the lost years that cannot be retrieved :

Owê mîner besten zît,
und owê mîner liehten wunneclîchen tage,
waz der an ir dienste lît !

Alas for my best time of life, and alas for my bright, delightful days, how many of them have I spent in her service !

There is a similar prelude to the song of praise beginning : " Diu mînes herzen ein wunne und ein krône ist ". This time the poet has been criticised on the ground that if he were really sad at heart with love-longing he could not sing so gaily : his sorrow must be fictitious !

Manger der sprichet : nu seht, wie der singet !
wære im iht leit, er tæte anders danne sô.

Many a one says : " Now look how he is singing. If he were in trouble, he would not do so."

But he does not care what they say : they are incapable of judging him, who was *born to sing*.

The situation visualised is that of the singer standing before his lady pouring out his love to her in songs which she accepts as mere compliment or entertainment. This gives a *double entendre* to lines like " klagete ich ir mîn jâmer, sô stuont ir daz herze hô,"—" If I lamented my grief to her, her spirits rose high,"—which on the surface implies heartless cruelty, but really means that she receives his lament impersonally and as a manifestation of his art to charm. Again when he mourns that " she never will believe what I say, how I love her and how my heart is at her service," the reference is to his self-discovering song. For she is so high above him and so far removed that there is no more contact between them on her side than the greeting he has to share with one and all. Yet he has " loved her from a child," and so the picture includes a tender retrospect of days when she was nearer to him and when she, who is now his noonday sun, was his bright morning star.

The vision of courtly love which unfolds itself in the songs of Heinrich von Morungen—only the *tageliet* falls outside its range—attains its most spiritual phase, first, where he thinks that Love " who gives the world increase of joy " brought him his lady in a dream and he gazed his fill on her beauty, seeing her as one exalted beyond all other women save that her winsome mouth was " ein lützel versêret,"—a little bit saddened ; and secondly, where, like Dante, he transports his love to the life beyond. " Sweet gentle slayeress, why will you slay my body, when I love you so deeply, in sooth, lady, before all other women ? Do you think that if you kill me I shall then nevermore behold you ? No, love of you has conquered me so fully that your soul is the mistress of my soul."

49

*Sach ieman die frouwen*
*die man mac schouwen*
*in dem venster stân ? . . .*

Has anyone seen her
With royal demeanour
Stand at her casement ?
The fair one bereaves me
Of care now, and leaves me
Too blithe for abasement.
She shines as the sun when
He hails the bright morrow.
While she was hidden, then
Needs must I sorrow.
Now I am glad again.

Is some one within, pray,
Whose wits have power to stay
His staggering sense ?
Let him go seek me now
Her of the crown-lit brow
Who is gone from hence,
That she come and comfort me
Ere I depart.
Love and love's cruelty
Break my poor heart,
Dig a swift grave for me.

Let this be written small
After my funeral
Upon a stone
How dear she was to me,
And what slight care had she
To think thereon.
Then may the passer-by
Mark my sad end,
And that great wrong descry
Which doomed her friend,
Stricken by her, to die.

*Ez tuot vil wê, swer herzeclîche minnet*
*an sô hôhe stat, dâ sîn dienest gar versmât . . .*

Deeply he grieves, who has set his heart's affection
On one so high above him that his service weigheth nought.
His foolish dream has taken a wrong direction
Where no complaint of his can stir an answering thought.
He is a wise man who with sure election
Serves where the worth of his service can be savoured,
And turns to one by whom his suit is favoured.

I have great need of favour, could I find it,
For the woman of my choosing is throned above the sun,
My pain incurable so she be not minded
To look on me again, as she of old has done.
She has been dear to me from earliest childhood ;
For her sake only did I first draw breath.
If she be angered, God knows, this is death !

Whither is it vanished, my bright star of morning ?
Alas, what could I hope for since my glorious sun uprose ?
She is too far above me, too regal in her scorning,
And long hours must pass before the sunset close.
Fain would I live to see the sweet approach of evening,
When she would descend to solace me again,
For I have gazed myself half blind in vain.


*Diu vil guote, daz si sælic müeze sîn . . .*

The fair and gracious one, blessed be she !
Ill thrive the watchers, by whose jealousy
Her light is hidden from the world, and so
We must content us with the afterglow !

I grieve until the long night pass away
When I shall see her rising with the day,
The lovely sun that shines so joyously
I cannot brook a cloud 'twixt her and me.

Cursed be they who guard her out of sight
Whom God created for the world's delight,
Nor aught forbade her beauty to behold !
What is the use to us of buried gold ?

*Owê, sol aber mir iemer mê*
*geliuhten dur die naht . . .*

Alas ! shall ever I see again,
Gleaming athwart the night,
Whiter than driven snow,
Her body bright ?
Thus were my eyes deceived,
For I believed
It was the moon's clear ray
That shone.
Suddenly day
Broke, and the night was gone.

" Alas ! and will he ever again
Be here when the dawn turns grey,
So that we need not rue
The approach of day—
As when he made lament
The last night he spent
Lying by the side of me.
Anon
Day suddenly
Broke, and the night was gone."

Alas ! she kissed me in my sleep
Times beyond all telling.
Her cheek was wet with tears
From her eyes welling.
Gently I bade her cease,
And she, at peace,
Her arms about me, lay
Held fast.
Suddenly day
Broke, and the night was past.

" Alas ! how often has he stayed
His wondering gaze on me !
My white arms he unbared
So lovingly.
It was a deep surprise
That his rapt eyes
He could not draw away.
At last,
Too soon, the day
Broke, and the night was past.

52

# ALBRECHT VON JOHANSDORF

The Bavarian poet Albrecht von Johansdorf has a quality of his own, so honest and so lovable that we could not afford to miss him. To the freshness and charm of his style is added the quiet thrill of being able to perceive, without error, the impress of a fragment of factual truth.  His more individual poems, a precious few, are undoubtedly songs of experience : one cannot read them with an open ear and fail to know this.  Except for Walther von der Vogelweide, no Minnesinger has left a confession so candid as Albrecht von Johansdorf in the four Crusading songs which bring out the earnestness of his religious purpose and the equal earnestness of his loyal and sensitive love.  There is no external evidence here, as in the case of Friedrich von Hausen, not even a sure clue to the Crusade in which von Johansdorf took part.  Possibly that of 1197 : opinions vary.  The documents containing his name yield only the bare fact that he was a ministerialis of Wolfger, Bishop of Passau ; but this at least indicates his social sphere, and we may reasonably assume some measure of encouragement or interest on the part of Wolfger, conformable with what is otherwise known of that prelate as a good friend of singers.  For the rest our single source of knowledge is the poetry of Albrecht himself, from which we are able to sense a man of grave temper and deep feelings, capable, however, of lively and graceful plays of fancy along with those more serious poems which reveal to us a phase of his own life.

It is best, or at any rate most convenient, to take these poems in the order in which they are arranged in *Minnesangs Frühling*.

> Ich hân dur got daz kriuze an mich genomen
> und var dâ hin durch mîne missetât . . . (MF. 86, 25)

I have taken the Cross in God's name, and go out yonder to make atonement for my sins . . .

This consists of a single stanza, and is a brief, plain statement of the poet's thought.  He has taken the Cross, and is anxious for the woman he leaves behind.  She is greatly troubled, he says, on his account.  He prays God to keep her honour safe while he is absent : if this is granted, he desires no more.  But if she should fall away and be corrupted—*sül aber si ir leben verkêren*—then let him die out yonder.

His concern for his lady's honour is a new and arresting point, implying a natural nearness of relationship and an absence of the courtly code.  Greatly as he adores her, he does not set her on a

53

pedestal : she is in fact more woman to him than lady, and the word *wîp* occurs in his diction far oftener than *frouwe*. In the phrase of Walther von der Vogelweide, she is *friundin unde frouwe in einer wât*—friend and lady in a single dress—and is all the more appealing.

> Mich mac der tôt von ir minnen wol scheiden,
> anders nieman : des hân ich gesworn . . . (MF. 87, ₅).

Death, indeed, may sever me from her love, no one else : this have I sworn . . .

This strikes a happier note than the foregoing. The general impression is one of frank-hearted confidence and ease, and is pleasantly enhanced by the caressing lilt of the dactylic rhythm. Only death can sever her love and his. He feels no doubt of her integrity, declaring that he who would slander her to him is not his friend. She is perfect in goodness of nature as in high birth and breeding. " God be gracious to us both ! " Then we catch a glimpse of a charming scene, where he comes to see her in his Crusader's dress, and she, the fair and good one, propounds to him the old riddle, how will he then journey over the sea and yet remain here ?—the traditional paradox of the body which goes away leaving the heart behind. Two lines of the stanza are missing : the last, " ê was mir wê, dô geschach mir nie so leide "—" I suffered before, never so much as now "—which the editors print as part of the poet's narration, might perhaps be construed as spoken by the lady, giving point to her lover's rejoinder that what she feels as sorrow is potential joy. " Nu mîn herzefrouwe, nu trûre niht sêre,"—" Now my heart's lady, grieve not so sorely,"—he answers, and seeks to comfort her with the thought of the Crusader's glory and of death that is a prelude to eternal life.

This song, contained only in A, is imperfectly preserved. In addition to the two lines missing in the second strophe, the conclusion of the third is corrupt in form, though, happily, the sense is clear.

> Ich und ein wîp, wir haben gestriten
> nu vil manege zît . . . (MF. 87, ₂₉).

I and a woman, we have been at strife now for some time . . .

In this it is evident that the course of true love had not run smooth. They had quarrelled, and the breach had already lasted some time, and still she remained obdurate, refusing to make peace and professing herself glad at his departure, because this would leave her free. And he swears that she is mistaken, he will never let her go. Nothing can shake his love for her, though he may never see her again, he is hers till death. Then, with the same protective gesture as once before, he prays for her safety and honour. " I never wake but this is my first prayer, that God may take care of her in this life, give her joy in the life to come. And may this befall me too."

Two other stanzas composed in the same metre deal with the more general aspects of the Crusade. But the personal note is renewed in the last line :

> Ich meine die da minnent âne gallen,
> als ich mit triuwen tuon die lieben vrouwen mîn.

I mean those who love without gall, as I faithfully love my dear lady.

> Die hinnen varn die sagen durch got . . . (MF. 89, $_{21}$).

They who journey hence may say in God's name . . .

This poem has three stanzas, of which the first two are charged with religious fervour, and contain a pungent attack on all who hold back from the Crusader's calling. The third stanza sinks from the height of that stern argument to a more personal level,—confession of the poet's own vacillation, of the unhappiness which now at last has driven him to face the issue with new strength of will, finally of the one sin he refuses to put away, because to him it is in reality a deep and sacred thing, and worthy of God's blessing.

> ich minne ein wîp vor al der werlde in mînem muote.
> got hêrre, daz vervâch ze guote !

I love a woman more than all the world in my soul. Lord God, turn that to good !

The Crusader's problem is solved, not by rejection of the human tie but by its inclusion in the things of the spirit, its withdrawal from the intellectual plane on which the conflict between earthly and heavenly love has meaning.

With the help of these four personal poems, we can also detect other signs of subjectivity which are less obvious, as for instance behind the generalised statement :

> Swer minne minneclîche treit
> gar âne valschen muot,
> des sünde wirt vor gote niht geseit,
> si tiuret und ist guot.

He who harbours love in lovesome fashion with stainless will, he shall not hear his sin told in God's presence : such love ennobles and is good.

Individual, too, in the light of the more personal poems, is the poet's insistence that, just as he loves his lady solely and singly—

*einfaltecliche*—she for her part must be expected to deal singly and honestly with him, " not for love's sake but because it is only right ".

The contrast between his own single love with its scant reward and the double loves of others lies also behind the daringly asked problem : " Can one, without breach of good form, if to do so were not inconsistent, offer allegiance to two women, separately and in secret ? "—A problem meant for a man's ear, as shown by the imperious question : " sprich, herre, wurre ez iht ? "—" speak, sir, would it be any harm ? "—and the supposed reply : " It may be allowed to men, but not to ladies ".

It is possible, on technical grounds, to separate the songs of Johansdorf into an earlier and a later group ; but Kurt Halbach,[11] who has worked out this distinction in detail, overstates the artistic disparity between the two. The earlier songs are not, as he described them, " unbeholfen ", " stammelnd ", or " hölzern ". The few slight formal defects which can be pointed out weigh little against their effortless mastery of natural and expressive phrase. Nor is there any break in the continuity of the poet's thought. One passage sheds light on another, regardless of what the time-interim may have been. The crusading poems of the earlier group are one in thought with the more musically mature song (given complete in C) which opens : " wie sich minne hebt daz weiz ich wol," — " how love begins, this I know well "—with its rounded summary of the poet's personal view (MF. 91, $_{22}$).

> Swâ zwei herzeliep gefriundent sich
> und ir beider minne ein triuwe wirt,
> die sol nieman scheiden, dunket mich,
> al die wîle unz si der tôt verbirt.

Where two loving hearts grow close acquainted and the love of both becomes one single troth, no one shall sever them, methinks, so long as death spares them.

We may note the personal insight expressed by

> dâ gehœret manic stunde zuo
> ê daz sich gesamene ir beider muot.

Many an hour is needed before their two wills are gathered into one.

This song has four stanzas. The first three are put into a woman's mouth ; then comes the poet's personal appeal. " She whom I serve and always mean to serve must surely understand what I mean. If I said more, it would be too much. I will let it depend on her goodness. I have need of her favour ; and if she will, I am glad, and if she will not, my heart is full of pain."

[11] Kurt Halbach : *Walther von der Vogelweide und die Dichter von Minnesangs Frühling*, 38 ff.

The courtly tone, which is almost absent from the earlier group, suggests itself here, but not so as to veil the essential candour. Halbach sees in this poem the influence of Walther von der Vogelweide. To me the whole thought is so very much Johansdorf's own that there can be no question of influence, rather of a meeting-place between kindred views. But, indeed, the stability of Johansdorf's conception of love goes further than Walther's unsatisfied probing. In the former there is a certainty of conviction which, despite all differences of temperament and of intellectual range, makes a link with Wolfram von Eschenbach. Yet there is no direct connection, only a casual affinity between.

> die sol nieman scheiden, dunket mich,
> al die wîle unz si der tôt verbirt

and these lines of Wolfram's *Titurel* :

> diu zwei kunnen sich dâ niht gevirren
> wan mit dem tôde al eine ; anders kan daz nieman verirren.

The two cannot part from one another, except in death : no one else can put that love astray.

> Sæhe ich ieman der jæhe er wære von ir komen ... (MF. 91, 36)

If I saw one who could say he was come from her . . .

In a stanza of ten lines, the lover declares that he would welcome anyone who brought him news of " her ". If it were his deadliest foe, this would not matter. " He shall have me a whole year for friend."

Nature-symbolism, which plays so dynamic a part in the songs of Morungen, is well-nigh absent from those of Johansdorf. But his feeling for Nature discloses itself simply in the refrain *froide und sumer ist noch allez hie*—" Joy and summer are still all here "—more vividly in his delightful picture of flowers and grass spreading a variegated glory of colour under a linden tree. " White and red roses, blue flowers and green grass, brown, yellow, red again, clover leaf besides, all these colours lay outspread beneath a linden tree ; birds sang in its branches ; that was a lovely spot. It lay all beautiful with long and short stalks growing side by side." Like Walther, he sends his lady news of the season's beauty, hoping she may reward him, doubtful whether she will.

This song has two stanzas. Disconnected from them in theme is a third in the same metre, one which, whatever its immediate bearing, serves aptly as an apologia from the unconventional singer who had so often worn his heart upon his sleeve. " God knows well that I have never forgotten her since I left the land. I would never have dared sing these songs of her, were she not very pure and free of all blame. She must allow me to speak of her virtues . . . "

Codex C contains two poems by Johansdorf which are unlike the rest. (MF. 92, $_{35}$ and 93, $_{12}$). The first is a little song of two stanzas on the relation between *minne* and *zuht*, love and good-breeding, the latter being personified as *Frou Zuht mit süezer lêre* (with sweet teaching). The second is a dialogue between a knight and his lady, and is based on a Provençal model. It illustrates, very pleasantly, the foregoing abstract theme of *zuht* and *minne*. The manner of it is graceful, deft, and delicately playful. In the first strophe the situation is indicated and the dialogue opens. " I found the lovely one unguarded and alone." She asks him, what does he mean, coming there by himself. He answers : " Lady, it just so happened ", and the conversation continues, he persistently trying to gain his point, but so modestly, so discreetly and tentatively that she is able each time to take advantage, either with quick retort or with skilled evasion. A momentary lapse into tenderness on her part—" Who has driven you, dear man, to such a pass ? "—gives him his opportunity, but she repels the flattering deduction all the more sharply. At length, she appears to yield, telling him he shall not go unrewarded. He asks, what this means, and she, withholding the more tangible meed he looks for, coolly replies : The gain to your honour !

In contrast to this *jeu d'esprit*, there is, finally, a last Crusading poem, one which stands apart from the others through its greater detachment, its sense of achievement and poise. It presents, like the foregoing, an objectified picture of womanhood, but of a different type. In the one, a volatile and charming coquette, in the other, a woman after Albrecht's own heart, true and tender. She is introduced in the third and fourth strophes : the first two give other facets of the situation, focussing our attention, first, on the whole Crusading army, then on the individual soldier and lover. There is, to start with, a general exhortation for men to join God's service beyond the sea, not impassioned, like that earlier diatribe against the unwilling, but calm and firm. The personal aspect is then envisaged, but again, without unrest or passion. " Love, let me free ! Thou must leave me for a while without affection . . . When I have fulfilled God's enterprise, then be welcome to me once more ! But if thou wilt not separate from my heart (which, perhaps, cannot be prevented) then if I take thee with me into God's land, let Him be asked to give half the reward to thee." And now we hear the woman speaking. She wonders how she can bear to let her beloved go, how she will play her double part, show a smiling face to the world while her heart is sad within her. And the imminence of the last farewell comes over her. " Ez nâhet : er wil hinnen varn,"—" The time draws near : he will have to go."

Her faithfulness is commended. Such a one can do the impossible thing, send her heart across the sea with her loved one, while she remains at home and thinks in silence of his great peril. " If my heart's love is alive or if he is dead," says she, " may he be safe in the keeping of Him for Whose sake he, sweet man, has renounced the world."

---

*Ich und ein wîp, wir haben gestriten*
*nu vil manege zît . . .*

I and a woman, we have striven,
And the breach is still unhealed.
My heart by her enmity is riven,
Yet she disdains to yield,
And thinks, because I journey hence,
That I shall leave her free.
God from Hell's torment grant me no defence,
If that my will should be !
Howso the sea wax angry and the strong waves roar,
Through it I will cleave to her the more.
But she,—the faintest mutter of far-off thunder
Would shake her loyalty.
Now say, is hers or mine the victory ?
No power can pluck my thoughts and her asunder.

I know not, whether I shall see
Her, face to face, once more.
All I confess of her in truth comes free
And true from my heart's core.
Her out of all women I cherish,
This in God's name I vow.
Body and soul ere I perish
To her command I bow.
I never wake, but this is my first prayer,
That God may keep her honour in His care,
And bless her earthly life and gentle fame.
Then in Thy realm to be,
Give her, Lord, joy everlastingly.
As it befall her, be it unto me the same !

*Die hinnen varn, die sagen durch got . . .*

They who fare hence may in God's name aver
That Jerusalem the fair city and the holy land
Never needed help more truly.
Fools make mock at that lament, and stir
Up laughter, saying : " Without them, could not the Lord's right
    hand
Alone deal vengeance throughly ?
Let them remember now that He for us in anguish died :
There was no need for Him to be thus crucified,
But that His pity bowed itself to save us.

He who cares nothing for the Cross and Grave in their sore plight,
Shall stand ungraced and naked in His sight !


In what, think ye, can such a man believe,
Or who shall come at last to help him in his dying day,
Who to God's cause his help denies ?
So far as I can for my part perceive,
Unless, indeed, it be a lawful hindrance bars his way,
I think, he sinneth otherwise.
Now what avails to speak of Cross and Grave ? the heathen horde
Think they can silence us with one contemptuous word,
That God's Mother was no Maiden holy.

He whose heart burns not at that impious defiance,
Where and with whom, alas, seeks he alliance ?


With me, at least, my cares have this way wrought,
That I would gladly purge my will of all low weaknesses,
Whereof my heart has not been quit
Ere now.   For often in the night a thought
Assails me : if I stay behind, how shall I make redress,
That God so deign to pardon it ?
Even so, I do not know of many sins whereto I cleave,
Save one, but this is all too dear for me to leave,
I could renounce all sins but that alone :

I love a woman more than all the world deep in my soul.
Lord God, direct that to a blessed goal !

*Sæhe ich ieman der jæhe er wære von ir komen . . .*

If I saw one who could say he was come from her,
I would bless him, though he were my foe.
Had he robbed me of all else, her messenger
Should for this his punishment forego.
He who but speaks her name
Has me to friend
From now to a full year's end.
What scathe or shame
To flay me he had wrought
Should be but nought.

# REINMAR VON HAGENAU

The Viennese court poet Reinmar von Hagenau has the distinction of being the first Minnesinger whose fame is recorded by his own generation. Two notable poets, Gottfried von Strassburg and Walther von der Vogelweide, bear witness to him. We find also, that the number of songs ascribed to him in the MSS. far exceeds the output of any other singer of the age before Walther. In his influence on the next generation Reinmar, as master of the courtly love-lyric at the height of its sophistication and charm, competes very equally with Neidhart von Reuental, founder of the new school of rustic poetry which is the antithesis of the courtly kind.

Walther commemorates the passing of Reinmar in an elegy nobly inspired by a profound sense of loss. " Reinmar," he exclaims, " what fine art perishes with thee ! " We do not doubt the sincerity of this because of the old rivalry between the two. It was a mixed relationship which, at this distance of time, it is impossible to assess correctly. Walther's earlier songs show him in Reinmar's debt. When from assimilation of his senior's technique, he went on to the higher delight of parody and to bold opposite treatment of similar themes, and when Reinmar answered him back in his own style, it may well be that all this was a mere contest of rival wits, enjoyed by both, and that there is no need to interpret a telling hit as a sign of rancour. Such contests we know were already part of the poets' game in Provence. It must be admitted, however, that this between Reinmar and Walther was based on an essential difference of outlook. For while Reinmar continued to represent the patient sad lover, serving his lady without hope, it would almost seem without wish, for reward, Walther extols the fortunate lover, and expects the lady to play a more generous part. " Minne," which Walther identifies with " wunne,"—gladness—, Reinmar identifies with " riuwe,"— grief (MF. 188, $_{34}$). With all this radical difference, there is yet no unequivocal sign of hostile sentiment, nothing to compare with the bitterness of Gottfried's attack on Wolfram, or with Walther's own attitude towards the poetry of low degree.

In the end, any differences between the dead man and the living were of little account compared with their common ground. Walther, less narrowly a courtier than Reinmar, is none the less court-bred, with a deep veneration for all that is gracious, decorous and harmonious. It is characteristic of himself and of his own social ideal, that the song of Reinmar's which he singles out as sure of undying fame is the one in praise, not so much of a single woman as of womankind : " Sô wol dir, wîp, wie reine ein nam ! "—" Hail to thee, woman, how pure a name ! " The inspiration lives on in his own famous song on the priority of the name " wîp "—woman—over " frouwe "—lady.

Woman is the highest praise of all women, and bestows greater honour than that of lady, to my thinking.

It is usual, though not strictly necessary, to read a note of detraction into these lines of Walther's elegy :

> ich wil bi mînen triuwen sagen,
> dich selben wolte ich lützel klagen :
> ich klage dîn edelen kunst, daz s'ist verdorben.

I will say by my troth, thyself would I lament but little : I make lament for the noble art which has perished with thee.

That might mean : The personal loss is small compared with that of a great artist. The other implication is, of course, possible too.

Gottfried von Strassburg also pays tribute to Reinmar, referring to him, however, not by name but as the nightingale of Hagenau, leader of the whole choir of lyric singers whose delightful art he describes in metaphor as " der liebe vogelsanc," the sweet song of birds. Who (he asks) will now take the lead, since " diu von Hagenouwe " is hushed in death ? The answer follows : " diu von der Vogelweide ". The passage occurs at the end of that novel and interesting excursus of Gottfried's *Tristan*, in which the poet turns aside from the story to give a survey of his fellow-poets. Two groups are distinguished : the *varwære* or painters (epic poets), and the *nahtegalen*, nightingales or singers. Bligger von Steinach, of whose literary output no more than a few rather mediocre lyrics are left, here takes his place among the *varwære* as a narrator of rare distinction and charm, it would seem, one whose art was akin to Gottfried's own. Heinrich von Veldeke and Hartmann von Aue are highly praised, Wolfram von Eschenbach is scornfully and harshly abused. Of the nightingales we hear that they were many in number : only the two leaders are singled out.

Reinmar's identity with the unnamed singer of Hagenau is a certainty beyond all doubt. There is simply no other whom Gottfried could have had in mind. That he alone should connect the Viennese court poet with his Alsatian home of Hagenau has a natural reason, they being both of the same soil. Elsewhere Reinmar is designated simply as *Her Reinmar*, or as *Reinmar der alte*, not because of his age but to distinguish him from later poets of the same name, Reinmar von Zweter and Reinmar der videler. His Rhenish origin links him with Friedrich von Hausen, to whose art his own is affiliated, showing the same marked analytical trend, though with a far greater degree of formal artistry and of intellectual finesse.

The year of his death is unknown : we can only assign it an indefinite date within the first decade of the thirteenth century. Gottfried's *Tristan* was still in the making; the fame of Wolfram's *Parzival* was in the ascendant, as Gottfried's diatribe bears witness ; Walther had not yet made his second entry into the political arena, and was still occupied with songs of nature and of love.

In Reinmar's life at the Viennese court there is one landmark : the death of his patron Leopold V, Archduke of Austria and Styria, in 1194. Reinmar composed a dirge for that occasion, putting the words of his lament into the mouth of the Duke's widow. This poem has been highly praised. Personally, I find the touches of beauty in it too deliberately studied, the emotional effects too forced. The words

> dô man mir seite er wære tôt,
> zehant wiel mir daz bluot
> von herzen ûf die sele mîn

When I was told he was dead, the blood immediately welled up from my heart and smote upon my soul

are for Reinmar unnaturally strong, while on the other hand the interjectional brevity of

> er ist nu hin. waz töhte ich hie ?

He is now gone. Of what use am I here ?

is unnaturally simple. The poem is interesting as the first known threnody in German verse, and is an act of ritual decorously performed.

The Crusading poems ascribed to the poet in C would, if genuine, refer to the Crusade of 1190, in which his patron the Archduke Leopold took part. Reinmar would thus have been one of his lord's contingent. The authenticity of both these poems (MF. 180, 28— 182, 3) has been denied or doubted, partly because the testimony of C, indubitably wrong with regard to a number of the poems it ascribes to Reinmar, is thus always open to question if unsupported, partly because these particular poems are isolated in theme from the rest of Reinmar's work, and accordingly very different.

Granted the occasion, however, one would scarcely expect even Reinmar to treat his religious theme with the same graceful dallying as is typical of his treatment of courtly love. The solemnity of the event and the traditional attitude towards it must have evoked an appropriate earnestness of tone. The arguments of Carl von Kraus miss this cardinal point. Approaching both poems independently,

I feel there is a strong case against Reinmar's authorship of the first (MF. 180, $_{28}$), not so much on account of the borrowed thoughts and uncharacteristic metre—both possible by adoption—as that there is nothing by which to recognise his style and tone. Both here and in MF. 184, $_{31}$ ff. there is a downright force of utterance completely foreign to the prevailing trend of Reinmar's art. The one word which in any way recalls him to us is simply *trûren*, and that by itself hardly counts. The poem may well be later than 1190, for while most of the thoughts are reminiscent of Friedrich von Hausen or Heinrich von Rugge, there is one phrase suggesting a nearer relation in time with Walther von der Vogelweide. The expression *lop und êre und dar zuo gotes hulde*—praise and honour and the grace of God—recalls the triple union of *guot, êre* and *gotes hulde* in the famous context of Walther's first political poem of 1198.

It is otherwise with the second Crusading song (MF. 181, $_{13}$). The type of metrical structure, the delicate phrasing, the sequence in the ideas and the faint yet clear provocation of the ideas themselves, all this is reminiscent of Reinmar. The poem presents a fastidious point of moral duty : is that man to blame, who, having taken the Cross, cannot hinder his thoughts from straying ? Thoughts are free !

I find myself here at odds with Professor von Kraus.[12] His premises seem to me wrong, and I cannot accept his view of the poem itself. "Unser Dichter "—that is, the supposed anonymous—" ist von dem, was er sagt, ergriffen ; Reinmar als wahrer Artist steht über dem Inhalt seiner Klagen. Der eine ist schwer und gemütvoll wie Wolfram, der andere geistreich und beweglich wie Gottfried." It is facile to assume that Reinmar's detachment in dealing with the Amor Cortois presupposes an equal detachment in the face of an experience incomparably more real and urgent. The emotional response is no more than one would naturally expect. At the same time there actually is, along with true depth of feeling, a vein of cool reasoning which resembles no other poet's way more than Reinmar's. What von Kraus means by going out of his way to mention Wolfram one cannot think.

And this moves me to criticise further. There is no wish on my part to depreciate one whose studies of Reinmar are long leagues ahead of my own somewhat casual knowledge of this most difficult and elusive poet. But it is a hazardous task to try and establish a final canon of Reinmar's authentic work and von Kraus, so I think, errs on the side of a too precise and arbitrary estimate of the poet's limits. Heart and mind cry out against his rejection of some of the choicest gems of Reinmar's art. I think especially of the suave and gracious *mîn ougen wurden liebes alsô vol*... (MF. 194, $_{17}$), of the exquisite *aller*

[12] Carl von Kraus : *Die Lieder Reinmars des alten*, I, 75.

*sælde ein sælic wîp* . . . (MF. 176, ₅), and of its little sister-song *frouwe tuo des ich dich bite* . . . (MF. 190, ₂₇). In *aller sælde ein sælic wîp* . . . the peculiar delicacy of Reinmar's persuasive, evasive, evocative language attains its acme. One can more justly claim that this is Reinmar at the height of his art than that he has been surpassed by a gifted anonymous. The poem has the rarefied sweetness of chamber music, and is perfect in the sequence of its vague entreaties, its discreet admissions, its soft enquiries, tapering to a dulcet close in " frouwe, nam des iemen war ? "—" Lady, did anyone perceive it ? "

One must admit a strong doubt in the case of the beautiful and, for Reinmar, surprisingly spontaneous *Hôhe alsam diu sunne stêt daz herze mîn* . . . (MF. 182, ₁₄). This, found only in C, is rendered suspect by the impure rhyme in the second stanza, *lîp : gît*. The spontaneity, if at first hearing more suggestive of Morungen than of Reinmar, is not in itself a sufficient ground for rejection. Reinmar, too, has occasional moments of *élan*, nowhere more so than in his delightful *ich wæn mir liep geschehen wil* . . . (MF. 156, ₁₀)—preserved in both B and C, and accepted by von Kraus as authentic. Here the lover has cast away all care. His heart dances, his spirit soars aloft for joy, like a falcon in flight or an eagle wheeling in the air. Between him and his lady no bar of inequality remains. " Good it is to be with her. Lord God, grant me that I may see her and relieve all her care, that if she be in any trouble I may lighten it for her, and she do the same for me. Then may we rejoice together. O well for me then if the night is long ! how should I grow weary ? " It is the nearest Reinmar ever gets to Walther's conception of love as *zweier herzen wunne*—the joy of two hearts—and of an equal sharing.

But the melancholy note prevails. A poem like this is but a transient interlude in the long continuous cult of hapless love. Unlike Heinrich von Morungen, whose songs are so full of light and movement, Reinmar, to use his own phrase, sees love almost always " in bleicher varwe,"—in pale colour—and seldom deviates from one static position, that of the lover devoting himself to his lady's service : the same old theme of unrequited love, of a patience and loyalty which stands the test. The general impression, after a first, or even after a second reading of Reinmar's poems is one of cloying monotony ; but the more intensely he is studied, the more one learns to value the fine precision of his elaborate and graceful art. The monotony then disappears. That static position is viewed from so many angles and is shown with so many slight variations, not concrete details but the elusive and provocative details of abstract thought, that it grows endlessly fascinating. The whole is governed by a cool and courtier-like temperament which has its own persuasive charm. Intellectual subtlety takes the place of emotional fervour : it has been well said that the theme is not so much the lover's feelings as his thoughts about his feelings.[13] The language is disarmingly simple, both in the choice of words and in the individual statement : the effect of subtlety lies in its tortuous syntax, in its retardations and evasions. The style, with its predilection for conditional clauses, for understatements and pregnant queries, mirroring not what was but what might have been, is a perfect means of expressing the discretion and diffidence, the self-abnegation and well-bred patience of the conventional type of courtly lover. This central rôle is not, however, the only one. The lady sometimes speaks in her own person, and her volatile presence is a foil to her lover's gravity. Also, the relation between these two is crossed, to a greater extent than with Heinrich von Morungen, by the singer's relation to his audience, and this gives an outlet for little defensive thrusts and parryings, such as have no place in the lover's pacific part.

Towards the audience the singer adopts a disdainful and slightly hostile pose. Their superficial desire to be entertained, their obtuse unawareness of the living theme behind his song, their raillery and banter, all these elements are brought into play and made to seem, in relation to the poet's sanctified life, like the sport of waves harmlessly chafing against the shores of an enchanted isle. Reinmar's treatment of his auditors and critics is not without humour : incapable of laughter, he has a whimsical eye for the absurd. As, for instance, when he affects a bored impatience with those who keep on asking his lady's age, implying that she must be getting on in years, he has been singing the praises of her so long !

This gay undercurrent quickens perceptibly in the speech of the lady herself. The idealised mistress of Reinmar's idealising lover turns out, in conversation with his messenger, an accomplished flirt. What one can guess from the strain she habitually puts on her lover's patience is translated here into more realistic terms. We discover a sprightly bundle of feminine contradictions. Affectation and tenderness, captiousness and inward self-esteem, ambiguities, vacillations and whims with a shrewd sense of power behind them, all these elements join in the dance together. The two *Botenlieder* (MF. 177, 10—178, 1) yield the quintessence of Reinmar's courtly wit and are the liveliest things he has left us. The genre itself may be looked upon as a bequest from the older Austrian love-lyric : the *botenlied* was, we remember, one of the favourite forms of the younger Dietmar. It was not cultivated by Friedrich von Hausen and other poets of the Rhenish group, or by Heinrich von Morungen. Reinmar is the first courtly singer to introduce it afresh ; and it gives it a new

---

[13] H. Schneider : *Die Lieder Reinmars des Alten* (Deutsche Vierteljahrschrift für Literaturwissenschaft und Geistesgeschichte, 1939), 341.

and arresting turn by allowing the lady scope for self-dramatization. The messenger plays a minor part. In the first *botenlied*, where he comes direct from his master and so brings news, there are questions to be answered to which, mindful of his master's interests, he gives brief and carefully weighed replies. In the second he stands at attention, listening as the lady tells him what message he is to take back. The process is long and involved : six stanzas of varying statements are needed for all she has to say and unsay. But while she does most of the talking, the messenger's presence, if unobtrusive, is fully realised. To no other could she have posed so profitably or spoken her mind so freely. As sharer of her lover's confidence and as one trained to decorous and discreet behaviour, he fulfils to a nicety the rôle which is a complement to her own. We see him lending a receptive ear while she tells him, first, what he is to say when he meets his master, then, what he must keep secret, and again, how, if such and such a question is asked he must answer *thus*, and so on, until finally she breaks off with the most maddening of anti-climaxes :

> dune solt im nimmer niht verjehen
> alles des ich dir gesage.

Thou must never say a word to him of all I have told thee.

All this in a light conversational tone, with nimble sentences and words of daily use, and with a general effect as of a leaping stream of clear water, broken into froth and dusky eddies by the chafing of its pebbly bed.

As the *botenlied* receives in Reinmar's hands a new character so also he suggests a new point of departure for the *tagelied*, without going so far as to evolve a separate form. The lover is imagined lying sleepless and alone at peep of dawn. " Whenever day draws near, then I dare not ask: Is it day ? That is because my lament is so great that nothing can help me. I remember how differently I used to feel, formerly, when care did not weigh on my heart as now : always in the morning the song of the birds cheered me. Unless her help come to me in time, summer and winter are both too long for me." And the last line of the lament renews its first thought : " seldom do I desire the day to dawn ".

Something may be said both for and against Reinmar's authorship of the song which begins so hopefully with an open-air glimpse of summer (MF. 183, $_{33}$) :

> Ich sach vil wünneclichen stân
> die heide mit den bluomen rôt . . .

The colourful opening, in which praise of the violet is added to the more customary mention of *bluomen rôt*, and the song of the night-ingale follows, is unlike the usual manner of Reinmar's muse. Still this reason against is not final. His adoption of the *botenlied*, different though his development of it is from the primary form, shows one link with the older Austrian lyric ; here perhaps is another. An acquaintance with the songs of Dietmar von Aist, a passing submission to their picturesque treatment of nature as a background for love, might account for this prelude. Charming as it is in itself, there is no organic bond with the ideas which follow. The vital relation between love and nature, manifest in the older lyric and realised by both Heinrich von Veldeke and Walther von der Vogelweide, lies outside the peculiar range of Reinmar's mind. A decorative effect is the most he can here attain.

The poem just considered is, if authentic, a mere episode in the general development of Reinmar's art. It is as a master of intro-spection that he excels : the inner life of the lover is his kingdom. Lacking as he does the transcendent vision of Heinrich von Morungen, he fascinates us by his command of the ritual and theory of courtly love. In this, his own particular line, we can trace an increase of power. The highest level is reached in *Als ich werbe und mir mîn herze stê* . . . (MF. 179, 3), a genuinely fine poem in which there is not a single weak line. The seven stanzas of which it consists form a satisfying sequence, the metrical structure is beautifully effective, and there is an impassioned depth of tone. In contrast to the minuet steps of earlier poems, Reinmar here achieves a noble freedom of movement, culminating in the bold upward sweep of one really splendid strophe, in which the image of the falcon is used in a new way :

> Ich bin als ein wilder valke erzogen,
> der durch sînen wilden muot als hôhe gert.
> der ist als hôhe über mich gevlogen
> und muotet des er kûme wirt gewert
> und fliuget alsô von mir hin
> und dient ûf ungewin.
> ich tumber
> lîde senden kumber
> des ich gar schuldic bin.

I have been reared as a wild falcon, whose wild will impels him as high as he can go. He (my wild self) has flown so high above me and desires what he scarcely will be granted, and thus flies away from me and serves where hope is barren. I, simple fool, suffer grievous longing, for which I only am to blame.

Throughout this song there is a ring of reality, as of an actor so steeped in his part that it has become second nature. How much sincerity, may we suppose, lies ultimately behind the whole of

Reinmar's choice and courtly masquerade ? His art forbids a solving
of that problem. Yet, though his fine-spun eloquence betrays
nothing of his own inner secret, he at least testifies that the love he
made his theme was a vital truth. It had, he said, a meaning for
every man. " For," so runs his charming declaration of faith, " no
one lives in the world but he may find his heart's queen :

> wan nieman in der welte lebet
> erne vinde sînes herzen küneginne.

---

### *Des tages dô ich daz kriuze nam . . .*

The day on which I took the Cross,
I kept my thoughts in close control,
As well beseemed that holy sign,
And as a pilgrim pure of soul.
I hoped I might so bind them to God's will,
They would not swerve, nor cease His service to fulfil.
But now they tend to break away,
As they were wont, and wander free.
And this is not my case alone,
But troubles other men than me.

I well might keep my vows unscathed,
But that unruly thoughts prevail :
When I should praise the God to Whom
I have sworn service, there they fail
To help me in my need, and jeopardize
My soul's salvation, harking back in treacherous wise
To those old joys whereof a taste
Lures me to do as once I did.
Maiden and Mother, give me grace,
For these I cannot all forbid !

Nor would I quite forbid free range
To thoughts (they have their own domain),
But rather give them leave to go
Thither, and straight return again.
So may they bear a greeting to our friends,
Turn back, and help me for my sin to make amends,
And may they be forgiven all
Wherewith, before, they wrought me ill !—
Natheless, I fear, they are not to trust,
And often will confound me still.

*Ein rede der liute tuot mir wê . . .*

One thing they say displeases me :
Indeed, it almost puts me in a rage.
They keep on asking me my lady's age,
And want to know, how old is she,
Because I have been serving her so long.
They say it to incense me.
May the sweet mistress of my song
For that ill-mannered question recompense me !

*Ich hân 'ir vil manic jâr
gelebt, und si mir selten einen tac . . .*

I have lived full many a year
For her sake, she for mine scarce even a day.
My head will soon be white, I fear,
With all this trouble.   I am growing grey
Beneath her tyrannous yoke.
She well might vent her anger for a change on other folk.

Does she suppose, I can avert
My mind from her, all for a touch of spleen ?
No matter how she do me hurt,
Destined I am, as I have always been,
To live on the assurance
Of ways to serve her, hoping that she may yet end my durance.

*Frowe, tuo des ich dich bite . . .*

Lady, do as I entreat thee,
That I still may be
Blest in the felicity
That flows from thee !
Only one custom thou
Shouldst leave behind.
Alas, why must thy deeds
Prove thee unkind ?
Surely thou knowest none
Who careth for thee more
Than I have done.

Let my heart rejoice to hear thee
Saying words that please.
Truly I have well earned
The right to these.

71

If for love it cannot be,
Suffer it no less,
Sweet woman, in token of
Thy power to bless !
Ere I from thee shall turn,
There is no fortune that
I would not spurn.


*Sage, daz ich dirs iemer lône . . .*

" Say, and take reward of me for ever,
Hast thou seen the dear man then of late ?
Is it true, and does he live as fairly
As they say, and as I hear thee state ? "
" Lady, I saw him.   Glad and well is he,
And high of heart, if this your gracious will should be."

" I will never seek to scant his pleasure.
Let him drop *one* theme : so much were good.
This is my request to-day and always.
Certain things there are must be withstood."
" Lady, to speak so far you have no call.
He says :  what must befall him he will let befall."

" Yes, but has he promised then, good fellow,
To refrain from song, unless it be
That I wish it so, and ask to hear it ? "
" Lady, such were his last words to me.
Surely you must have heard the same before."
" Alas, the effect, if I command it, will be sore ! "

" Yet, if I continue to forbid it,
I shall lose my blessing with his praise,
And the people will begin to curse me
When I rob them of his lovely lays.
This is the weariest problem I have known,
Whether to do it, or to leave the deed alone.

" That we women cannot by conversing
Win a friend, but his demands increase,
Riles me.   Love I will not.   Constant women
Hate the restless ways that murder peace.
Yet if I were inconstant (I am not)
And he had left me, I would leave him on the spot."

# WALTHER VON DER VOGELWEIDE

The place we should assign to Walther von der Vogelweide as lyricist, his actual rank as Minnesinger, is, despite his pre-eminence, difficult to decide.   Gottfried von Strassburg names him Reinmar's successor as leader of the choir of nightingales ; and Gottfried most certainly knew more of the Minnesinger's art than we do.   A perfectly schooled musician, he must have been also a perfect judge of that side of the Minnesang which (with few exceptions) is lost to us. The lyrical art of his age was to him not simply words, but words and melody—*wort unde wîse*—while we are cognizant of the words alone. And this imperfectly.   Though the language lives as we read it, we know that we cannot regain more than a part of its original movement and life.   We know, too, that many an apt phrase must have referred to some unknown trick of circumstance which gave it colour.   All this might be said of other poets of the time besides Walther : to him, however, it applies more urgently, in view of the contemporary verdict which challenges our own.

For myself I will say that, while Gottfried's verse sings and makes melody and enchants the ear with liquid syllables, in Walther's I am chiefly aware of a finely expressive speaking voice, resonant and incisive.   His output of purely lyrical verse, of poetry that sings itself, is small as compared with his far greater output of poetic oratory.   That, I think, is a fair and generally received impression. Gottfried's description of him as a singer of unrivalled priority means two things.   First, a highly developed musical art, a gift for fine melody matching the varied excellence of his metrical technique. This we must accept without question, though on trust.   The tunes which have been preserved, isolated survivals of differing date,[14] are insufficient criteria of the kind of melody Gottfried had in mind. His reference is to *der minnen melodîe*—melodies of love—and to these only.   Ignoring that wealth of theme which for us is one of Walther's chief signs of greatness, Gottfried, intent upon the one theme to which his own art is dedicated, refers to the lost harmonies inspired, so he says, by the Goddess Love—*diu gotinne Minne*— dwelling on Mount Citheron.   Our second inference follows from the first.   This eulogy must point to the period in Walther's life when the lyrical strain ran clearest : the period of his most delightful songs, such as " Under der linden " . . . and " Muget ir schouwen waz

---

[14] For a succinct account of this subject, s. K. Plenio : *Die Überlieferung Waltherscher Melodieen* (Beiträge zur Geschichte der deutschen Sprache und Literatur, 1917, 479 ff.).

dem meien Wunders ist beschert "... The didactic streak so heavily present in his earlier love-poems had, with his entry into public life (1198—1204), found satisfying scope in dealing with larger problems than the Amor Cortois. It may well be that this diversion of moral force into other and wider channels set free the lyrical impulse and moved him to sing of love easefully, winningly and lightly. The flowering of Walther's art as a Minnesinger lies, coinciding with Gottfried's *Tristan*, between the first and second phases of his contact with political life : the year 1212 marks, we may say, the close of his summer season, the approach of winter. If he continued to sing of love, it was in the studied and intellectual guise of poems like

> Ob ich mich selben rüemen sol,
> sô bin ich des ein hübescher man . . . (L. 62, $_6$ . . .)

to which, as its last lines refer to the Emperor Otto, a relatively late date may be assigned.

His was not an unchequered summer. With his temperament, the sunniest weather was quickly clouded, though, on the other hand, gleams of a saving grace of humour that never left him could light up his bleakest hour. Dissatisfaction and morbid sensitiveness are combined in him with resiliency and a power to take refuge in serene and innocent beauty.

And since, following Gottfried's lead, we are thinking of him first as lyricist, we may ask ourselves what was the source from which his lyrical inspiration sprang. Love undoubtedly, but not, as Gottfried suggests, love of woman. His purest perceptions, his happiest feelings are derived from a deeply sincere love of Nature, this being no conventional background but rather the living foreground of the songs best attuned to *der minnen melodie*.

He sees flowers and clover competing as to which grow the faster. Or he sees the flowers sprouting out of the grass, laughing up at the dancing sun, while the little birds make melody in the best tune that they know ; and when he turns from this picture of a perfect May morning, presenting in rivalry to it a fair lady of high degree, her gay and gracious qualities are enhanced by the strength of the challenge. It is no small thing for her to outshine what had seemed to be "half heaven". And the challenge takes on a more imperious ring as the idyllic picture shown in the first strophe widens into one of the royal splendour of May holding high festival, so that the choice lies between this personified power and "noble ladies". That the latter are assumed to win so sharp a contest becomes an audacious compliment which is yet saved from the imputation of unreal flattery by a sudden outbreak of the personal note :

Her Meie, ir müezet Merze sîn
ê ich min frouwen dâ verlür !

Sir May, you must change to March sooner than I would lose my lady there !

In *Under der linden* the two human figures, a girl and her lover, are
so harmonised with the landscape which enfolds them that they
become part of Nature. Strewn roses mark where they lay and a little
bird shares their secret.

Muget ir schouwen waz dem meien
wunders ist beschert . . . (L. 51, 13 . . .)

— Can you see what wonder working power is bestowed on May ? . . . —

is a song in praise of May, and of May only. There is no other
ascendancy here but his. He is a doer of wonders, a magician he
well may be since, wherever he passes, no one grows old for all things
renew their youth. Human beings, birds and trees and flowers are
steeped in the same bright unison of joy. Only one thing jars : the
cruel scorn of a lady whose red mouth debases itself to laugh at her
faithful lover. She alone, in her heartless beauty, is out of tune with
the May season ; and he, through her, is denied his share of blessing.
He appeals to her to look around and see, how the whole world
rejoices : will she not relent and give him " one little joy " ?

*In einem zwivellichen wan* . . . (L. 65, 33 . . .) turns on a conven-
tional lover's problem, whether or not to quit his lady's service.
The point of interest is the blade of grass with which he plays a
child's game in order to solve his problem : *si tuot, si entuot, si tuot,
si entuot, si tuot*—she does, she doesn't, she does, she doesn't, she
does.

*Uns hât der winter geschadet über al* . . . (L. 39, 1 . . .) is a song
in dispraise of winter, season of dearth and cold. If only one could
sleep through it ! But summer will come again, winter will yield
the victory to May.

The trials and boredoms of winter, along with contrasting memories
and hopes of summer, form the subject of a satirical song of crasser
quality than those just considered:

Diu werlt was gelf, rôt inde blâ . . . (L. 75, 25 . . .)

The world was gay-coloured, red and blue . . .

Sexual love is absent from both these winter songs, as from

Dô der sumer komen was . . . (L. 94, 11 . . .)

When the summer was come . . .

Here in the midst of the usual pleasant landscape, by the side of a clear spring, under the cool shade of a linden tree and lulled by the nightingale's song, the poet falls asleep and dreams a dream.

Walther's attitude towards Nature includes side by side with his love of warmth, sweetness and light a keen aversion to those rougher aspects which he associates especially with winter. Not that they are absent at other times too. The crow which dominates the winter landscape with its unmusical caw also breaks and disperses the spell of the summer dream. The loud-croaking frogs which put the despairing nightingale to silence are disturbers of summer peace. Again, just as the contemplation of winter is lit up by thoughts of returning summer and so made bearable, the contemplation of summer in serious moments brings with it a poignant sense of impermanence and decay. " I am one who has never spent half a day with unbroken joy. Whatever joys I have experienced till now, I have been deserted by them. No one can find joy on earth but this must pass away like the bloom of flowers. Therefore my heart will desire false joys no more " (L. 42, $_7$ . . .). Here, as in one of his latest poems, the summer season wears a treacherous aspect : its transient joy is a symbol of the vanity of human life. He feels this more and more as he grows older. Even so, the beauty of the lyrical note is not harshened.

> Zâî wie ich danne sunge von den vogellînen,
> von der heide und von den bluomen, als ich wîlent sanc !
> swelch schœne wîp mir denne gæbe ir habedanc,
> der lieze ich liljen unde rôsen ûz ir wengel schînen.
>
> (L. 28, $_{4-7}$).

Ah, how I would then sing of the little birds, of the field and of the flowers, as I used to sing ! If then any fair woman gave me her thanks for that, I would let lilies and roses bloom from her cheeks.

Thus the poet exclaims, thinking that the rest for which he hopes after his years of wandering will give him back the lost mood of summer. That wish remained unfulfilled. The elegiac sadness taking its place grows to a pitch of grave loveliness as he resumes his parable of the short, uncertain life of man :

> Aller arebeite heten wir vergezzen,
> dô uns der sumer sîn gesinde wesen bat ;
> der brâhte uns varnde bluomen unde blat ;
> dô trouc uns der kurze vogelsanc.
> wol im der ie nâch stæten vroiden ranc ! (L. 13, $_{21}$ . . .).

We had become oblivious of all stress and travail when Summer invited us to be his retinue. He brought us quickly passing flowers and leaves : then the brief song of birds deceived us. Well for him who always strove to win imperishable joys!

Elsewhere, the imperfection of life presents itself to him under the symbol of the rose which is never without a thorn.

Ja bræche ich rôsen wunder, wan der dorn . . . (L. 102, 35).

I could have pulled a wondrous wealth of roses but for the thorn.

In this line Walther reveals his cardinal weakness. Elsewhere, to suit the occasion, he depicts himself as one whom good luck eludes : Fortune, he says, distributes her gifts among others and turns her back on *him* !—the petitioner's pose. Here, he candidly probes the inner cause of his life's shortcomings : the inevitable mistrust by which his happiness is thwarted. From that he is never free. Among his love-songs are two in which, as with Albrecht von Johansdorf, personal experience forms an immediate theme. In a girl of low degree he had found what he missed in high-born ladies, a warm and affectionate heart ; yet he cannot be sure that she will remain true always. And the second song shows the rift between them deepening, because her modesty keeps her at a distance and he thinks she cares less for him than he for her (L. 50, 19 . . . .).

The more we consider his personality, the more we feel how very much he stands outside the charmed circle of the Amor Cortois. This, for him, is no longer a cult, but a social phenomenon ; and he treats it, as he does other social phenomena, with intellectual acumen, with seriousness and vigour, and with a ready play of wit and humour. Apart from some journeyman's work, his poems on the theory of love are stimulating and, from the light they shed on their social background, informative. We value them, not for their lyrical quality (of that there is little) but for their intellectual substance and succinct expression. They are to be classed as *Minnelehre*, not as *Minnelyrik*.

The contemplation of one idealised type is not his purpose. He distinguishes sharply between two types of women, the good and the worthless, that is, between those who are honest, kind and faithful, and those who are unstable and callous. But he is equally just towards his fellow-men. If he dispraises false women, it is not to give a handle to men who are just as bad. So he warns good women, *guotiu wîp*, to avoid all *rüemære und lugenære*—boasters and liars—the kind of false lover who steals a woman's trust in order to brag of his conquest (L. 41, 13). The type is one recognised also by Hartmann von Aue and, before him, by Heinrich von Melk. Walther, however, does more than condemn the obvious and common vice of the *rüemic man*. In one of his later poems he applies the lash unsparingly to a fault more readily condoned but just as harmful, the levity of those young fools who talk love's language and do not feel it.

77

" Huetet ir iuch, reinen wîp, vor kinden berget iuwer jâ :
sô enwirt es niht ein kindes spil."

" Be on your guard, women of pure heart, withhold in front of childish boys
your consenting 'yes' : then there will be no child's play." (L. 102, 5-7.)

Walther's scholastic attitude of mind evinces itself in the sym-
metrical ordering of his ideas, which he arranges preferably in pairs,
sometimes, to mark a more striking effect, in triads. In the last
case, one concept is generally set over against the other two. Thus
*gotes hulde*, God's grace, is shown to outweigh *guot und êre*, wealth
and honour ; while in another context *êre und gotes hulde* are opposed
to *guot*. Again, in formulating his three chief wishes, of which the
third is uppermost in his mind, Walther links together the first two,
which are *gotes hulde und mîner frouwen minne*, " God's grace and
my lady's love," and dwells longer upon the third, which is *der
wünnecliche hof ze Wiene*, " the delightful court of Vienna ".

His twofold combinations are many and varied : sometimes there
is antithesis, sometimes a mating of ideas to form a new concept,
sometimes a mere joining of kindred terms. He compares the words
*wîp* and *frouwe*—woman and lady—deciding that " woman is the
highest name of all women," and states his reason why. Again, he
expresses his own desire for " friundin unde frowen in einer wæte."
—" friend and mistress in a single dress "—that is, in one person, lady
and love complete. He asserts on one occasion that his lady is
*zwir beslozzen*, shut off in two different ways, *hie verklûset, dort
verhêret dâ ich bin*, now cloistered from him in bodily separation, now
isolated by her own rigid pride ; and he wishes he could possess
both keys, that of her actual presence and that of her inner mind.
To himself he attributes two social graces, *zwô fuoge*—he is gay when
others are gay and sad when they are sad. And in a somewhat bitter
estimate of his lady's merits, he recognises in her two faults and two
graces, the same number of each, yet lets us know that the faults
weigh heavier. " She does her foes no harm and hurts her friends " :
that is all, and it is enough. Her compensating merits are likewise
two, *schœne und êre*, beauty and the honour of high rank, and of what
worth are these ?—mere show !

He is also the first to discriminate between two kinds of love,
*hôhiu minne* and *nideriu minne*, high love and low love, in neither of
which can be found satisfaction or peace, for both run to extremes.
By the first is meant love which aspires beyond its reach, the homage
paid to a lady of high birth, with all its train of passionate longings,
unfulfilled desires. By the second, love on the physical plane, mere
sensuous love, which leaves behind more pain than it was worth.
The context does not necessarily imply love for one of low birth,

though this is its natural corollary. The poet, having now suffered from both extremes, would fain find, if he could, the golden mean. He has been *vil nâch ze nidere tôt*, almost dead from having gone so low, and is *nu aber ze hôhe siech*, now again sick from striving too high.

His complete ideal of love is defined in characteristic phrase as *zweier herzen wunne*, the delight of two hearts. For, if unshared, one heart alone cannot hold it, it becomes then a burden too heavy for one to bear. Or, to quote from another passage : " Love must be mutually shared, so mutually that it passes through two hearts and through no more than two ".

This conception of love, in which Walther differs from Reinmar, coincides with that held by Gottfried von Strassburg, in so far as the stress lies on its twofold sharing. But Gottfried realises that mutual relation, the mystical union of two in one, far more deeply than Walther. Even though, as he says, he himself had scarce any experience of his own to draw from, his prophetic mind makes clear to him all it means. In Tristan and Isolt, his ideal lovers, he realises to the core that mutual sharing. " Love in those two had knit two hearts together with the bonds of her sweet magic, and with such great mastery, such wondrous power, that so long as they lived they remained in thrall." And this all-complete love is not joy alone, not unrelieved sorrow, but a sharing of both joy and sorrow ; it is bitter as well as sweet, and the bitterness of its pain makes its pleasure sweeter. " He who never suffered because of love has never known love's joy." Against the deeper insight revealed by Gottfried Walther's dictum that " Love is love if it pleases, if it hurts it is not really love " sounds trite and shallow. But that reading would be unfair. We know Walther too well. His insistence on the bright side of love, his denial of what is bitter, are the instinctive impulse and recoil of a sensitive nature which longs keenly for the one and dreads the other. If this is weakness, it is at any rate not shallowness. All the same, a weakness which, in one direction, limits the poet's range.

Gottfried, in praising Walther, gives no hint of this limitation : indeed, he fully approves of the happier trend which he seems to associate with the new lead of the nightingales' choir. " May they bring to a joyous issue their mourning and their sad lament, and may this happen in my time ! " Perhaps, though he does not say so, after the long-drawn-out melancholy plaints of Reinmar, a change was welcome.

As we consider these two, Walther and Gottfried, we feel that, in reality, Gottfried, not Walther, was the nightingale of perfect note. His romance of *Tristan* is as much song as story and has been rightly spoken of as a *Hohelied der Minne*, a high song of love, *canticum*

79

*canticorum.* The lyricism pervading it is its essence, by which the story lives. And it may be observed that the theory of love, which in Walther's treatment appeals primarily to the intellect and is primarily didactic in tone, is transformed by Gottfried into a musical theme, which grows and ebbs and grows again with refluent melody. But indeed, Gottfried's lyrical art surpasses that of the Minnesingers, Reinmar, Walther and the rest, in this special sphere. He alone, in treating of the theory and doctrine of love, transcends the intellectual approach and becomes as passionately fervent as in singing of love's experience. The distinction between *Minnelehre* and *Minnelyrik* which we recognise with Walther is non-existent in Gottfried. For he raises the doctrine of love to its highest power and wings it with music.

Walther has, on the other hand, some claim to the title *varwære* or painter, which Gottfried uses to designate epic poets. The pictorial side of his art is well developed and is one of its greatest charms. His most characteristic love-songs appeal as strongly to the eye as to the ear. From the faintly hyperbolical, full-length portrait of a beautiful woman in *Si wunderwol gemachet wîp* . . . (L. 53, ₂₅ . . .) to the living and shining pageant of May in *Muget ir schouwen waz dem meien* . . . his poetry abounds in pictures which are delightfully hale and lucid, and which give an impression of colour and substance that is the antithesis of Reinmar's phantasmal shapes of song. Walther's style is altogether less visionary than that of either Reinmar or Heinrich von Morungen. And while he làcks Morungen's gift for evoking a single pure abstract mood by rhythm and symbol, he has his own gift for interfusing situation and mood in the creation of a new and palpable effect.

Walther's flair for conjuring up instantaneous pictures gives colour and point to his treatment of the theory of love. But he also enlivens this in a special way, by his vivid and ever-ready personification of abstract qualities. In particular, the personified figure of Love—Frou Minne—is imagined with great zest and humour. She is represented as *der diebe meisterinne*—as a prime thief and burglar—whose entry no locks can resist. She conquers young and old ; no one's wit is a match for hers ; and her arrows stick deep. She has her tribunal, her high court of appeal, to which her votaries come demanding justice. In all these traditional rôles she becomes an individual being, more dynamic and forceful, indeed, in Walther's songs than his typical Court ladies, false or true. His wittiest presentation is when he depicts her as a coquette of mature age pretending to be young, romping with the young folk and despising those of forty, though in fact she herself is far older, old enough to take herself in hand and behave *als ein bescheiden wîp*, as a sensible woman.

The opposite process is using an abstract noun to mask a person. Asked what his lady's name is and asked too often, Walther replies: " I am so tired of this, I will tell you all what it is, then please leave me alone. *Genâde und Ungenâde*, Favour and Disfavour, my lady has those two names." More original and daring is his use of the name Hildegund, introduced as the last bold word of a bold conclusion :

Mînes herzen tiefiu wunde
diu muoz iemer offen stên, si enküsse mich mit friundes munde.
mînes herzen tiefiu wunde
diu muoz iemer offen stên, si enheiles ûf und ûz von grunde.
mînes herzen tiefiu wunde
diu muoz iemer offen stên, sine werde heil von Hildegunde.

My heart's deep wound, this must always stay open, unless she kiss it with a friend's mouth. My heart's deep wound, this must always stay open, unless she heal it up and heal it thoroughly. My heart's deep wound, this must always stay open, unless it be made whole by Hildegund.

The audience would have instantly grasped what that name signified. Its connexion with that of the poet is easily inferred from their being linked together before in the famous old German saga of Walther and Hildegund. What sounds a confession is really a captivating piece of masquerade.

The personal, the confessional element in Walther's love-poetry is, from the very nature of that kind of poetry, more ambiguous than when definite events of his life or definite relations to patrons and rivals gave him stuff to work in. His courtlier love-poems, his *Lieder der höheren Minne*, must primarily be regarded as songs of compliment or of social instruction and entertainment. From these, however, there emerges one vital fact, that the graceful formalities of the Amor Cortois were inadequate to a nature bent on the full reality of erotic passion. Where the personal note breaks through, whether as a reflex of immediate experience or of a strongly conceived characteristic pose, it expresses the kind of lover Walther was, a proud, exacting, dissatisfied lover, one, too, who seldom forgot for long his main function as mentor. The altruistic patience of Reinmar's ideal lover was something he neither felt nor wished to feel. He is tenacious of his rights as man and of his rights as singer. If, in return for his song, he asks of ladies no more than that they should give him a fair greeting, *wan daz si mich grüezen schône*, and they deny him that, why then, he will make an end. There is certainly a ring of personal just indignation in the emphatic lines :

Ich wil mîn lop kêren

81

an wîp diu kunnen danken :
waz hân ich von den überhêren ? (L. 49, 22-4).

I will transfer my praise to women who know how to thank : what have I from
the over-proud ones ?

This, in Codex C, is suitably followed by the converse of his revolt,
his confession of love for a girl of low degree. His mind dwells on the
thought of one who had given him the substance of love for its un-
satisfying shadow. He addresses her as *Herzeliebez frouwelin*, and
invokes God's blessing on her. Who she was remains obscure, more
probably a Court attendant of low rank than, as has been supposed,
a girl from a neighbouring village. The song addressed to her is
filled with a feeling of very great tenderness, all the more winning
from its restrained simplicity of phrase. It expresses a sensitive
reaction to the mockery of those who scorn this girl of low degree,
and an answering scorn in vindication of his love for her, as he shows
up the shallow pretensions of her detractors. Finally comes a lurking
fear lest, after all, her love should change, and a protesting cry : " Owê
danne, ob daz geschiht ! "—" Alas then, if that should happen ! "
We are present at the inception of a new kind of poetic vision.
This simple girl, who in her lovable sincerity is as true a lady as any
of her prouder sisters of high rank, is not only a figure from life but
at the same time the embodiment of a new ideal. The second stage,
at which the experience blossoms out into independent creation, is
attained and perfected in the limpid beauty of *Under der linden* . . .
(L. 39, 11 . . .) and *Nemt frouwe disen kranz* . . . (L. 74, 20 . . .). The
third stage, when the vision detaches itself from one poet's experience
and passes into the general stream of tradition, is absent, and with good
reason. The delicate conception of low-born ladyhood was eclipsed
by Neidhart von Reuental's vivid picture of the sensuous, high-
spirited village girl whose attraction lies in her untamed exuberance.
Walther's ideal, however, is not quite isolated, for while in the Minne-
sang there is nothing else like it, Hartmann von Aue, in *der Arme
Heinrich*, has created a kindred figure with the same fresh, virginal
appeal.
*Under der linden* . . . and *Nemt frouwe disen kranz* . . . are pastorals.
The central figure in both is peasant girl. In *Under der linden* . . .
it is she who speaks, tells of the tryst between her and her lover, out
in the field, under the linden tree, and of how when he saw her come
he greeted her as a noble lady, as *hêre frouwe*. In *Nemt frouwe disen
kranz* . . . the lover speaks and tells of two meetings.[15] The first,

[15] The arrangement of the strophes here followed is that which Wilmanns
adopted in his smaller edition of Walther's poems (*Sammlung Germanistischer
Hilfsmittel* v).

when at a dance—we assume, on the village green—he met a beautiful young girl who greatly charmed him. He gave her a chaplet of flowers to wear, saying that if he had precious stones to give he would adorn her head with those. She accepts his gift with bashful grace. " Her cheeks grew red, as when the rose blooms by the lily. She cast her bright eyes down, then bowed gracefully to me : that was my reward." He now lost sight of her, and all the summer through kept trying to find her. At last it seemed that they had really met. They went out into the field to gather flowers. From the trees beside them blossoms fell showering down upon the grass; and being in that " rich dream "—for a dream it was—so filled with gladness, he laughed for joy, day dawned, and he awoke.

With this dream-ending we may bid farewell to Walther's love-songs. For it makes a fitting close. Love, at the best, had never been to him more than a fleeting dream. In the end, his sense of the world's impermanence grown trebly strong, he felt, on looking back, as though his whole past life had been a dream, from which he has wakened to find all familiar things he cared for gone, or so changed that he does not know them. As this world fades, the other world draws nearer, and he looks for the life to come.

This mood of other-worldliness, this *Jenseitsstimmung* by which he is finally ruled, lies deep within him. Though rare in his earlier poems, it is yet potentially present. Like Hartmann von Aue, he is conscious of two disparate worlds and strives to reconcile them, but with a higher sense of dedication to that end than Hartmann, and a more stubborn valour. As Hartmann is part monk and part knight, Walther, though he would have refused to be so called, is *clericus* no less than courtier. That he must have received a clerical education is certain; and while, like many others, he ultimately preferred a free secular life to taking orders, his religious training determined his whole way of thought. Though he ranks himself as one of *uns leien*, his religion is not that of a layman : its accusing righteousness reveals the preacher, its intellectual clarity the schoolman. We can most readily see him as a product of a Cathedral school : this would explain his affinities with the *scolares vagantes*, to which Burdach first drew attention, as well as the ease with which he fitted into his place at court. He could scarcely have been, as Hartmann probably was, convent-bred.

*Gotes hulde*, God's grace, though he once links it in his wish with *mîner frouwen minne*, my lady's love, in reality comes first. Where he contemplates the nature of God and justifies His ways to men, or where, more personally, he ponders the relation to God of his own erring and honest soul, and trusts in Him, here it is that we penetrate to the depths of his being and learn the sources of his faith and courage.

*Herzeliebez frouwelîn . . .*

Sweetheart, young mistress mine,
God bless thee this and every day :
Could I some wish define
Greater than this, for thee, I'd pray
For words to utter it; what can I say more
Than this, that no one cares for thee as I do : whence my heart is sore.

They tell me, I do ill to address
My song to one of low degree ;
But they reveal their wit the less,
Who thus disclaim what love should be.
Let us not heed their jibes, they do not know
Love's meaning, they who are in love with wealth and with fair out-
ward show.

Beauty tends to cruelty :
Of Beauty's wiles let all beware.
Love can fill the heart with glee :
Beauty with Love may not compare.
Love makes a woman beauteous to behold.
Beauty has not the gift to make her lovable, if truth be told.

As I have borne, so let me bear,
And still continue to endure.
Thy fortune and thy face are fair,
Let no one speak of thee as poor !
Whate'er they say, I love thee in such measure,
The ring of glass thou gavest me would I not change for a queen's
treasure.

If thy heart be leal and true,
I shall not suffer doubt, nor dread
Lest thou shouldst give me cause to rue
My love, and wish its vows unsaid.
If it be otherwise, then let us go
Our separate ways alone ; but ah, what pain, if that were really so !

*Uns hât der winter geschât über al ...*

Winter has done us great harm everywhere.
Field and forest are withered and bare,
Hushed every voice that made melody there.
O to see girls playing ball on the fair
Open road, and to hear songs of birds in the air !

Would I might sleep until winter were o'er !
Waking, I grieve, and my anger is sore
At his wide sovereignty dreary and hoar.
May will most surely defeat him once more :
Flowers I shall pluck where the grass lieth frore.


*Under der linden an der heide ...*

Under the linden tree in the field,
Where the bed of us two had been,
Strewn beautifully, flowers and grass
May even now be seen.
Down by the wood in a dale,
Tandaradei,
Sweetly sang the nightingale.

I was come into the meadow ;
My true love came before.
He received me as his lady !
I am blest for evermore.
Did he kiss me ? a thousand times, this !
Tandaradei,
See how red my mouth still is.

Then did he make so richly
A couch of flowers gay.
In his heart there is laughter
Who chances to come that way.
By the roses he will find,
Tandaradei,
Where, so soft, my head reclined.

That he lay by me, were it known,—
God keep that from me !
What he did with me, never a one
Know this, save I and he,
And a little bird so true,
Tandaradei,
That may share our secret too.

*Mit sælden müeze ich hiute ûf stên* . . .

Thy blessing on me as to-day
I wake, Lord God, and go my way,
Thy care be over me where'er I ride !
O Christ, reveal to me the power
Of Thy great goodness hour by hour,
And for Thy Mother's sake be near my side !
As the holy Angel stayed
By her and Thee, when Thou wast laid,
God of old and Babe new-born,
Close to ox and ass in manger lowly,
Whereof the Blessed Gabriel,
Ministering to Thee, took no scorn
But tended Thee and watched Thee well :
So tend me also, that Thy will most holy
Cease not with me to dwell.

*Swer ane vorhte, hêrre got* . . .

Whoso, Lord God, being bold to say
Thy Ten Commandments, finds a way
To break them, for true love has failed to care.
Thy Fatherhood most men confess :
He who regardeth me as less
Than brother gives on meaning to that prayer.
From the same substance we are made ;
We grow alike ; our daily bread
Passes into our bodies, whence we thrive.
Who then can tell the master from the man,
When their bare bones, by worms bereft
Of differing flesh, alone are left,
Though he had known them both full well alive ?
Christian, Jew and heathen serve His plan,
Through Whom all souls survive.

*Mehtiger got, du bist sô lanc und bist sô breit . . .*

Most mighty God, Thou art so long and art so wide,
If we were to think accordingly, that labour tried
Would be in vain. Our measurements fall short beside
Thy power and everlastingness. My case alone
Tells me how many others also strive to think thereon.
With no avail. It lies beyond the scope
Of all that we dare meditate or hope.
Thou art too great, Thou art too small. No mind can reach
So far. Thrice foolish he who essays to span that breach !
Will he aspire to know what law and sermon cannot teach ?

*Owê wir muezigen liute, wie sîn wir versezzen . . .*

Alas, we idle people, we have sat down unheeding
Between two joys on the sad and lowly ground !
We had forgotten how to toil and strive, nought needing,
While liberal Summer all our wishes crowned.
To flower and fleeting leaf our lives were bound :
Bird-song ensnared us with a dream of mirth.
O well for him whose joys outlast the earth !

Alas for the tune which the cricket gaily taught us,
When we should have made provision against the winter's chill !
Had we struggled with the ant, what high honour this had brought us
Of peace and calm plenty we should now possess our fill.
This was ever the world's distempered will :
Fools have always mocked and spurned the wise.
These shall be judged according to their lies.

Alas, what honour from the German land is driven !
Clear wit and manly prowess, gold and silver gain,
He who has these, and lags with guilt unshriven,
Shall he not look for Heaven's reward in vain ?
Angels there, fair ladies here his worth disdain.
Stripped, arraigned in the eyes of God and Man,
Let him face the double sentence, if he can !

Alas, there comes a wind, know that and mark it surely,
Whereof we hear the baleful tidings told and sung.
This shall pass through all kingdoms of the earth in fury.
Palmers and pilgrims lament with sorrowing tongue.
Trees, towers in headlong ruin to the ground are flung,
Heads blown from off the strongest of the brave.
Now let us flee for refuge to God's grave !

87

# WOLFRAM VON ESCHENBACH

Wolfram von Eschenbach, pre-eminent as epic poet, has also his own distinctive line as Minnesinger. Of the eight songs which are certainly his,[16] four represent the genre of the Provençal *alba* : a significant choice on his part, since this is the most dramatic form of mediæval love-lyric. Its objectivity, its concentration upon a strong and sharply defined situation, its inherent passion, are native air to a poet who cared far more for the *vita activa* than for the graceful subtleties of courtly love. Wolfram is the first Minnesinger to adopt the fully developed type of the Provençal *alba*, in which the figure of the watchman is added to those of the secret lovers, either as the impartial herald of dawn or as the friend who warns them of its approach and urges them to part since night is over.

Kurt Plenio, in his scholarly investigation of Wolfram's songs,[17] found by basing his chronology of them on metrical grounds that the four *tagelieder* arranged themselves in this order :[18]

(1) Ez ist nu tac daz ich wol mac mit wârheit jehen
ich wil niht langer sîn . . . (L. 8).

(2) Den morgenblic bî wahtærs sanc erkôs
ein frowe, da si tougen
an ir werden friundes arme lac . . . (L. 1).

(3) Sîne klâwen
durh diu wolken sint geslagen,
er stîget ûf mit grôzer kraft . . . (L. 2).

(4) Von der zinnen
wil ich gên, in tagewîse
sanc verbern . . . (L. 5).

With this grouping, Plenio was able to show that the watchman comes more and more into the foreground, until finally he dominates the scene. In (1) he is never named. In (2) there is mention of his song: he himself takes no part in the action. In (3) he plays a very strong personal part. This poem consists of a dialogue between him

---

[16] The eighth song as preserved contains in addition to three authentic strophes three which some imitator had added. A ninth song attributed to Wolfram in A and C is unquestionably spurious.

[17] K. Plenio : *Beobachtungen zu Wolframs Liedstrophik* (*Beiträge zur Geschichte der deutschen Sprache und Literatur*, 1916, pp. 47—127).

[18] The arrangement of the songs in Lachmann's edition of Wolfram is indicated by a prefixing of the letter L.

and the lady, he admonishing, she insisting that he has wakened them too soon. The farewell between her lover and herself is described without words from either. In (4) the watchman stands out in masterly relief: two long strophes are spoken by him in monologue. In the third strophe the parting is described, and this time a few words are given to the knight, the lady is silent.

We will consider these songs in more detail.

While the first song is mainly composed of a dialogue between the lovers, I cannot for all that endorse Plenio's view that the watchman is not yet present. The opening lines, in which the coming of day is announced, are according to Plenio spoken by the knight: " Die Mahnung *ez ist nu tac* ist hier dem Ritter selbst in den Mund gelegt." Can this be so ? The lady's reply, where she speaks of her lover in the third person, seems more fittingly addressed to the watchman (or to herself), and the fact that just after this her companion is said to be lying asleep—*der was entslâfen dô*—surely shows that the warning cannot have come from him. One may concede that the watchman's part is small : his warning uttered, he is no longer there. It must also be confessed that the sentence *ich wil niht langer sîn,* literally, " I will no longer be," comes more naturally from the knight, on whose lips it would be interpreted " I will stay no longer," though in fact he does not usually display such haste. Spoken by the watchman it could only mean " I will delay no longer (*i.e.* it is time for me to give warning)," while the phrase *ze leide mir*—" to my grief "—though this again would come more naturally from the knight, is not impossible as a mark of sympathy from the lovers' friend. The reasons against the watchman as speaker of those first lines weigh less than the sheer unlikelihood of the knight himself announcing the dawn, then falling asleep again.

In all four songs there is great dramatic power, and the unconventional metres are so shaped—in the first song, indeed, so rough-hewn—as to give an effect of bold realism.

The sacrifice of lyrical sweetness to rugged dramatic power is most evident in the first of the four songs. As in the opening lines :

Ez ist nu tac      daz ich wol mac      mit wârheit jehen
ich wil niht langer sîn.
diu vinster naht      hât uns nu brâht      ze leide mir
den morgenlîchen schîn.

The internal rhymes, harsh in themselves and occurring at abrupt, short intervals, strike an opening discord. Day is here, and the spell of night is suddenly broken. The effect is renewed in the *Aufgesang* of the second strophe, with similar-sounding rhymes and the same pattern, the discord being renewed as the lover starts up from sleep:

dô daz geschach     daz er ersach     den grâwen tac,
dô muose er sîn unfrô.

When it happened that he beheld the grey day, then was he far from glad.

In this song the *Aufgesang* reveals each time a new phase of the situation, smiting it out in lines that ring heavily and in abrupt succession. First comes the watchman's warning, by which the lady alone is roused. She clasps her sleeping lover in her arms and he awakes. A passionate farewell follows. Then he departs and she is left alone. The second part of the strophe, the *Abgesang*, in each case amplifies the new phase, representing in its somewhat irregular structure the unstudied forms of natural speech. End-rhyme is half abandoned: there are no rhymes in lines 3—5 or in the last line but one. The four-beat line, the most customary sentence-unit, predominates as norm. The longer lines convey a heightening of emotion and an access of imaginative power. As when the lady speaks of him whom she would gladly shelter in her eyes—

den ich in mînen ougen gerne bürge,
mohte ich in alsô behalten.

Or when the knight exclaims :

wie ist diu naht von hinnen alsô balde ?
wer hât si sô kurz gemezzen ?

How has night sped away from us so swiftly ! Who has measured it so short ?

Or when the lover's close embrace is described in this hyperbole :

ob der sunnen drî mit blicke wæren,
sin mohten zwischen si geliuhten.

If there had been three suns with shining ray, they could not have shone between them.

Or when the knight speaks his last farewell :
Dîn wîplich güete neme mîn war
und sî mîn schilt hiut hin und her und her nâch zallen zîten !

May thy womanly goodness take care of me and be my shield to-day hence and hither and afterwards at all times !

The first strophe of this song may now be quoted in full :

" Ez ist nu tac     daz ich wol mac     mit wârheit jehen
ich wil niht langer sîn.
diu vinster naht     hât uns nu brâht     ze leide mir
den morgenlîchen schîn."
" Sol er von mir scheiden nuo,
mîn friunt, diu sorge ist mir ze vruo.

ich weiz vil wol, daz ist ouch ime
den ich in mînen ougen gerne bürge,
mohte ich in alsô behalten.
mîn kumber wil sich breiten.
owê des, wie kumt ers hin !
der hôhste vride müeze in noch wider an mînen arm geleiten."

" Now it is day, when I may well declare in truth that I will no longer tarry.
The dark night has brought us, to my grief, the morning light." " If he, my friend,
must now depart, that call has come too soon upon me. I know well, it is the same
for him, whom I would gladly shelter in my eyes, if I could so keep him. My
trouble grows big. Alas, how will he get away ? May the protection of the
Highest guide him back to my arms again ! "

In the second song (L. 1) there is a more regular strophic pattern
and rhyme sequence, but with the same general effect of impromptu
in the strongly varying lengths of line and in the varying pausation
and overflow. This naturalistic handling of the metre befits the
sense. Its casual form is entirely right for the inevitable sequence of
the recorded moments, for the involuntary impulse determining the
woman's words—the man's are not given—and for the live and start-
ling realism of the final picture.

Let us take, as a fragment of illustration, the woman's first speech :

" . . . Owê tac.
wilt unde zam daz freut sich dîn
und siht dich gerne,
wan ich eine. wie sol ez mir ergên ?
nu enmac niht langer hie bî mir bestên
mîn friunt. den jaget von mir dîn schîn."

" Alas Day, wild and tame rejoice in thee and see thee gladly, save I alone.
What shall happen to me ? Now my friend can stay here with me no longer.
Thy light chases him from me."

The third *tageliet* is magnificent : that is the least we can say of
this superb dramatic lyric. Both dramatically and lyrically it stands
on a higher plane than the two we have considered. Lyrically, be-
cause the elements of the metre are harmonized : the movement of
the verse, while free and flexuous, has an assured and ordered rhythm.
It is a proud, strong movement, and conveys something more than
the human side of the story, though this is as tense as ever. For over
and beyond it we can sense the lordly, untarrying, relentless advance
of Day. The language, too, has a nobly sustained resonance of tone
and is rich in splendid phrases. As, for instance, when in the opening
lines, under the image of an eagle or falcon ready for flight, the watch-
man describes the approach of day :

> sîne klâwen
> durch diu wolken sint geslagen,
> er stîget ûf mit grôzer kraft,
> ich sihe in grâwen
> tägelich als er wil tagen,
> den tac . . .

His claws have struck through the clouds, he mounts up with great strength :
I see him dawning, as is his daily wont to dawn, the day . . .

Or again, when the watchman urges the lady to let her lover go :

> er muoz et hinnen
> balde und âne sûmen sich :
> nu gip im urloup, süezez wîp.

He must away swiftly and without delaying. Now give him leave, sweet woman.

Or in

> ez ist nu tac : naht was ez dô
> mit drucke an bruste din kus mirn ab gewan.

" It is day now : it was night when, breast close to breast, thy kiss received him
from me."

Dramatically also, this poem stands higher than the other two.
In those, the lovers realise their position and accept without question
the necessity of the hour. They curse the day which brings their
night to an end ; they make the most of their intense farewell ; yet,
for all their grief at parting, they know that it has to be. But now the
situation expands. The watchman enters the scene, armed with a
sense of duty which comes in conflict with the blind wilfulness of
unreasoning love. He takes thought for the lovers' welfare and is
opposed. Seeing the day break, he has come to fulfil his pledge :
to lead hence in safety the gallant man he had let in the night before.
The lady answers him : " Watchman, these are the same unwelcome
news thou always bringest as it draws towards day. By my troth
I bid thee, I will reward thee for it as far as I dare, let me keep my
dear companion with me here." Then he, disregarding a request
so fatal, again urges her to let her lover go. Yet, though the moment
is crucial, he does not speak roughly to her. Though firm, he shows
great tenderness to her in her crying need. " He must depart
swiftly and without delaying : now give him leave, sweet woman.
Let him then love thee afterwards secretly as now, that so he may
keep his honour and his life. He entrusted himself to my good faith,
that I might bring him hence again. It is now day : it was night
when, breast close to breast, thy kiss received him from me."
Still she resists, maintaining that he always wakens them too soon.

" Before the morning star rose or the daylight shone, thou hast often torn him away from my white arms, not from my heart."

We may here assume that the watchman goes back to his post. And now, immediately, as the day shoots its ray through the window and the watchman's song rings out, she is seized with alarm for her companion's sake. And just as before she had been foolhardy, now he, the valiant knight, undeterred by the peril that hangs over him, will not suffer the watchman's warning call to cut short their deep and passionate farewell.

In this brief, concentrated drama there are, we may say, four actors. For, in addition to the three human figures, the watchman with his wise fidelity and the reckless lovers, there is also Day itself, so powerfully conceived that we feel a superhuman presence, irresistible and fateful, forerunner and champion of the hostile human forces which are not named.

In the fourth *tageliet* (L. 5) the effect is nearer to that of pure lyric, the metre with its preponderance of short, crisp lines suggesting the actual song, the *tagewîse*, with which the watchman is wont to salute the dawn. Suggesting as though in anticipation, not reproducing : the watchman, prologizing, defers his matitudinal song. Standing alone on the battlements, he contemplates his duty to the lovers, theirs to themselves and him. Now it is time for him to go down and warn them. They, seeing it behoves them to love with honour, must give ear to his counsel. He, the guardian of their lives and their good name, will do his best to help them. And now he calls to the knight in ringing tones :

" ritter, wache, hüete dîn ! "

" Knight, awake, be on thy guard ! "

Then he addresses them both directly, in strong assertions which admit no gainsay. Knightly honour is at stake ; sorrow at parting and hope of a future meeting must give way to that. And now the sky brightens and the danger of discovery grows apace :

" ein sumer bringet
daz mîn munt singet,
durh wolken dringet
ein tagender glast.
hüete dîn, wache, süezer gast ! "

" A summertime brings that whereof my mouth sings, there darts through the clouds a radiancy of dawn. Be on thy guard, awake, sweet guest ! "

The parting described in the third strophe is needed for completion, but is eclipsed in imaginative daring by the first two.

It is characteristic of Wolfram that in his *tagelieder* the martial side of knighthood comes into play. When the lover declares that his lady's goodness will be his shield to-day and at all times, we hear the forecast of Parzival's thought about Condwiramurs and of his advice to Gawan :

> " friunt, an dînes kampfes zît,
> dâ nem ein wîp für dich den strît :
> diu müeze ziehen dîne hant,
> an der du kiusche hâst bekant
> unt wîplîche güete."     (*Parzival* 332, ₉ . . .).

" Friend, in thy hour of conflict, let a woman maintain the fight for thee, may she guide thy hand, one in whom thou hast found purity and womanly kindness."

In the *tageliet* stress is laid on the knight's valour as shown by his fearless prolongation of love's farewell while the danger quickens. We are told that

> der ritter ellens niht vergaz . . .

the knight forgot not his valour

and that

> swie balde ez tagte,
> der unverzagte
> an ir bejagte
> daz sorge in flôch . . .

However swift the dawn, the dauntless man took such award from her as put their cares to flight.

Not since Kürenberg's lover called for his horse and armour, had the martial note in the Minnesang been thus decisively sounded. Heinrich von Morungen in his *ich wil eine reise* . . . uses war as a fiery symbol. Here knightly valour and knightly honour are objective realities ; and this secret nocturnal love is an adventure of the chivalrous life involving both.

But this dark flame of dangerous and secret love, however strongly imagined, is not Wolfram's ideal. His fifth and last handling of the theme is in the spirit of one beyond reach of its glamour. This is in the song

> der helden minne ir klage
> du sunge ie gegen dem tage . . .       (L. 4)

which has *tagwîsz* written against it in the margin of B by a late hand, and which might well be called a *tageliet* of a new kind. But it really is a bridal song, praising the serene happiness of wedded love which can bear the full light of day. The song is undoubtedly a reflex of Wolfram's own personal experience as bridegroom, and being unique in the history of the Minnesang may be quoted in full :

der helden minne ir klage
du sunge ie gegen dem tage,
daz sûre nâch dem süezen.
swer minne und wîplich grüezen
alsô enpfienc
daz si sich muosen scheiden,
swaz du dô riete in beiden,
dô ûf gienc
der morgensterne, wahtær, swîc, dâ von niht gerne sinc.

swer pfliget oder ie gepflac
daz er bî liebe lac
den merkern unverborgen,
der darf niht durh den morgen
dannen streben,
er mac des tages erbeiten :
man darf in niht ûz leiten
ûf sîn leben.
ein offen süeze wirtes wîp kan solhe minne geben.

For secret love thou wast ever wont to sing lament towards day, the bitter after
the sweet. Whoever thus received love and a woman's greeting, that they had to
part, whatever thou didst then advise them both, when the morning star rose,
watchman, be silent, of that no longer choose to sing !

Whoever is or has been used to lie by his love without hiding from spies has
no need to hasten away because of morning, he can await the day : there is no need
to lead him out thence at his life's peril. An openly known, sweet wedded wife
can give that kind of love.

This view undergoes no change. Wolfram must have been a
most happily married man. Wherever he refers to his own family
life, it is in a warm, affectionate tone ; nor is there ever a trace of
matrimonial bickering among his wedded couples, and only one case
of jealousy (Orilus). Over and beyond this, he sees marriage love
as a part of the great social order, honoured in the sight of men.
Its legality sets it higher than the love which has recourse to guile.
Less vehement, it burns with a steadier flame, and does not scorch
but warm. Nor does it lack adventure. Its permanence means, no
mere idle security, but a life-long sharing of life, a testing and prob-
ing, as the channel in which it flows widens and deepens. Where
there is this perfect union, death alone can part :

diu zwei kunnen sich dâ niht gevirren
wan mit dem tôde al eine : anders kan daz nieman verirren.

The two cannot part from one another, except in death : no one else can put
that love astray.

This last testimony is put into the mouth of the old king Titurel, looking back from the wane of life over a fair and fruitful past (*Tit. 5*).

From this we return to Wolfram's lyrics. These include three songs of courtly love, in which the well-worn theme of the lover's service is conventionally re-stated. It is plain that the young poet's heart is not touched thereby. So, while he offers no new ideas, his originality vents itself in new fancies. He gives a novel turn to the old conceit of the lover being able to see his mistress at all times, absent or present, by night as well as by day, exclaiming " How like an owl I am ! My eye sees her in dark night "—

> wie bin ich sus iuwelnslaht :
> si siht mîn ouge in vinster naht. (L. 3)

He speaks vividly of his lady's help eluding him, flying swiftly past him, wilder than a deer, *snel für mich, wilder danne ein tier*. In his description of her, wondering at her hard heart, he sees her softly moulded breast, which can vie with a year-old hawk's for beauty. Of that same hard heart he declares that he might sooner supplicate a flint to crumble (L. 8).

These are mere brilliant fancies. They are outshone by the inspiration of two most beautiful stanzas, in which the many times praised month of May leaps to life at the touch of winged words. All the old-time phenomena, singing birds and burgeoning leaves and flowers, are renewed in new language. No poet before this had named flowers bursting forth and leaves shooting in such pregnant phrase as *ursprinc bluomen, loup ûz dringen*, or called the gleam of bright flowers *der bliclîchen bluomen glesten*. Others had praised the sweet singing of birds ; no other as yet had said that " all the May season they rock their children with song "—" al des meien zît si wegent mit gesange ir kint ". Yet the beauty of May, expressed so potently, is not the main theme : in the midst stands the poet himself, glorying in his own transcendent gift of song. Birds cease to sing before summer is well over ; he can sing when frost lies on the ground and, he bids his lady mark, without her guerdon. When May was here, " then the nightingale slept not, but now I am still awake and sing up the mountain and in the vale,"—

> Dô slief niht diu nahtegal :
> nu wache aber ich and singe ûf berge und in dem tal. (L. 6)

This elation is somewhat belied by the sober conventional tone of the three stanzas immediately following. It is best to regard these not as continuation but as another and inferior song in the same metre. There is really no logical link between them and that enchanting pæan. The proud independence of the poet who declares he can sing without woman's guerdon foreshadows the spirit of a famous song lost to us. It was a *rüegliet* or taunting song, and was a bitter fruit of the poet's experience, the indignant outburst of one of Amor's scorched votaries against a lady who had played him false. While the song is lost, we have his full commentary on the effect it roused. This is given in *Parz.* 114, ₅ ff. in a personal digression interposed between Books II and III. Here, briefly and haughtily, the poet restates his consciousness of his worth as singer :

> ich bin Wolfram von Eschenbach
> und kan ein teil mit sange.

I am Wolfram von Eschenbach, and have some skill in singing.

And, he goes on to say, there is one woman I refuse to praise. My anger towards her is unrelenting. She has done me such wrong, I cannot choose but remain her foe. Therefore the rest of them treat me as *their* foe. Although I am sorry they hate me, still, it is their women's way, and must be borne with, since my words carried me too far and I said what went against myself, which will likely not happen again. All the same, let them be wary how they attack me, they will find I can offer strong defence. I know how to judge their ways and their behaviour. Every pure woman shall find in me a champion bold to praise her ; I am grieved to the heart if she suffers. The praise of that man limps and is lame, who rejects all ladies because his own has failed him. . . . Then, the knight in him extinguishing the singer, he goes on to state what service they may look to receive from him, not with song but in knightly combat with shield and spear :

> schildes ambet ist mîn art :
> swâ min ellen sî gespart,
> swelhiu mich minnet umbe sanc,
> sô dunket mich ir witze kranc.
> ob ich guotes wîbes minne ger,
> mag ich mit schilde und ouch mit sper
> verdienen niht ir minnen solt,
> al dar nâch sî si mir holt.

The service of the shield is my birthright. Wherever I put not forth my valour, if any woman loves me for my song, I think her judgment poor. Be it that I desire a good woman's love, if I cannot with shield and with spear earn her love's guerdon, may she favour me as I deserve (*i.e.*, not at all).

The notorious song which was the starting-point of this excursus had another sequel. Among Wolfram's lyrics is a very simply built song of three stanzas (L. 3), of which the first two are linked together in thought, forming no more than a pleasant affirmation of the courtly lover's correct approach to love. The first ends with that quaint simile of the owl which we observed before. The third stands apart, introducing an entirely new thought, and has been recognised as belonging to a later occasion, as, in fact, a brief apology for the offence caused by the taunting song. It is a disarming answer, innocent and good-humoured in tone, and the simple metre is exactly right :

> Seht waz ein storch den sæten schade :
> noch minre schaden hânt mîn diu wîp.
> ir haz ich ungerne ûf mich lade.
> diu nû den schuldehaften lîp
> gegen mir treit, die lâze ich sîn.
> ich wil nu pflegen der zühte min.

See, what harm could a stork do the crops : the women have even less harm from me. I am loath to burden myself with their hatred. As for her who has trespassed against me, I will let her be. I will now take care of my manners.

Thus the affair is dismissed, lightly, as befits a man of sense and humour. But it had been bitter earnest, and the memory of it died hard. Wherever Wolfram mentions false women, he grows severe : it is as though the old hurt rankled. Yet among his female characters there is no false type : all his women are true. And it is with a sense of having made full atonement that he turns at the end of *Parz.* Book VI to his audience, saying : Have I not done well, have I not made retribution for that harsh song which was meant for one woman only ? I have told you of Belacane and of Herzeloyde, of Jeschute, Ginover and Cunneware, and have shown you their true hearts.

He had also, in the story of Parzival and Condwiramurs, shown knightly service and the bitter-sweet stress of love-longing woven into a romance of marriage, and had sent his hero forth on his long quest fortified by his wife's love, and believing her unseen presence to be his shield in battle.

-------

> *Den morgenblic bî wahtærs sange erkôs*
> *ein frowe dâ si tougen*
> *an ir werden friundes arme lac . . .*

Morn, and the watchman's song that hailed it, broke
The slumbers of a lady where she lay
Secretly in her noble friend's embrace.
The joy that filled them both was driven away.

Her bright eyes dimmed ; her face
Grew wan again.   She spoke :
" O Day, both wild and tame rejoice in thee,
And see thee gladly, save I alone.   What shall become of me ?
My friend can stay no longer here.   Thy light
Hunts him away from me, out of my sight ! "

Day thrust its brightness through the window-pane.
They, locked together, strove to keep Day out
And could not, whence they grew aware of dread.
She, his beloved, casting her arms about
Her loved one, caught him close to her again.
Her eyes drenched both their cheeks.   She said :
" One body and two hearts are we.
Nought is, can mar or separate our mated fealty.
From that great love of ours my heart lies waste,
Save when thou comest to me, and I  to thee make haste."

Thus did the sorrowing man take swift farewell :
Their fair smooth skins drew closer, closer yet.
This the sun saw and shined upon :  a kiss
From a sweet lady's mouth, with eyes all wet.
How they lay twined in the intricacies
Of blended lips, breasts, arms and thighs, whose art can tell ?
If a shield-painter could have limned them there,
Where they lay clasped, no other picture could have been as fair.
Yet was this last love-bliss of theirs pierced through
With grief.   Their faithful love was all too true.

# HARTWIG VON RAUTE

For this gifted poet the most suitable place is here, after Wolfram von Eschenbach.  A single translation may help to give some idea of his form and style.

### Ich wil versuochen . . .

I will make essay
Whether she perchance may
Give me leave to renew
My hopes, and pursue,
Longer than I yet have done, her love.   Then if she
Receives this bounteously,
My joy will soar to greet that season of delight,
My spirit attain such height
That it were wondrous strange
If my heart checked its range,
If for joy it did not leap to the very skies,
And a high new song devise
Of such sweet doing
In sweet melodious wise with rapturous wooing.

# NEIDHART VON REUENTAL

The originality of Wolfram, as shown in his treatment of lyrical forms, goes well with that of two other Bavarian poets, Hartwig von Raute and Neidhart von Reuental. Of the former too little has survived, of the latter, perhaps, too much. What is left of Hartwig von Raute is a handful of songs, just four, and we are lucky in the chance which has preserved even these. The first is conventional except for the last four lines, which stand apart and have their own separate theme. The other three, composed of single stanzas, are songs not of love-longing but of love-rapture, daring and beautiful in their technique and of an inspired buoyancy of tone.

The poetry of Neidhart von Reuental may be called epoch-making. Whatever its unknown antecedents, it represents a breaking of new ground in the history of the Minnesang. The village pastoral which Neidhart brought into fashion is a new and original genre : while it has affinities in French and Latin pastoral poetry and implies their priority, it is in many ways different from both. What it may have derived from earlier folk-song remains conjecture ; but the view that there *was* a connection need not be dismissed as " romantisch-conservativ."[19]   In the songs of Neidhart as in many of the *Carmina Burana* the chief inspiration is the movement of the country dance ; and folk-dancing is never far removed from folk-singing. The drawback is that, at this period, the only popular dancing songs extant are a few anonyma interspersed with the Latin love-songs of the *Carmina Burana*, and these, though primitive in style and tone, are not necessarily of popular origin ; they were most likely composed by the *scolares* themselves. There is, however, among them, one genuine folk-song : a four-line stanza meant to be sung by girls in chorus, as round they go in the ring-dance with joined hands :

> swaz hie gât umbe
> daz ist allez megede.
> die wellent âne man
> allen disen sumer gân.

What goes round here, that is all maidens.   They want all this summer to go without a man.

This, one need hardly say, is too elemental to help in the discovery of Neidhart's antecedents.   Probably to a great extent it was he himself, who by his natural genius achieved the transition from the

[19] W. H. Moll : *Über den Einfluss der lateinischen Vagantendichtung auf die Lyrik Walthers von der Vogelweide und seiner Epigonen im 13ten Jahrhundert*, 109.

primitive dancing song to the stylised pastoral which he created to amuse the court. The intermediate stage would have been the songs which he made for his rustic friends. The rôle of song-maker assumed by him as part of the masquerade must have had foundation in fact. It could not have been otherwise, given his intimate share in the open-air dance which pulses through his wonderful summer songs.

The time has gone past for interpreting Neidhart's poems as biographical records. Their realistic data, above all, their disarming nomenclature are now seen as a new and daring form of masquerade. Of the general underlying facts we can still be sure. We know that the poet took part in village festivities, that few details of the life he saw there were hidden from him, and that he had swung and sung to the rhythm of the country dance. We may also guess that he had, in his dealings with village girls, kissed and teased and wrangled and made amends ; but the story of his flirtations contains none can say what proportion of truth to fiction. The same must be said of his feuds with the village churls. Malicious and hostile relations lay behind his satirical pictures ; but his life was not one unending series of feuds with adversaries whose names are legion, Engelmar and Engelher and Engelwan, and Engelram, Engelbolt and Engelber, Hildebolt and Hildemar, Berewin and Berewolf . . . these names, selected at random, may give some idea of the lengthening string. They are more than any one man could have tackled. That flirtations and feuds went together, the first occasioning the second, .is again an established pose. Another reason for the peasants' war suggests itself as more likely than that of love. Neidhart probably began satirizing the lower class not out of pure malice but simply to amuse the higher. For himself and his courtly audience, the upstart villager, ludicrously aping his betters, was fair game ; and Neidhart spared none of his points. But he could not lead a double life. His village associates knew of his jibing songs and took practical vengeance. They burnt his crops and damaged his means of livelihood and made life burdensome, so Neidhart informs us, and this time he speaks plain truth. Such hard facts were no part of the masquerade. And his attitude towards his despised opponents becomes coarsely hostile. While his earlier satires show good-natured hilarity, the later ones are steeped in cold venom.

The name Neidhart — actually Nîthart — exactly fits the poet's rôle as enemy of the peasant, as *Bauernfeind*, by which he lived on in legendary tradition long beyond his time.[20] It was therefore more likely to have been a nickname conferred on him, rather than his own baptismal name. As *her Nîthart* he is first referred to in Wolfram's

[20] *Nît* .. malice, enmity.

*Willehalm*, 312, ₁₂₋₁₄, which shows that by the year 1212 or somewhat later his fame had ripened. The title *her* confirms his knightly rank. He himself never gives his name but calls himself *der von Riuwental* (Reuental). A place of that name has been pointed out in modern times in the vicinity of Freising, but since Neidhart once mentions *Landeshuot* as adjacent locality, it is more feasible to identify his small estate with Reintal in the neighbourhood of Landshut. His conversion of this to the symbolic name of Riuwental—vale of sorrow—can be easily explained by the meagre resource it furnished. At the same time, it is used in the earlier songs with a confident ring which belies the literal meaning. When troubles increase, the meaning becomes more patent. As a poor man Neidhart, in spite of his knightly training, was clearly at no great advantage compared with the wealthy farmers, whose well-stocked houses and broad acres entitled them to look down on him for his lack of means, just as he looked down on them for their lack of manners. He was, after all, no aristocrat, merely a poor gentleman whose status as ministerialis was legally lower than that of the landowning peasant. It was a competition between *guot* and *êre*, between wealth and that real though elusive thing called honour, particularly elusive in Neidhart's case, since he does not seem to have had any code or ideal. His sincerest feeling is a love for his own native soil, an intense local patriotism which must at one time have made a close bond between him and his peasant friends. In 1217 he took part in the Egyptian Crusade of that year as member of the contingent raised by the Duke of Austria. His Crusading songs—if one may call them so—have no trace of religious fervour. They are filled with an unhappy sense of exile, as though all the time he were longing to be at home. He tries to put a good face on it, saying they keep up their spirits ; afterwards, speaking of things out there, he remarks rather grimly : " We scarcely exist ; more than half the army is dead ". He pictures the season of May in his own dear country, and wishes he had the chance of singing to his friends, for, says he, *die Walhen*—Italians or French—have no use for my song. He sends, or imagines himself as sending a messenger with greetings for his wife and friends.

We assume that Duke Lewis of Bavaria, his overlord, was also his patron ; but the vogue he started spread far beyond its original nucleus, as Walther's lament for the decay of courtly singing, *hovelîchez singen*, bears witness. Duke Lewis died in 1231 : we are not certain whether it was he or his successor Otto who deprived Neidhart of his fief, but the misfortune occurred, we may say, about the beginning of the thirties. It was a heavy blow, and from the poet's point of view undeserved. *Ich bin sîn verstôzen gar âne schulde* —" I am ousted from it without any cause," he says, and again, *ich hân des mînen herren hulde verloren âne schulde*—" I have lost my lord's favour without cause (i.e. by no fault of mine) ". That the offence he gave to his rich peasant neighbours had much to do with it can be gauged from the close of this revealing song. He admits then :

> mir ist vil leide daz ich von Eppen und von Gumpen ie so vil gesanc.

I am very sorry I ever sang so much about Eppe and Gumpe.

He migrated to Austria where he enjoyed the liberal patronage of Duke Frederick surnamed " der Streitbare ", the successor of Leopold VI. The rest of his life was spent in close connection with the Viennese court. From Frederick he received a small fief near Melk on the Danube, and for this he returns grateful thanks, qualified by the remark that it would be all right, were it not for the huge rent he has to pay, *wan der ungefüege zins*. His old age is rather sad : there is something so withered and joyless in his outlook, and the poetic impulse is on the wane.

Neidhart is pictured in the illustrated Heidelberg codex as standing with a garland of flowers in his hand, in the midst of a rather unruly band of peasants clamouring for a song. And that represents very well what he must have been like in his prime, when the flame of his genius burned strong in him.

For he had been a poet of genius. His beautiful summer songs are filled with a surge of Dionysian ecstasy and are most magically alive.

His poetry falls into two groups, *Sommerlieder* and *Winterlieder*, songs of summer and songs of winter.

The annual May festival, held since time immemorial to celebrate the coming of summer, forms the setting of the *Sommerlieder*. The song usually begins with a picture of the return of May, and one hears in this prelude echoes of the old nature-worship which still clings unconsciously to the primitive rites of the season. May comes marching into the land as a royal lord. He leads the wood by the hand. Winter is driven back. Field, meadow and wood put on their best array, which the May has sent them. The trees which had been bare and grey now have their new twigs thronged with singing birds : from them the May takes tribute.

From this live setting the situation springs, generally in dramatic form. Sometimes there is a dialogue between a girl and her mother. The girl is all in a flame to join the dance. The mother warns her to beware of men, they are all deceivers, she tells her, and she tries to keep her at home, but in vain. Once it comes to a free fight between the two. On another occasion the mother confiscates her daughter's dress and shoes. In a song of richer content this is bettered: the daughter defies her mother, tells her to be quiet and bluntly asks her, *Wâ nu slüzzel?*—" Where now is the key?" Not getting it from her, she goes and forces open the chest where her dress is stowed away, shakes it out, puts it on and draws it in with a girdle, and now she is off and is tossing her parti-coloured ball to her lover, him of Riuwental! For it is a favourite device of the poet's to introduce himself in this way, always as the pick of the gathering, as a lover of courtlier make than the average loon. One time the mother mentions a more suitable match : *der junge meier muotet dîn*—" The young farmer has a mind to you ". The girl thinks scorn of that notion. Sometimes there is a dialogue between two girls, and here the best effect is obtained by contrast. One girl is down in the dumps, she has evidently been crossed in love and has no heart for the dance and no use for the men. The other is full of gay spirits, for *her* lover is simply perfect : he is, of course, von Riuwental. Sometimes the intoxication of May affects both old and young, and we hear of an old woman who all the winter had lain bed-ridden now leaping like a ram and rushing to take part in the dance with the youngest. Or the parts of mother and daughter are reversed : the former, leaping like a kid, tells her daughter to bring her her array, she is going to dance with the rest, and the daughter reproves this levity as unbecoming. The gusto of the poems is superb. The love which Neidhart treats of is very far removed from love's dream : all the sexual impulses are awake and unashamed. There is no reserve or modesty in this headstrong and lusty love, which feels itself as a part of the great joy of Nature, as a manifestation of the mating season, frank and inevitable.

The *Winterlieder* describe the dances which take place indoors when snow is on the ground. But the dance does not seem to be the essential feature of the winter festivity, in fact, the houses of the peasants were as a rule too small to afford space for dancing. There were exceptions : Megenwart, we hear, had one of those " large rooms ",—*Megenwart der wîten stuben eine hat.* But essentially the winter songs are *Spottlieder*, songs of jest and mockery. The chief feature of the winter sports was a rude altercation ending in blows. In the winter songs there is a rough masculine element, whereas in the summer songs the young girls take the lead. It is thought that originally the men were accustomed to meet alone, and to indulge in coarse jesting and interplay of words as they diced and drank. Certainly it is here that we feel the presence of Walther's *Frou Unfuoge*—Dame Discourtesy : but the best of the winter songs are, all the same, good entertainment and very clever. They are full of fresh realism, an interesting feature of this being the introduction of numerous proper names, which gives it all a familiar air. For instance :

> Wer nach Künegunde gê, des wirt enein :
> der was ie nâch tanze wê :
> ez wirt uns verwizzen, ist daz man ir niht enseit.
> Gîsel, ginc nach Jiuten hin und sage in zwein,
> sprich daz Elle mit in gê.
> ez ist zwischen mir und in ein starkiu sicherheit.
> kint, vergiz durch niemen Hadewîgen dâ ;
> bit si balde mit in gân . . .

An analysis of this song (No. 18 in Keinzel's edition) is the best way of illustrating the type.

First, the winter landscape is described, a counterpart of that in the summer prelude. All is drear and melancholy, cold and silent. The first line, which sounds like an invitation to out-of-door sport, *kint bereitet iuch der sliten ûf daz îs*—" boys and girls, prepare yourselves sledges for the ice "—stops short of any such fulfilment. Arrangements are now made for the holding of a dance indoors. What is the most suitable place ? " Megenwart has one of those big rooms." That will do splendidly. Whether Megenwart approves or no seems not to matter : his *daughter* does. " It is his daughter's wish for us to come there." The girls' forces are mustered. " Decide, who is to go and tell Kunigund : she was always aching for a dance. We shall be well blamed if *she* is not told. Gisel, go along to Jiute and tell the two of them,—say that Elle must go with her. There is a strong contract between me and them. Girls, for any sake don't forget Hadewig ; tell her to make haste and come. One custom may be laid aside : they may leave their foreheads bare." There follow some details of the women's dress. To have the neck well covered is more important than to deck one's head. After this the fun begins. The girl Geppe is dancing with Gumpe. Eppe tries to pull her away from him. The threshing staff which he carries —strange company manners !—gives him odds ; but Master Adelber intervenes with his rod and stops the fray. Then (the logic must take care of itself) all this, we are told, was about an egg which Ruopreht found. Ruopreht threatened to throw this at Eppe (evidently taking Gumpe's part). Eppe answered him rudely back, saying " tratz ! " Ruopreht aimed the egg at his head (which was bald), and it all ran down him. Then there was another scuffle. Friedliep wanted to dance with Gotelind. So did Engelmar. To cut the tale short, I will tell you (says Neidhart) how it all ended. Farmer Eberhart had to be fetched to put a stop to it, before they had torn out one another's hair. The silly ganders !

If the matter is rough, it makes good farcical sport.

Engelmar, mentioned here for the first time, becomes subsequently one of the most important figures in Neidhart's crowd. Opinions vary as to what biographical value there is in the triangular situation with Neidhart, Friderun and Engelmar ; nor does Neidhart give us a clear relation of the incident on which it depends. Few will probably go so far as H. Schneider, and regard the whole thing as mere allegorical fiction.[21] Neidhart's realism served as a masque, yet not so as to justify the denial of potential truth : our difficulty is in drawing the line between truth and fiction. The story, pieced together, amounts to this. Neidhart and Engelmar were rivals for the love of Friderun. Neidhart had had some priority. This was lost to him when, in the midst of the open-air dance one May festival, he being absent, Engelmar sprang to the side of Friderun and snatched from her a mirror pocketed in her dress. This evidently meant more than the theft itself. It was an assertion of ownership, and meant that Engelmar took possession of Friderun and Neidhart lost her. The event then became to him a symbol. He depicts it as the turning-point of his life, and as representing the triumph of *unfuoge*, the defeat of him, the penniless gallant, by the overbearing, overdressed, insolent peasant. From now on he changes his pose completely. He is now no longer, as in the songs of his prime, the courtly and debonair knight the girls admire. His supremacy over their hearts is gone. He is the defeated rival of his inferiors, giving vent to his hatred of them in spiteful satire.

Neidhart's later poems undoubtedly show a great falling-off in quality. This is especially true of his Austrian period, though the deterioration had begun before. One might say, winter had come ; but the effect is rather that of a rotten-ripe autumn, as compared with his summer prime. Sociologically, his later satires are full of meat and very interesting, but this does not cover up his decline as artist. The songs are structurally loose, and metrically monotonous. The long line of six or seven feet is all too frequent, and is pounded out with a heavy regularity of cadence which makes it tedious. So for instance :

> Die selben zwêne die gehellent hin nach Engelmâre,
> der gewalticlîchen Friderûne ir spiegel nam.
> tretzic unde hœnic sints an allen ir gebâren,
> die selben zwêne dörper Giselbolt und Engelrâm.

The same two follow up the tune of Engelmar, who took by force her mirror from Friderun. Defiant and disdainful are they in their whole behaviour, the same two rustic churls Giselbolt and Engelram.

A new and crude experiment is that of parodying the language of

[21] H. Schneider : *Helden- Geistlichen- und Ritterdichtung*, 420.

courtly love, then, unexpectedly, applying it to some village wench, for whom such high-flown praise is ludicrously unfitting. Lines lifted from Reinmar and from Heinrich von Morungen give point to the incongruous effect.

Like Walther, though without his sustained and deeply felt seriousness, Neidhart often laments that the world has changed and is a sadder and a worse place than as he had known it. And it is in direct imitation of Walther's *Frou Werlt*, Lady World,[22] that he personifies *Werltsüeze*, the World's Sweetness, or, as we may say, World's Delight. But he does so in his own way, playing a game of mystery with his hearers, in order to spring a surprise upon them in the end. He begins with the usual touch of winter. " They complain that this is the sharpest and hardest winter there has been for a long time." In the same way *he* complains of his lady's hardness. He has served her without stint all his life. No one need blame him if he desert her now : she has never tried to reward him, not by the worth of one hair. Then he breaks out into vituperation. It is not enough to have called her cold and callous. No, she is an infamous strumpet. All the virtue she appeared to have when he first knew her has fallen from her. She has changed for the worse and her court is thronged with shameless, worthless people. For God she does not care ; to him who loves good she exhibits spite and hatred. Why should he continue to serve such a one ? His lady's honour has gone lame and staggers ; it has tumbled down into a pool of filth and none but God can cleanse it. Eighty new melodies had he sung in his lady's service. This is the last he will ever again sing to her, this lament for having served her. And now, there be many who will wonder who she is, this lady whom he had singled out in song and had once praised so highly. " Her name is World's Delight. May the Lord God release me from her ! "

This poem, with its line of development running through it, is structurally one of the best of the later songs. It is also one of the most vital. The feeling is sincere : the deliberate rhetorical effect which the poet achieves does not belie his real earnestness. But the theme is renewed once only, and this time it is followed, incongruously, by a further display of the old satiric vein which always paid him. For, says he, when I turn my mind to sorrow, some one comes and says, Sing something else, something we can enjoy. And so back he goes to his ridiculously dressed-up village churls.

Elsewhere there are serious undertones, and references to the un- happy state of the land at large show, for his old age, a widening of

---

[22] This poem (L. 100, 24) is a dialogue between Walther and Frou Werlt, in which he resists her blandishments, says he now knows the truth about her, and bids her a final farewell.

horizon. But the last of him brings a final and welcome recrudescence of the old sense of joy, as he invokes the summer scene and calls on the friends of his youth to join the dance :

Liebiu kint, nu vreut iuch des gedingen
daz got mit sîner güete mange swære kan geringen.
uns kumt ein schœniu sumerzît
diu nâch trûren vröude gît.
ich hœre ein vogellîn singen

In dem walde sûmerlîche wîse.
diu nahtigal diu singet uns die besten wol ze prîse,
ze lobe dem meien al die naht.
manger leie ist ir gebraht,
ie lûter, danne lîse.

Dâ bî lobent diu merlin und die zîsel.
ûf Hiltrât Liukart Jiutel Berhtel Gundrat Geppe Gîsel !
die zement wol an der meien schar.
Vrômuot sol mit samt in dar ;
diu ist ir aller wîsel.

Dear children, rejoice now in the hope that God with His goodness can lighten many a trouble. To us there comes a lovely summer season which will give joy after grieving. I hear a little bird singing in the wood its summer melody. The nightingale sings her best tunes nobly all night long in praise of May. Her warbling is in many keys, always clear, then low. And the blackbirds and finches join in the praise. Up, Hiltrat, Liukart, Jiutel, Berhtel, Gundrat, Geppe, Gisel ! These are fit members of May's company. Glad-heart shall come there along with them: she of all them is leader.

From this poet of the unscrutable mask we are content to receive, first and last, what we know to have been the truest part of him, the fadeless assurance of his " eternal summer ".

---

*Ine gesach die heide
nie baz gestalt . . .*

I never saw the field
In lovelier bloom.
Sunrays the green leaves
Of the wood illume.
With joy, in both we hail the May's advance.
Maidens, now take hands,
And merrily haste to meet the summer-time in festive dance.

Praise unto May is given
By many a tongue.
From many a bank and brae
The flowers have sprung
Where but a short while since no flowers had been.
The budding limes are green,
And gentle maids, as you have heard just now, in the dance are seen.

They are care-free and filled
With joy's excess.
You maidens clothed with charm
And loveliness,
Adorn yourselves, and let Bavarians praise,
Let Franks and Swabians gaze
Enraptured ! Lace the dainty smocks you don for holidays !

" For whom shall I adorn me ? "
A maiden said.
" The drowsy fools see nothing !
My hopes are dead.
Honour and joy the world accounteth strange ;
The men seek nought but change ;
Women of whom they might be proud come not within their range."

" Not so," her playmate answered.
" We shall not need
To say farewell to gladness.
Of men, indeed,
Many there are who value women's best
And comeliest ;
And I am wooed by one who can drive sorrow from the breast."

" Let me behold that worth
To me unknown !
The girdle that I wear
Shall be thine own.
Tell me the name of him who loveth thee
With such fine constancy !
I dreamt last night thy thoughts were fixed on one of fair degree."

" He whom they call the knight
Of Riuwental,
Whose song is the delight
Of one and all,

He is my friend.  Nor shall he lack reward.
For him, my heart's adored,
I will array me.  Hence, and come along, the dance is toward ! "


*Und hân ich indert heime . . .*

And if some place I have a home,
Where may it be ?
The swallow with a speck of loam
Has more than me.
For this is all she needs to form
A cot to last her through the summer warm.
God give me a house with sheltering roof
By Lengebach, and proof
Against the winter's storm !

# SELECT BIBLIOGRAPHY

The following list is necessarily very imperfect. But the scope of the subject makes it impossible to recall everything of importance without running to inconvenient length. The reader desirous of fuller information may be referred to the bibliography supplied by Ehrismann : *Geschichte der deutschen Literatur bis zum Ausgang des Mittelalters, Zweiter Teil, Schlussband, München*, 1935, pp. 180—286.

## EDITIONS OF TEXTS

K. Bartsch : *Deutsche Liederdichter des zwölften bis vierzehnten Jahrhunderts.* Siebente Aufl. besorgt von W. Golther, Berlin, 1914.

F. H. von der Hagen : *Deutsche Liedcrdichter des 12ten, 13ten und 14ten Jahrhunderts,* 4 Teile. Leipzig, 1838. Nachdruck, 1923.

F. Keinz : *Die Lieder Neidharts von Reuenthal.* Leipzig, 1910.

Lachmann und Haupt : *Des Minnesangs Frühling* (MF), Leipzig, 1859. Vierte Auflage bearbeitet von F. Vogt, 1922.

Lachmann : *Die Gedichte Walthers von der Vogelweide.* Zehnte Ausgabe herausgegeben von Carl v. Kraus. Berlin, 1936.

F. Pfaff : *Die grosse Heidelberger Liederhandschrift in getreuem Textabdruck.* Heidelberg, 1909.

—— *Der Minnesang des 12. bis 14. Jahrhunderts* (Kürschner, Deutsche National-Literatur VIII). Stuttgart, 1895.

F. Pfeiffer : *Abdrucke der Liederhss.* A und B. Stuttgart, 1843-4.

W. Wilmanns : *Walther von der Vogelweide* herausgegeben und erklärt. Vierte vollständig umgearbeitete Auflage besorgt von V. Michels. Halle, 1924.

## BOOKS AND ARTICLES DEALING WITH THE MINNESANG

K. Bielschowsky : *Geschichte der deutschen Dorfpoesie im 13ten Jahrhundert.* Berlin, 1891.

H. Brinkmann : *Geschichte der lateinischen Liebesdichtung im Mittelalter.* Halle, 1925.

—— *Die Entstehungsgeschichte des Minnesangs.* Halle, 1926.

K. Burdach : *Reinmar der Alte und Walther von der Vogelweide.* Leipzig, 1880. Zweite berichtigte Auflage mit ergänzenden Aufsätzen über die altdeutsche Lyrik. Halle, 1928.

—— *Walther von der Vogelweide.* Philologische und historische Forschungen I. Leipzig, 1900.

—— *Über den Ursprung des mittelalterlichen Minnesangs, Liebes-romans und Frauendienstes.* Sitzungsberichte der Preuszischen Akademie der Wissenschaften, 1918; reprinted in *Vorspiel* I, pp. 253—333. 1925.

G. Ehrismann: *Die Kürenberg-Literatur* (Germanisch-romanische Monatsschrift. 1927).

—— *Geschichte der deutschen Literatur bis zum Ausgang des Mittelalters,* Zweiter Teil, Schlussband. München, 1935. pp. 180—286.

K. Halbach: *Walther von der Vogelweide und die Dichter von Minnesangs Frühling.* Stuttgart, 1927.

A. Jeanroy: *Les Origines de la Poésie Lyrique en France au Moyen Age.* 1904.

—— *La Poésie Lyrique des Troubadours* (2 tomes), 1934.

C. von Kraus: *Die Lieder Reinmars des Alten* (3 Bände). 1919.

—— *Die Lieder Heinrichs von Morungen.* 1925.

—— *Walther von der Vogelweide. Untersuchungen.* Berlin, 1935.

H. Menhardt: *Zur Lebensbeschreibung Heinrichs von Morungen* (*ZfdA*, 70, 209—234). 1933.

—— *Heinrich von Morungen am Stauferhofe?* (*Ibid.* 73, 153—260). 1936.

F. Michel: *Heinrich von Morungen und die Sprache der Troubadours* (Quellen und Forschungen, 38). 1880.

W. H. Moll: *Über den Einflusz der lateinischen Vagantendichtung auf die Lyrik Walthers von der Vogelweide und die seiner Epigonen.* 1925.

K. Plenio: *Beobachtungen zu Wolframs Liedstrophik* (Paul Braune Beiträge 42, 47—128). 1917.

—— *Bausteine zur altdeutschen Strophik* (*PBB* 42, 411—502 and 43, 56—99). 1917-8.

—— *Über Walthers und Reinmars Herkunft* (*PBB* 42, 276—280).

H. Schneider: *Helden- Geistlichen- und Ritterdichtung* 365—449. Heidelberg, 1925.

—— Eine mittelhochdeutsche Liedersammlung als Kunstwerk (*PBB* 47, 225—269). 1923.

—— *Die Lieder Reinmars des Alten* (Deutsche Vierteljahrsschrift für Literaturwissenschaft und Geistesgeschichte. Jahrgang 17, Heft iii, 312—342). 1939.

A. Schönbach: *Die Anfänge des deutschen Minnesangs.* Graz, 1898.

—— *Walther von der Vogelweide.* Dresden, 1890. Neu bearbeitet von H. Schneider, 1923.

F. R. Schröder : *Der Minnesang.* I. Die Forschung. II. Das Problem (Germanisch-romanische Monatsschrift 1933).

A. Schulte : *Die Standesverhältnisse der Minnesinger* (*ZfdA* 39, 185—251).

E. Sievers : *Heinrich von Morungen* (*PBB* 50, 331—351). 1927.

F. Vogt : *Geschichte der mittelhochdeutschen Literatur* I, 137—156. Berlin u. Leipzig, 1922.

W. Wilmanns : *Leben und Dichten Walthers von der Vogelweide*, Bonn, 1882. Zweite vollständig umgearbeitete Auflage besorgt von V. Michels. Halle, 1916.

G. Wolfram : *Kreuzpredigt und Kreuzlied.* (*ZfdA* xxx, 89). 1886.

# APPENDICES

## Appendix I

# WOLFRAM VON ESCHENBACH AND THE PARADOX OF THE CHIVALROUS LIFE

It has become a commonplace of literary criticism to contrast the dualism of Hartmann von Aue with the organic unity of Wolfram von Eschenbach's view of life. The distinction is undoubtedly just, provided it is not pressed too far. There is certainly a difference of mental trend. Hartmann, with his strong predilection for the study of opposites, is peculiarly qualified to deal with antitheses, in small things as well as great. Hence his masterly use of stichomathia as a vehicle for expressing the quick interplay of contrasted temperaments and wills. So, most effectively, in *Erec* 4059—83, where the choleric, point-blank enquiries of the enraged Graf alternate with the grudging, aggravatingly short replies of the houseowner whose privacy he has so rudely invaded. Or again, in *Erec* 9025—48, where the hero encounters the heavy blustering threats of his huge enemy with cool retorts of imperturbable self-assurance. Hartmann thinks readily in terms of conflict. The *Büchlein*, his earliest work, consists of a debate between the heart and the body. *Erec* and *Iwein*, each with a congenial theme derived from its French source, deal with the rival claims of knightly prowess and sexual love. The last and strongest of the crusading songs proclaims the victory of heavenly over earthly love, the one envisaged as real, the other as counterfeit. The triumph of Hartmann's art in depicting a conflict of opposites is in *Gregorius*, where the vocation of knighthood is brought into direct rivalry with that of the ecclesiastical and monastic life ; and the boy Gregorius contends with his spiritual father, pleading the cause of chivalry against the abbot's appeal to the higher claim of the religious way of life.

Defeated at first, it is the latter which ultimately wins. Although Hartmann expresses his own ideal in the words of Gregorius :

> Ritterschaft daz ist ein leben,
> swer im die mâze kan gegeben
> sone mac nieman baz genesen.
> er mac gotes ritter gerner wesen
> dann ein betrogen klôsterman  (1530—35)

in the tale of Gregorius himself, this ideal is foredoomed to frustration, because the tragic fatality in store for him demands from him not *mâze* but the entire sacrifice of the chivalrous life for one of world-renunciation and penance. The pendulum, however, swings back in the tale of " der arme Heinrich ", to whom, redeemed by the grace of God from pride and self-will, the opportunity denied to Gregorius is freely granted, that of living the chivalrous life with *mâze* and as a true *gotes ritter*, or knight of God.

Wolfram thinks naturally in terms of fellowship and concord. Such conflicts as arise in the course of his story are seldom, if ever, deliberately planned by him, nor does he introduce contrasts so sharply obvious as those of Hartmann. Yet, for all that, Hartmann, working within narrower limits, is able to solve his differences the sooner. The simple plot of *der Arme Heinrich* gives him means sufficient to solve the problem raised in *Gregorius*. And the call of the Crusade becomes at the same time a promise of how to win both the praise of the world and the soul's salvation,—" der werlde lop, der sêle heil ".

On the other hand, Wolfram, out of the fullness and depth of his experience, discovers a discord which strikes at the very heart of humankind, nothing less, indeed, than the old universal enmity between love and death. Of this there are signs already in *Parzival*, though not enough to disturb its ordered synthesis or dim its clear-shining optimism. It is otherwise when we come to *Willehalm*. To interpret this rightly, we must not rest content with the vantage-point gained in *Parzival*. That finely harmonised view of human life expressed in the earlier work meets with a far rougher challenge in *Willehalm*. From this epic of war to the death there rings out a dissonance more profound than anything within the more limited range of Hartmann.

Let us reconsider the ground which the two poets have in common.

Both share, with differences of perspective and treatment, the same sphere of chivalrous life, and like-mindedly regard it as a life of *êre âne gemach*, honour without ease,—that neat antithetical phrase we owe to Hartmann. Both take into account, though the angle of approach is different, the religious life of world-renunciation, the *vita contemplativa* which has its place together with the *vita activa*. Both look for a unifying principle of life. Hartmann's watchword is *mâze*, self-discipline, temperance ; Wolfram's is *triuwe*, the bond of fellowship in which *fides* and *caritas* are united. Still, it must be remembered that Hartmann, too, recognises the value of *triuwe*, and that Wolfram lays stress on *kiusche*, purity, and *diemüete*, humility, which are the foundations of *mâze*.

To both, the besetting sin of the chivalrous life is *superbia* or *hôchvart*. Hartmann demonstrates this in " der Arme Heinrich ", Wolfram in the case of Anfortas, thinking of whom Trevrizent says that " hôchvart ie seic unde viel",—pride ever sank and fell, and of Parzival, in the angry stubbornness of his revolt against God's dispensation.

In the chivalrous life Hartmann discerns a rivalry between its two main factors : the love of man and woman, and the fighting-man's thirst for knightly prowess and honour   In both *Erec* and *Iwein*, the solution is by the same characteristic rule of *mâze*, more consistently, however, in *Erec*. In neither of these stories, as told by Chrestien de Troyes and retold by Hartmann, is the solution too difficult : time with the teaching of experience provides the key.   But could Hartmann have handled the problem (solved in *Erec*) in the form in which we encounter it in the *Tristan* of Béroul, when, in his forest exile with Iseut, Tristan wakes to the realisation of the knightly honour he has sacrificed to his love, and resolves on a partial recantation beyond his power to maintain ?   The answer is certainly No.   Hartmann's imagination, at home with the fortunes of Erec and Enite, could never have grasped the tragic dilemma of that other pair of fated and passionate lovers.   A similar limitation appears if we compare his Iwein with Wolfram's Gahmuret.   As Iwein fails to keep tryst with Laudine, so Gahmuret forsakes Belakane, in each case for the same abstract reason, predominance of the claims of knightly honour over those of love.   But where Iwein errs through mere forgetfulness, Gahmuret acts with his eyes open, renouncing his love because the fighting-man's urge toward prowess has the stronger pull.   Iwein, as Hartmann conceives him, is more the victim of circumstance—and of his lady's unreasonable hardness of heart—than of any moral conflict within himself.   There is nothing in his character to hinder him from attaining the golden mean, whence the account of his ordeal lacks any deep significance.   Gahmuret, fated to love and fated to do his love violence in response to the stronger side of his nature, is a far more dramatic figure than the mild and virtuous Iwein.   With Gahmuret, it is useless to think of *mâze* : he is too eager and too passionate.

Because his view of life is so wide and varied, Wolfram transcends those juxtapositions and clear-cut differences which are the main concern of Hartmann.   Where Hartmann loves to separate and oppose, Wolfram tends to co-ordinate.   But again, because Wolfram's sympathies are stronger, his understanding of human nature more penetrating than Hartmann's, the problems he discloses are in more direct relation to the compulsive forces of human passion, and are therefore more vitally real.

The co-ordination of love and knightly honour is perfectly achieved in the marriage of Parzival and Condwiramurs.   Yet in the relation of those two interacting factors there lies a potential seed of tragedy.   The life of the fighting-man, inseparable as it is from danger and hazard, that strenuous life of *êre âne gemach*, is always shadowed by the menace of sudden death; and death may be a glory to the man, but to the woman whose life is bound up with his, and indeed to all of those left who love him, wife, mother, or father, an intolerable grief. Thus the relation of love and knightly honour becomes in the last resort a tension between love and death. In this fundamental fact lies the major crux of the chivalrous life. The temptation of *superbia* may be overcome, but the sorrow of the bereaved is unanswerable.

Or, at least, it can only be met with a resigned fatalism :

> alsus vert diu mennischeit,
> hiute vreude, morgen leit. (*Parz.* 103, 23—4)

Thus fares mankind : joy to-day, grief to-morrow.

In the first two books of *Parzival*, in the story of Gahmuret the Angevin, Wolfram gives an incisive picture of the short-lived glory of knighthood, and of the great sorrow which falls to the lot of women because of it. Not only Gahmuret, that splendid and reckless knight-errant, is predestined to fall in battle, but so also did his father, his brother, and his father's father die before him. In this kind of hereditary doom there is nothing new, nor in the figure of the mourning woman, one of the oldest in literature, yet here, each individual case of the common lot brings with it a fresh stab of reality. Schoette, widow of Gandin and mother of two sons, Galoes and Gahmuret, comes vividly before us in one short scene of memorable pathos. Bidding farewell to the younger son before he sets out on his travels, she says to him : " Son of King Gandin, wilt thou stay with me no longer ? Alas that I ever bore three ! Thou art also thy father's child. I have buried the strength of my heart, the delight of my eyes . . . ". Later, the death of her elder son, and the continued absence of the younger, caused her heart to break. Kaylet, in giving news of this to Gahmuret, states without rhetoric the simple truth :

> Dô ir erstarp Gandîn,
> und Gâlôes der bruoder dîn
> und dô si dîn bî ir niht sach,
> der tôt ouch ir daz herze brach. (92, 27—30)

The briefly recorded fate of Schoette is a prelude to the fully told tragedy of Herzeloyde, the saddest, surely, of all Wolfram's women. Well might Sigune tell her son that " thy father bequeathed her sorrow ". Whatever joy she had had must have been short-lived. In the beginning of her married life lies a premonition of its ending, through her acceptance of the condition her husband imposed on her, not to hold him back as his first wife had done, but to let him have his fill of fighting. Eighteen times, we are told, he returned to her fresh from combat, before he passed oversea to fight for his friend the *baruc*, and for six months she heard no news of him.  That ordeal she endured with a queen's courage (102, 23—103, 10), then, all at once, " the sword-blade of her joy snapped asunder at the hilt " A strange prophetic dream descends upon her, and goads her into anguish, just before the arrival of Gahmuret's squires and pages, bringing news of their lord's death.   From that moment her life is blighted.   Not even the birth of her son can bring her a lasting joy, for with her love of him is mingled the dread of his growing up to share his father's fate.   Their idyllic life in the forest, on his side so full of sunshine and high spirits, is for her an anxious and, finally, useless struggle to avert his destiny.   The time comes when he rides away and leaves her, and in losing him she loses all that binds her to life.   In that supreme agony—" der werlde riwe aldâ geschach "— death comes suddenly upon her.

Then, at the very last, the death-pang gives place to a realization of the life beyond it.   " Thus she, who was a root of goodness and a stem of humility passed on the way that brings to bliss."   And that suffices.   The story turns back to young Parzival, setting out on his first adventurous journey.

It is, however, artistically fitting that the close of Book III is in grave harmony with its beginning.   This time it is the old knight Gurnemanz, interpreter and teacher of chivalrous custom, who acknowledges, with dignified grieving, the harsh award of the chivalrous life.   The loss of his three sons, " die ellenthaft gestorben sint ", is a sorrow unhealed by time.   Then, with the coming of Parzival, a new hope had sprung up, that the boy would stay and marry his young daughter and be the light of his old age ; but this " fourth son " is lost to him as well.   " Ah, you have been too quick to ride away and leave me mourning !   Alas that I cannot die, since the fair maid Liaze and the land I give with her content you not ".

Gurnemanz recalls the death of each of his sons with an economy of language which gives all the deeper emphasis to its pathos.   In the case of two, Lascoyt and Gurzgri, the circumstances are taken from *Erec*.   Lascoyt is killed by Iders in contest for the prize of the Sparrowhawk, Gurzgri by Mabonagrin.   Both times, the situation is transformed in its removal from the plane of romance to that of tragedy.   Here is no fortunate issue for a brave young knight encountering fearful odds, but a stroke of stern realism : the odds prevail.   The death of Gurzgri is described in more detail than the rest : to the young man's fate is added that of his wife and mother. " Mahaute rode beside him in her beauty ; her proud brother Ehcunat had given her him to wife.   To the high city of Brandigan he came riding, in the direction of Schoydelacurt.   There his death was not averted : Mabonagrin slew him there. Therefore Mahaute lost her radiant hue, and my wife, his mother, lay dead."

Thus the conclusion of Book III matches its beginning. But Herzeloyde as woman, and Gurnemanz as man, wear their rue with a difference. She, for her part, repudiates the life of chivalry as a hostile element which has lost all value. He, to whom knighthood remains an unalienable heritage, accepts its rough award with resignation. " Sus lônt iedoch diu ritterschaft."

The idea of chivalry as exacting a heavy toll is especially stressed in the first three books of *Parzival*, yet does not give them their dominant tone. The general impression is one of overflowing vitality, both in the short-lived manhood of Gahmuret and in the boyhood of Parzival. This happier strain continues undisturbed in Book IV. From Book V onward, there emerges another kind of sorrow, the more subtle agony of a life-in-death. But this lies outside the scope of the present study.

There remains the figure of Sigune, in whom the sorrow of bereavement is shown with great intensity. Grief for the death of her lover is made still more unbearable by the anguish of remorse, because she herself had, unknowingly, hastened his end. Like Herzeloyde, she withdraws from the world, but, left without any living tie, carries her renunciation further and becomes a recluse. Here is the angle from which Wolfram most naturally regards the religious as compared with the secular life. For those who have loved and lost and have no more wish for the *vita activa*, the *vita contemplativa*, the religious life of meditation and penance, is a haven of refuge. In this haven Sigune waits for the life immortal, when she and her lover shall meet to be no more parted. Her death, like that of Herzeloyde, is conceived as an end and a beginning.

Sigune's case can be compared with that of her father, Kiot. That of Trevrizent is different : he renounces the life of chivalry in the belief that this sacrifice is needed to win his brother's release from suffering. Even so, in the change from one kind of life to another, the breadth of his humanity gives scope for a firm hold on temporal things.

There is, despite the poignancy of its tragic moments, no place in *Parzival* where the poet, as distinct from his characters, appears troubled by doubts or misgivings. We have still to examine, tentatively at least, the attitude of mind revealed in *Willehalm*.

That is not easy. One of the baffling things in *Willehalm* is the interjectional abruptness of some of the thoughts uttered. More freely than in *Parzival*, in *Willehalm* the course of the narrative is strewn with Wolfram's own personal reflections and comments : yet this increased subjectivity does not facilitate our reading of the poet's mind, rather, it makes us realise the warring complexity of the ideas presented to us.

It can only be by substituting general and, I feel we must add, wishful impressions for close investigation, that the author of a recent and brilliantly-written essay on the ethics of chivalry,[1] F. W. Wentzlaff-Eggebert, sees in *Willehalm* a direct and consequent development of the point of view attained in *Parzival.*

> Jetzt (*i.e.* in *Parzival*) vollendet sich das Bild des deutschen Ritters im Sinne des Mittelalters ! Gott und der Welt dienen erscheint als höchstes Ziel, und so endet Wolframs Dichtung mit jener bekannten Lebens-Lehre, die deutlich zeigt, wie sich Ritterliches und Christliches ergänzen sollen . . . Aber das ist nicht die Summe von Wolframs Weltanschauung. Seine Gebundenheit mit der Zeit, sein tatkräftiges Im-Leben-Stehen verlangte noch eine Vertiefung des Themas. Sie beruht auf der Stellung zum gelebten Frömmigkeitsempfinden seiner Zeit : zum Kreuzrittertum. Erst *Willehalm* bildet den Höhepunkt von Wolframs Ritterethik. Ein Rittertum kampfer-probter, im höchsten Sinne männlicher Haltung und gleichzeitig frommen Herzens ersteht vor uns (p. 268).

These are fine-sounding words, but, instead of " Erst *Willehalm* bildet den Höhepunkt von Wolframs Ritterethik ", one may equally well affirm : " Erst *Willehalm* zeigt uns den wunden Punkt in Wolframs Ritterethik." How can it be overlooked that for Wolfram the " Idee des Rittertums "—however fervently he himself, as a son of his age, believes in it and does it honour—is crossed and complicated by that idea of human brotherhood in which his natural nobleness of feeling shows itself more Christian than the teaching of the Church Militant ?

It is without deliberate intent, simply because he could expound his material in no other way, that Wolfram's *Willehalm* expresses, on a magnified scale, that paradox of the chivalrous life of which there were glimpses in *Parzival.* On the one hand, the glory and thrill of battle, fanned to white-heat on the Christian side by belief in a sanctified cause ; on the Pagan side clothed in a dazzling excess of outward splendour. Against this, the cruel wastage of lives and the lament that follows.

This dichotomy is, of course, universal, and can be traced all down the ages, to the accompaniment of a courageous fatalism and an ever-recurring lust for vengeance. But, in the age we are consider-ing, the association of chivalry with an ethic attuned to the Church's teaching sharpens the discrepancy between the glory of war and its ruthlessness. The crusader's ideal is an attempt to overcome the antithesis : in the conception of a holy war the fighting-man's energies are sanctified, the brutalities of his trade justified as means to a

---

[1] F. W. Wentzlaff-Eggebert : *Ritterliche Lebenslehre und antike Ethik (D.V.J.S.* 23 Jhg. 1949, 2/3).

righteous end. To the soldier of the Cross was offered the compensating promise of heavenly reward, not without the earthly satisfaction of being entitled to hate one's enemy with a whole heart and to rejoice in his downfall. The *Bataille d'Aliscans* has much of this vengeful spirit. It is to the honour of Wolfram that the grosser compensation of revenge and hate is denied him. He accepts, without flinching, the bounden duty of the Christian fighter to defend his Faith ; yet his sympathies go out to both armies. Inspired though he is to flights of eloquence when he thinks of the souls of the slain Christians borne to their reward in heaven, nevertheless, he grieves at the gloomier prospects of the resplendent Paynim, whose shining and variegated colours are like the luxuriant flowering of a field in May :

> nu gedenke ich mir leide,
> sol ir got Tervigant
> si ze helle hân benant. (20, 10—12)

Now I think it a great pity, should their god Tervigant have destined them for hell.

As in the *Bataille d'Aliscans*, the untimely death of the boy Vivians, the youngest hope of the Christian army, is deeply mourned. But here, on the Saracen side also, Tesereiz, the garland of love—" der minnen kranz ",—and Arofels, the Persian king, are singled out for eulogy and lament. So warmly are they imagined, that Wolfram not only expresses his own sorrow, but puts into the mouth of their slayer Willehalm, not indeed at the time but afterward and in retrospect, words of generous regret for the death of two enemies so noble (204, 15—205, 30).

Let it be said at once, that in *Willehalm* the " Idee des Kreuzrittertums " does not solve the antithesis of the fighting-man's chequered life. Nor does it lie within Wolfram's purpose to solve it. He views his material in the concrete, attracted by its potential nobility, its breadth and magnificence, and equally aware of its grimness. The theme he recognises as radically different from that of his earlier epic ; for now the fighting is such that, rightly named, it can only be called " mort ", that is, slaughter.

> swâ man sluoc ode stach,
> swaz ich ê da von gesprach,
> daz was nâher wol gelendet
> denne mit dem tôde gendet.
> diz engiltet niht wan sterben
> und an freuden verderben. (10, 21—26)

Wherever blow or thrust was given, whatever I spoke of this before was more often brought to a safe landing than ended with death. Here all is a matter of dying and of the loss of joy.

It would take too long to trace all the shifting moods in the poet's mind as he follows the storm-swept path of his story. They vary between two extremes. The fighting-man's exultation in the sheer joy of the contest comes into full play in the splendid battle-scenes of Books VII and VIII. That is the one extreme. The other is sorrow and pity for the carnage of war, exceedingly strong in one who was so great a lover of mankind, and embracing both sides of the struggle, Christian and Paynim. Compared with the clearer and steadier vision of *Parzival*, it would seem as though Wolfram now saw through a glass darkly, trusting, however, in the ultimate care of a divine Providence, and, like Gurnemanz, accepting this life as it stands :

> jâmer ist unser urhap,
> mit jâmer kom wir in daz grap.
> ine weiz wie jenez leben ergêt :
> alsus diss lebens orden stêt.—   (280, 17—20)

Sorrow is our beginning, with sorrow we come to the grave.   I know not the way of the life beyond : it is thus, that the course of this life is ordered.

There are, in particular, two passages which bear striking witness to a divided and questioning frame of mind. The one occurs in the first book of *Willehalm*, the other in the ninth and last.

In the first, Wolfram envisages, with a clarity so startling that he immediately reacts against it, the dilemma provoked by the love of Willehalm and Gyburg (30, 21—31, 20):

Arabele, Gyburg, one woman twice named, love and thyself are now interknit with sorrow : thou hast made a league with loss and harm. Thy love cuts the Christian cause to pieces ; they who defend that cause no less unsparingly cut down thy kith and kin. Of these, too, many shall therefore perish, unless He, Who sees into all hearts, prevent it. My heart declares that the reproach is thine (*mîn herze dir ungünste giht*).

Wherefore ?   I should first state what I found culpable, or where is my understanding ?   No blame lay with the queen, with her, who was once called Arabel and renounced that name in baptism for the sake of Him to whom the Word gave birth.   That Word came mightily down to a Maid (she is evermore a Maid), of whom He was born Who, without flinching, gave His life up to death on our account.   Whoever suffers in battle for His sake shall receive everlasting meed : him shall the singers welcome, whose music rings so clear. . . . I mean, in heaven the angels' melody : that is sweetest of all sweet song.

The dilemma, thus categorically thrust aside in an escape to the unassailable sanctuary of the Christian faith, does not cease to exist. Objectified, it re-appears in the mind of Gyburg, who, though she never swerves from nor repents the choice she has made, realises to the full its fatal consequences and, confessing herself the cause—" *ich trage al eine die schulde* ",—suffers with all her great and generous heart.

125

In the second of the two passages here singled out (450, 15—30), Wolfram, echoing words he had previously put into the mouth of Gyburg, asks the question :

Is this a sin, that those who were never taught the Christian faith were slain like a herd of cattle ? (*daz man si sluoc als ein vihe*)—

and answers thus :

I declare that it is a great sin : they are all God's handiwork, seventy-two peoples and tongues are His own.

And then, dropping that thought completely, and passing to another :

The admirat Terramer, with many a mighty king, would have brought all those peoples to the throne in Aachen and thence to Rome ; but this was thwarted by the swords of those who made head against it, and so sacrificed their lives that their souls, for this, now shine resplendent. . . .

It is impossible to overlook the hiatus between the two statements : what, then, is the implied connection ? Evidently, the aim of the second is to show, in fairness to the Christians, the desperate issue they had to face, and so to extenuate the lack of mercy which has just been condemned.

Contradictions such as these reflect the natural workings of a mind capable of perceiving both sides of a conflict, not, however, with intellectual detachment, but with an emotional sharing which retards the solution.

Wolfram expresses his feelings and thoughts both in his own person, and also dramatically : by the mouth of Gyburg, and later, when the war is over, by that of the victor Willehalm (459, 21—460, 26). Bernhart, duke of Brabant, brother to Willehalm, finds the victorious leader plunged in deep dejection, and upbraids him for it, saying in conclusion : " God has given thee great honour and has increased thy renown." To this Willehalm, looking his brother in the eye, returns the inscrutable answer : " got weiz wol waz er hât getân ",—" God knows well what He has done ", adding, because he feels how far the sacrifice outweighs the gain, that " dirre sic mir schupfentiure hât ervohten in dem herzen mîn ",—" this victory has wrought defeat in my heart." Yet, though he cannot bring himself to rejoice, he resolves to show a more cheerful front and to conceal his trouble, for

ez îst houbetmannes sin,
daz er genendeclîche lebe
und sîme volke trœsten gebe.—

" It is the captain's thought, that he must live courageously and give confidence to his people ".

126

But the chief exponent or, we may also say, the poetic symbol of the tragic dilemma is Gyburg, who, as *casus belli*, assumes responsibility for the war launched because of her, and whose heart leans to her own kindred as well as to the race of her adoption. She it is who declares that all men are equal in the sight of God, seeing they are all His handiwork, and who pleads for mercy to the heathen side, should the Christians win the day (306, 1—310, 26). The climax of her pleading is in these four lines :

> Ob der heiden schumpfentiure ergê,
> sô tuot daz sælekeit wol stê.
> hôrt eines tumben wîbes rât :
> schônet der gotes hantgetât.—

" If the heathen suffer defeat, then do as beseems salvation. Hear the counsel of a simple women, and spare God's handiwork."

Ethically, this is one of the highest moments, equalled only by the magnanimity of the closing scene, where, in a gracious act of atonement, Willehalm makes peace with his quondam enemy King Matrableiz, and bids him this farewell :

" I commend thee, King Matrableiz, to Him Who knows the number of the stars, and Who gave us the light of the moon. . . ."

There is small need to speculate why *Willehalm* ends with this scene of reconciliation and calm. Though more remained to tell, it may well be that Wolfram himself recognized the poetic fitness of such an ending, and, regardless of what posterity might think,[1] chose to carry the tale no further.

[1] S. Ulrich von Türheim, *Rennewart* 10255—63 :

> swer hât daz vorder leit gelesen
> diss buoches, der muoste wesen
> in clage als er ez gelas.
> als sîn danne niht mêre was,
> sô begunde er sprechen : 'owê !
> daz er uns niht des buoches mê
> in tiutsche hât gesprochen !
> er hât ez abe gebrochen
> dâ ez uns was aller beste.

*er hât ez abe gebrochen* : those words indicate plainly, that Wolfram, whatever his reason, left off where he did of his own free will.

Appendix II

# THE GERMAN CONTRIBUTION TO THE MATTER OF BRITAIN, WITH SPECIAL REFERENCE TO THE LEGEND OF KING ARTHUR AND THE ROUND TABLE[1]

The contribution which German poets made to the matter of Britain during the Middle Ages may be divided into two main categories. In the first place, texts which fill a gap in the literary tradition and help to establish lost sources. In the second, those valued for their own individual poetic worth. There is a third category larger than either of these which, in spite of its inferior quality, cannot be left entirely out of account : imitative works of secondary value in which stock situations and motives are renewed, sometimes not without skill, but without any notable breath of new inspiration. Such are hardly to be reckoned as forming a real contribution. The matter of Britain, viewed in its entirety, would be little the poorer if all these had vanished. Their very existence, however, bears witness to the magnetic power of the tradition from which they borrow.

Examples of all three categories may be found in the German renderings of the romance of Tristan. To the first belongs without question the *Tristrant* of the North German poet Eilhart von Oberge, composed about the end of the twelfth century, and invaluable as a reproduction of material which is otherwise lost. Graceless and mediocre in its treatment of a famous tale, it supplies, none the less, a complete account of the pre-courtly version of the romance of Tristan represented in Old French by a surviving third of the work of the Norman Béroul. Whereas Eilhart's account is complete, all that is left of Béroul's fine and spirited poem is the middle part. The *Tristan* of Gottfried von Strassburg belongs to both the first and the second category. As Eilhart to Béroul, or to some other poet of his class, so in similar yet different relation, Gottfried to " Tomas von Britanje " : that is to say, the Anglo-Norman poet Thomas of whose work only three fragments, covering the conclusion of the tale, survive. The courtly version which Thomas created has had a happier fate than the pre-courtly version represented by Béroul. The *Tristan* of Gottfried von Strassburg not only gives us, as do the other derivatives from the work of Thomas, material drawn from

---

[1] Read at a meeting of the Oxford Mediæval Society on 25 November 1948.

the lost major part of the source, reproduced with such fidelity that no link in the chain is missing ; it is, at the same time, a poetic re-creation harmoniously in tune with the spirit of the original source. We need not hesitate to go further. For Gottfried undoubtedly transcends his French master and is the finer artist of the two. In subtlety of thought and in magical beauty of style his version of the romance is unrivalled. But he did not live to complete it. His poem breaks off just where the first fragment of the source begins. Two later poets, one belonging to the middle, the other to the end of the thirteenth century, undertook, severally, to manufacture a con-conclusion, combining the material of Eilhart with a style imitated from Gottfried. Ulrich von Türheim, the earlier of the two, falls easily into the third category with a third-rate journeyman's performance. Heinrich von Freiburg, not unworthy of a place in the second category, belongs also mainly to the third. A poet of quality, he remains too much hampered by the dead hand of convention to allow his own ideality free play. Had he done so, he might have conceived a new and interesting variation of the theme. In contrast to Gottfried, who has given the story of Tristan and Isolt an im-passioned stamp of immortality, Heinrich von Freiburg is haunted by a plangent sense of the mutability and transitoriness of human happenings as opposed to the rigid finality of death, an attitude of mind which has its full scope only in the beautiful elegiac close. Here, passing in review the events of Tristan's life, he repeats and repeats the melancholy burden that death is the end of all. In Gottfried's thought of those two perfect lovers, life and death are joined together as one immortal memory, for " although they are long dead, their sweet names lives yet ", and

> ir leben, ir tôt sint unser brôt.
> sus lebet ir leben, sus lebet ir tôt.
> sus lebent si noch und sint doch tôt
> und ist ir tôr der lebenden brôt.

" Their life and their death are our bread. So their life lives, so their death lives. So they live still and yet are dead, and their death is the bread of the living."

In the German contribution to the matter of Britain the two major achievements are, indisputably, the *Parzival* of Wolfram von Eschenbach and the *Tristan* of Gottfried von Strassburg, so different as to be mutually exclusive, so that only by contrasting can we treat of them both together. Each, again, imposes its own limiting condition. The Table Round of King Arthur, in which the matter of Britain is otherwise centred, plays but a casual part in the pre-courtly version of *Tristan*, while in the courtly version of Thomas-Gottfried it has no longer any place at all. For this reason, the *Tristan* of Gottfried demands isolation. The *Parzival* of Wolfram with its teeming wealth of material demands, on the other hand, rigorous selection. Its source, the only one which can be proved, is the unfinished *Perceval* of Chrestien de Troyes ; but the matter of Wolfram's epic is incomparably richer than that of Chrestien. In particular, the legend of the Graal, with which the Arthurian legend is interwoven, assumes in Wolfram's epic such full significance that it claims to be considered alone. The realm of King Arthur and the realm of the Graal are two distinct though interacting spheres ; and the hero Parzival has a place in them both. But he belongs more positively to the latter. Despite his membership of the Table Round, he is never more than a guest at King Arthur's court, here today and gone tomorrow. His destined heritage is Munsalvæsche: it is there that his appointed goal is set. Then, too, the story of his father, Gahmuret the Angevin, which precedes his own, is no integral part of the Arthurian cycle. Connection is made by means of a genealogical tree : Gahmuret and King Arthur are given a common ancestor and ancestress from the two sons of whom their collateral lines are descended. There remain the adventures of Gawan ( = Gawain), who belongs so essentially to the Table Round of which he is the flower ; but here again we are faced with an unruly wealth of incident which drives us to concentrate on a narrower theme. There is scope enough and to spare if, within the matter of Britain, we limit ourselves to King Arthur, to the court of which he is the centre, and to the figures most intimately connected with him, leaving out of account, or at least merely touching upon, the adventures of individual knights in the lands outside his realm.

As starting-point let us take a remark made by Wolfram's young Parzival when he comes for the first time to Arthur's court, a child in mind and upbringing, ignorant of the great world. To the page Iwanet who has taken him in tow he remarks in bewilderment : " Ich sihe hie manegen Artûs "—" I see here many an Arthur ". For he has never before seen so many splendid-looking people all at once, each one he thinks must be Arthur, and as he rightly expects to see only one Arthur he is naturally much amazed by this multiplication. Iwanet laughs and explains.

This remark may be aptly applied to the legend of King Arthur in general, for even if there are not as many Arthurs as Parzival fancied, there are certainly more than one. Broadly speaking, we can distinguish three, if not four.

There is, in the first place, the Arthur of Geoffrey of Monmouth, an active and enterprising king who is the ruler of a great and expanding realm, a famous leader in battle, the beater-back of the invading Saxons, whose reign reaches its peak in the successful defiance of Imperial Rome. This is the Arthur of an older pseudo-historical tradition whom we can trace in bare outline from the first mention of him by Nennius in the ninth century until we come to the full-length portrait of Geoffrey of Monmouth about the middle of the twelfth. His picture remains unimpaired with the successors of Geoffrey, with Wace and Layamon. It has been preserved to English readers by Malory's *Morte Darthur*, notably in the opening events and in the close, in what Tennyson has styled " The Coming of Arthur " and " The Passing of Arthur ". Originally he is not only a battle-leader and the ruler of a splendid court, he engages also in single-handed adventures after the manner of a knight-errant. In Geoffrey's history he is the slayer of two giants. Earlier records speak of him as killing a dragon which had laid waste the land of Cornwall and as hunting a wild boar.

Then in the French romances from Chrestien de Troyes onward there emerges a second Arthur, the pacific and benevolent ruler of a court which represents the Golden Age of Chivalry. He is no longer a great actor, but rather the producer of a many-sided and loosely-built drama of shifting scenes, in which the knights of the Round Table play leading parts. King Arthur now represents the point of rest at the centre of a very busy sphere of action, both in regard to the court with its social pleasures and problems and to the adventures which go on outside. The priority which in Arthurian romance is given to the single-handed adventure of the individual champion over organized warfare does in fact necessitate this static position of the king. In the midst of all the romance there is this much realism. The king himself does not normally sally forth to seek adventure. That is not his *métier*.

One would expect, all the same, that this wise and steadfast Arthur at the centre of things would, if a crisis arose, show resource and enterprise. It is here, however, that we encounter a third Arthur. It is an Arthur, who, in the face of a formidable crisis, behaves in a foolish or in a faint-hearted way. We meet him at the beginning of Chrestien's *Lancelot*, in the events leading up to the abduction of Queen Guinevere. Though the flaw in his behaviour is lightly stressed, none the less it is clear that he has acted with criminal levity in the rash promise he made which resulted in the carrying-off of the queen. Gawain reproves him for it. "Sire," says he, " you have done a very foolish thing, which causes me great surprise." There is a similar situation in Chrestien's *Perceval* (859—1300),[1] containing the same kind of primitive and irrational folk-tale element. Here King Arthur's ineffectiveness in a time of crisis is very patent. Perceval when he comes riding into Arthur's

[1] In the edition of Alfons Hilka (Max Niemeyer Verlag 1932).

court finds the king buried in sorrowful thought, while the knights around are engaged in gay conversation, a strange uncourtly situation. The king finally explains that his worst foe, the Red Knight of Kinkerloi, has openly defied him here in his own court, has boldly robbed him of his gold goblet, and has added insult to this act of robbery by spilling the wine on the queen. The king admits in conclusion that he does not know what to do. Young Perceval kills the Red Knight and removes the peril with which neither the king nor any of his knights had known how to deal.

This third Arthur belongs to a different world from that of the first and from that of the second Arthur, a more primitive world where abnormal things happen and ordinary standards of conduct do not obtain. Chrestien understands this and quite rightly does not interpret King Arthur's weak conduct in ethical terms. He knows how to distinguish the atmosphere of the folk-tale from that of the sophisticated and courtly world in which he is at home, and treats it with matter-of-fact simplicity, as is meet. His objective presentation, however, is succeeded in due time by an attitude directly critical, in the author of the prose *Perlesvaux*. Here King Arthur is characterized as culpably neglectful of his royal honour. " For ten years was King Arthur in such estate as I have told you; nor never was courtly king so praised as he, until a slothful will came upon him, and he began to lose the pleasure in doing largesse that he was wont to have, nor was he minded to hold court neither at Christmas-time nor at Easter nor at Pentecost."[1]

In the German contribution this third Arthur (so far as I know) is not apparent. It is generally the second Arthur, the benevolent and gracious host, who is presented. But there is also, in the *Lanzilet* of Ulrich von Zatzikhoven,[2] a striking trace of the active and enterprising Arthur who belongs to an older tradition. This is in Ulrich's account of the abduction of Queen Guinevere, which is in many ways different from the account of Chrestien. Ulrich's *Lanzilet* as a whole represents a lost portion of the Old French literary tradition : in this, as in Eilhart's *Tristrant*, lies its specific value. It reproduces the matter of a French text which Ulrich, as he tells us, obtained direct from Huc de Morville, one of the hostages of Richard Cœur de Lion. The poem begins with the childhood of Lanzilet (Lancelot), telling how he was carried off by a water fairy, the Lady of the Lake, and brought up on an island inhabited only by maidens, how when he grew up he departed thence, had several

---

[1] From the English translation of Sebastian Evans : *The High History of the Holy Graal, Branch* 1.2.
[2] Ulrich von Zatzikhoven : *Lanzilet* (herausg. von K. Hahn 1845) ll. 4966—5360 and 6708—7444.

adventures, and ultimately arrived at King Arthur's court, where he took part in the rescue of Guinevere, not as a lover, simply as a loyal servant of King Arthur. There is no trace here of any close affection between Lancelot and Guinevere. The hero has his own wife Iblis, to whom he is devotedly attached. Arthur himself is the devoted husband of Guinevere and so far from playing the passive and inglorious part ascribed to him in Chrestien's *Lancelot*, he shows up very well. The ravisher, King Falerin " von dem verworrenen tan"—of the Tangled Forest—makes a surprise attack on Arthur and his knights while they are hunting the White Hart, overpowers them with superior forces, and carries off the queen. Arthur is in no way to blame : he resists stoutly, but the odds are too great. Several knights are killed and he himself is severely wounded. On his recovery he takes counsel on how best to effect a rescue. The enemy's castle is rendered impregnable by a thicket surrounding it which teems with serpents and other noxious beasts, and through which it is impossible to penetrate alive. At this point King Arthur's son Lôût (< Lohot or Lohut) arrives with a large army. We hear great praise of the young man, and incidentally, what seems a new variation of the Breton hope, how in the end, not in this story but long afterwards, both he and Arthur, father and son together, rode away into a strange land and were no more seen, and how the Britons wait always for their return. Lout, arriving, is much distressed about his mother the queen, and exhorts people in general to come to the aid of Arthur, for, says he, he deserves it well, no man ever came short who relied on my father's help. In the council, Tristan or, as he is here called, Tristrant, " der listige Tristrant "—the sage, the cunning Tristrant—advises the king to seek help from the wizard Malmik who dwells by the Misty Lake (*bî dem genibelten sê*). And now we find King Arthur himself taking part in a perilous adventure. His son Lout is left in charge of the kingdom while he and three others set out to visit the wizard Malmuk. Those others are Karjet (Gaheries), Tristrant, and Lancelot. It is a dangerous journey. The way lies across the Shrieking Bog and there are other danger-points as well. At the Shrieking Bog they are aided by the timely arrival of a certain knight of the Round Table who is generally little more than a name, " der wilde Dodines ", Sir Dodinas le Savage, usually found in company with Sir Segramors. Here it is told of him that he lived at King Arthur's court in winter, and in the summer roamed abroad seeking wild adventures, and in particular warring with the King of Ireland ; and that he rode a horse so swift that he could skim across the Shrieking Bog (*daz schrîende mos*) without so much as stirring up any mud. This Dodines now offers to guide King Arthur and his companions, and with his good help they reach the wizard's house. And here they get help from the wizard's beautiful daughter, who persuades her father to give them his powerful aid. And what he does is to put an enchantment on the serpents and other evil creatures guarding Falerin's castle as well as on everyone in the castle itself. So they are able to penetrate into the stronghold and rescue the queen. And so, says Ulrich, the noble king was released from all his troubles. Or nearly so ; for the wizard demands his price ; and thereby hangs a fresh hazard in which, however, the king this time is not directly concerned.

In Wolfram's *Parzival* we find a trace of Arthur in the role of knight-errant, but there is nothing traditional here. It is simply that Wolfram imagines Arthur in the second book of *Parzival*, in the time before he became king, as a young man who would naturally be swift to act. The situation is this. In the tourney of Kanvoleis, in which Parzival's father Gahmuret the Angevin, is victor, characters from the Arthurian cycle are introduced, and it is remembered that all this is a generation earlier than the main story. So Uther Pendragon is king, and although rather old is not too old to take part in the tourney. King Lot of Norway, the father of Gawan, is in his prime. Gawan himself is a little boy and is only allowed to look on, he is thrilled with excitement and longs to be a man. And Arthur is not here because he has gone off in quest of his mother, has in fact been absent for three years.[1] This anticipates the adventure of the enchanted castle (*Schastel Marveil*), which is achieved a generation later by Gawan. All that is told here is that a clerk, one skilled in necromancy, has run away with the queen, Uther Pendragon's wife, and that Arthur has run after them— " den ist Artûs nâch gerant ". So here is a chance glimpse of an active and enterprising Arthur, setting off to rescue his mother (as it happens, a wild-goose chase), just as in *Lanzilet* he takes part in the rescue of his wife.

Of the great battle-leader of Geoffrey of Monmouth the German poets have apparently no cognizance. That line of tradition seems to have been unknown. King Arthur as man of action is never more than a mere knight-errant. Of this kind of role there is a further example in an episode of that well-meaning but mediocre and formless poem, the work of the Styrian Heinrich von dem Türlin (*ca.* 1200), which bears the pretentious title of der Âventiure Krône, the Crown of Romances.[2] In the episode with which we are here concerned, the whole situation is extraordinarily naïve, equally so the conception

---

[1] 66, 1—8.

[2] Heinrich von dem Türlin *Diu Krone* (herausg. von G. H. F. Scholl, Stuttgart 1852).

of the worthy king. This naïveté is certainly not due to anything old or primitive in the elements of the story ; we can trace, in its ingenuous plot, the inventions of a crude but energetically fertile mind.[1]

Thus it is. King Arthur one day wakes up to find all his knights gone except three who have remained to keep him company. The rest have given him the slip, riding away at break of dawn to take part in a certain tournament, contrary to his will. It is too late to pursue them and bring them back. The king settles down meanwhile with his three companions. One winter day the queen finds him warming himself at the fire. She mocks his effeminacy, comparing him to his detriment with a certain bold knight who roams about in the winter cold clad only in his shirt, and singing love-ditties as though it were the month of May. King Arthur, anxious at once to redeem his character, sets out with his three companions to encounter that hardy stranger. Each one is posted in a different spot. The wandering knight comes on the scene, and details are given of his picturesque appearance. His arms consist of shield, sword, and spear ; he wears a chaplet of flowers on his head, is clad in a fine white shirt and scarlet breeches, without cloak or tunic, and is singing a joyous song. His name is Galozein. The three knights engage him severally and are each overcome ; but King Arthur succeeds where they fail. Having surrendered, the stranger declares himself to be the lover of Queen Guinevere, whom he claims to have known and adored long before her marriage to Arthur, claims in fact to be her rightful mate. The ensuing situation is naturally tense and vexatious ; and the king decides to bring it to a head (ll. 3313—5468). The story then turns upon the adventures of Gawein. When at length we return to King Arthur's court, the missing knights have come back, all but Gawein ; and with their approval the king formally arranges to do combat with his rival— a preposterously naïve situation. The combat commences, the king all eager for the fray,[2] but Galozein refuses to fight it out. The queen is now challenged to reveal the truth. She affirms that the stranger's tale is completely false, and that she is King Arthur's faithful wife. Arthur is satisfied, and Galozein departs in high dudgeon. Soon after this, the queen is carried off by another violent character (a variation of the abduction-theme), and is rescued in mid-

---

[1] This does not deny the presence of fossilized relics indicating an earlier stratum in the Arthurian tradition.

[2] Artûse wart vil schiere geholt
sîn ors, sper unde schilt.
sam ein vogel gereiztez wilt,
sîn herze gein dem kampfe spilt. (10570—10573)

forest by no other than Galozein. Having her in his power, he tries to force her into submission ; she resists while she can, and is just at the end of her strength when Gawein appears on the scene, engages that other in combat, and finally, after a long and bitter fight, knocks him out. The queen and Gawein return with the wounded prisoner to Arthur's court, where, on recovering, Galozein now admits that his story concerning the queen was a pure lie. The king, moved to mercy by his avowed repentance, forgives him, and Galozein becomes a worthy member of the court until, in due time, he is provided with a suitable bride (ll. 10113—12600).

This astonishing tale has two points of interest : the conception of King Arthur as fighting his own battles, in marked contrast with that of the *roi fainéant*, and the fact that the queen is involved in a triangular situation, which, while it turns out to be based on a false assumption, suggests the influence of the famous legend of the love between her and Lancelot.

Elsewhere, King Arthur appears, first in the romances of Hartmann von Aue, and then in Wolfram's *Parzival*, in his well-known pacific role as ruler of his court and as the benevolent host of Table Round. And the queen plays a similar part, that of a gracious and indeed perfect hostess. There is no hint by either poet of a relation other than marital, though Wolfram quite evidently knew Chrestien's *Lancelot*,[1] and seems also to have known of a lost French romance in which Iders had been her lover.[2]

Hartmann's *Erec* and *Iwein* are derived from the like-named romances of Chrestien de Troyes, and are in themselves epoch-making, but only in relation to German literature, not necessarily to the Arthurian cycle as such. Hartmann's *Erec* is, so far as can be judged, the earliest Arthurian romance in German. Its probable date is round about the year 1191 ; this at least has been a long-accepted *terminus a quo*. A lost Arthurian epic in Low Franconian is, on the evidence of other casually preserved fragments, not impossible, but if so, all trace has vanished. For us, as indeed for his own generation, the Swabian Hartmann marks the starting-point of a new line. Certainly it was he who gave the Arthurian legend its vogue in his own tongue, introducing not only the matter but also the knightly ethos which goes with it and gives it its peculiar value. His *Erec* and *Iwein* are more than the first Arthurian romances, they are also the first real romances of chivalry, in the German language.

The position of Hartmann as introducer of the Arthurian scene is

---

[1] *Parz.* 583, 8—11.
[2] See the author's article : " Ither von Gaheviez ", *Modern Language Review,* 1931.

aptly realised by Wolfram von Eschenbach, at the point where his young hero Parzival comes to King Arthur's court for the first time, an odd rustic figure joined with an odd companion, the fisherman with whom he has spent the night. Wolfram turns aside and addresses Hartmann von Aue, the author of *Erec*, as an old inhabitant of Arthur's court, as a master of ceremonies whose business it is to look after the young guest and see he is properly treated :

> Mîn hêr Hartman von Ouwe,
> frou Ginovêr iuwer frouwe,
> und iuwer herre der künc Artûs,
> den kumt ein mîn gast ze hûs . . .[1]

" Sir Hartmann von Aue, a guest of mine, is coming to see your lady Guinevere and your lord King Arthur. Ask for him to be safeguarded from mockery. He is not a fiddle or a rote for people to play on. Let them choose themselves another plaything : do this, or I for my part will soon make short work of your lady Enide and of her mother Karsnafide."

This in itself emphasises the position of Hartmann as pioneer. But the service he did his own literature does not imply a corresponding importance in the field of Arthurian legend as a whole. The question may well be raised, whether he did more than reproduce, in his own rather serious way, the excellent matter provided him by Chrestien de Troyes, whether he added anything of note to Chrestien's vivid descriptions of King Arthur's court and of the leading figures belonging to it.

On the whole—and this is true of both *Erec* and *Iwein*—there is a perceptible loss of vivacity. The court of King Arthur, seen through the soberer medium of Hartmann's temperament, is not nearly so lively a place, nor is the German poet able to give the same feeling of careless spirited high-breeding, the same air of easy elegance. Hartmann's presentation of good manners is more self-conscious and errs somewhat on the side of gentility. There is not the bold aristocratic freedom of speech we find with Chrestien and also with Wolfram. Hartmann has been praised for his deepening of the ethical side, not without reason, but to a greater extent than is his due. His long-winded comments are often no more profound than Chrestien's pungent sallies. Where Chrestien seizes the ethical point and expresses it in a swift aphoristic phrase understood by all, Hartmann turns it over and over. His reflective tendency comes out best in the soliloquies of Iwein, to the study of whom he brings a stronger pathos and a more intimate sympathy than Chrestien.

To the portrait of King Arthur as royal host Hartmann adds no

[1] 143, 21 ff.

particular trait. But we can give him credit for deepening that of Guinevere. Queen Guinevere for him is more than a gracious hostess, she is a woman of quick and warm sympathies. It is in relation to Enite, or Enid (as we may prefer to call her), that he brings this out. That relation is also depicted by Chrestien, but Hartmann has developed it further. Chrestien tells how Enid, coming to King Arthur's court in all her poverty, was instantly looked after by the queen, who dressed her and adorned her most beautifully, evidently taking the liveliest interest in Erec's young bride. Hartmann strengthens this charming relationship. Later on in the story, Erec and Enid, in the course of their unnecessary roamings, are invited to spend a night in King Arthur's camp. Here the two poets differ. Chrestien's Erec is a hot-blooded, impetuous young man, who never knows when he has had enough. King Arthur and the rest are convinced that he has had as much fighting as is good for him, he is weary and wounded, and they are all much concerned. King Arthur in particular looks after him like a father, puts him to bed, and sees that he has a good night's rest (ll. 3931—4280). Hartmann's Erec is a cold-blooded young man, so deliberate and calculating that although he has been through the same adventures as Chrestien's Erec, one feels he can very well look after himself. Hartmann's sympathies are with poor Enid, who is worn to shreds, we are made aware of her misery, and Queen Guinevere is aware of it too. In a passage of sixteen lines (ll. 5100—5115) it is related simply and clearly, and with such delicacy and rightness of phrase that we see it all, how Guinevere showed a " sweet will " in her reception of Enid, how she led her away from her husband, took her to her own private room, tended her, asked womanly questions, and when Enid told her of her troubles lamented with her. It is a pleasing and intimate sketch of the friendship between the older and the younger woman. Wolfram has caught the spirit of it where he makes Guinevere express her sorrow at having had to part with her " sweet playmate " Cunneware, whom, after she had left to be married, the queen never saw again.'[1]

A word may be said about Hartmann's treatment of the seneschal Keie (or Kay) in the opening scene of *Iwein*. Here the picture of Arthur's court, while derived from that of Chrestien, is so good that it can be placed on the same level. As for Kay, for once Hartmann's sober deliberate style is quite as effective as Chrestien's vivacity. Both pictures of Kay are good, different in kind rather than in degree. Chrestien's Kay is impetuous, brusque, and choleric; Hartmann's is cooler, more deliberate and self-possessed, the tone

---

[1] *Parz.* 646, 10—12.

in which he speaks is a sarcastic drawl. The contrast between him and his more active companions is, moreover, brought out by Hartmann with clear independence in his grouping of the six figures : the lazy, inert figure of the " unmannerly Kay " taking his ease on the floor, in contrast with the four knights seated and Calogreant standing to tell his tale.

There is again full equality between the two poets in the scene where Laudine's messenger (by Hartmann identified with her maid Lunete) denounces Iwein (Ivain or Yvain) in the presence of King Arthur and his court. Hartmann's rendering of the scene is at every point as forceful and trenchant as Chrestien's.

There are, both in *Erec* and in *Iwein*, several occasions where, on a hint from Chrestien, Hartmann shows a new delicacy of perception, or adds some telling detail of his own. Yet, when all is said, his contribution to the legend of King Arthur and the Round Table is, relatively, of minor importance. And this is still more true of his successors in that same field, Wirnt von Gravenberg and the rest. The German poets who follow in Hartmann's train get neither the superb brilliance and gallantry of Chrestien's presentation, nor the curious old-world glamour we find in the French prose romances, as also in the prose of Sir Thomas Malory. Instead, they continue to develop the moralising strain bequeathed by Hartmann, which, in their master's work, bears the stamp of his more interesting cast of mind. Even so, it is not here, in his Arthurian romances, but in his religiously toned narratives, *Gregorius* and *Der Arme Heinrich*, that Hartmann's strong moral trend is poetically right.

Pioneer though he is, the achievement of Hartmann as interpreter of the matter of Britain is nowhere near that of his great contemporary, Wolfram von Eschenbach. In the region common to them both, Wolfram far outstrips Hartmann. He also outstrips, not altogether perhaps but in the main, Chrestien de Troyes, and this because the world he creates is of larger dimensions. Although his chief concern is with the Graal, and although finally the glory of Munsalvæsche casts into the shade the lesser glory of the Table Round, none the less, he gives a picture of the latter which in its life-like humanity and breadth is unrivalled. The court of King Arthur as presented by Wolfram becomes in reality what is assumed for it in the poetic ideal, but is nowhere else worked out so fully, a complete symbol of the chivalrous life.

Wolfram's presentation falls into three stages, each of which corresponds to a definite stage in the life of his hero. The first is that of *Parzival* Bk. III. Here the boy Parzival pays his first visit to King Arthur's court. The story is essentially the same as in

Chrestien's *Perceval*, but the impression created is entirely different and more complex.

The story is at bottom a folk-tale with a simple-minded hero, and, to match his mentality, a primitive and rude conception of King Arthur's court, here a place quite different in type from the cultured and modernised court which Chrestien presents to us in *Erec* and *Yvain*. It seems as though, in this particular part of his new story, Chrestien must have kept close to his source and, recognizing that the primitive court suited this type of hero and this type of tale, pictured it as primitive.

Wolfram, on his side, achieves something more. With his strong realisation of the child's personality, he enables us to see King Arthur's court from two angles, as the seat of a mature aristocratic life and, at the same time, through the eyes of young Parzival, as the king's court in a fairy tale. The personality of the child is so completely alive that we are able to accept from his point of view the primitive features of the story, the Red Knight snatching up the gold cup from the Table Round, and Kay's beating of the damsel who laughed, and yet feel that the environment in which the tale is set is by no means primitive but, on the contrary, a sphere of life which the child does not yet understand.

The queen's page, Iwanet, forms a link between these two spheres. While he himself is quite sophisticated, he is still boy enough to enter into the feelings of another and simpler boy for the time being, evidently finding it good fun to instruct and direct the young greenhorn. So he helps Parzival to put on the armour of the Red Knight Ither whom he has slain in combat, and teaches him how to hold shield and spear. But as soon as Parzival has ridden away, Iwanet now thinks of the queen his mistress who had loved Ither as a friend, and goes to her in all seriousness, bringing news of his death. And the queen laments for one who had been the flower of perfect manhood.

We are left with an unsolved discord. Because the Red Knight whom Parzival has killed is no longer Chrestien's felon, but a generous and gallant man whose enmity towards King Arthur is no foreigner's hatred but an unhappy rift in an old alliance, therefore the tragedy of Ither's death falls as a black cloud across the sunlit levity of a fool's paradise.

It must be confessed that the dual presentation of Arthur's court raises more than one difficulty. What, exactly, was the nature of the feud between Arthur and his kinsman Ither? That question is imperfectly solved. But at least King Arthur is cleared from the slur of unmanly weakness depicted by Chrestien. It is the sad thought of an earlier and kinder relation which stays his hand.

For the rest, in this part of the story, Arthur is shown as the kind of king the boy expects to find, friendly and affable and not at all proud. And while other qualities are added, these remain. It is true that wherever, in mediæval tradition, we meet with King Arthur, he is, almost invariably, an obliging and accessible monarch. But Wolfram brings out his complete lack of pride in a very explicit way. He speaks of him once as " der unlôse Artûs niht ze hêr "— the modest Arthur who was not too grand ; and there is a good example of this absence of grandeur when, in a later phase of the story, his young nephew Segramors comes bursting into his tent in the early morning with an urgent request which cannot wait. The king and queen are asleep ; and Wolfram now adds a lively touch of his own to what Chrestien gave him. For Segramors snatches away the coverlet and wakes them both up ; and they laugh at his wild behaviour.[1]

About this good-humoured Arthur who sees a joke Wolfram makes a mild joke of his own. He calls him " der meienbære man "—the man of May—because, says he, everything told about him seems to have happened at Pentecost, in the blossoming May season.

There is the same shrewd humour in Wolfram's illuminating comment on the seneschal Kay. Kay, according to Wolfram, had been much maligned ; he was really a very useful fellow, and King Arthur would have done badly without him. For Arthur's court was a place which drew to it all sorts and conditions of men, both good and bad, and Kay's sharp tongue did useful work in driving away the undesirables. Then, turning to his patron, Landgrave Hermann of Thuringia, Wolfram says : " Lord Hermann, you could do very well with a seneschal like Kay, to keep *your* court in order !"

These humorous touches are very human, and fit naturally into the life-size conception of Table Round which, with preliminary sketches in Books IV and V, is worked out to its fullest extent in Book VI. This is when, a year later than his first visit, Parzival again comes into contact with King Arthur's court, this time on equal terms. He has proved himself a most valiant knight, has put away childish things, and with honourable welcome takes his place in the adult company of Table Round, until " Cundrie with harsh words " drives him forth to seek the Graal, and he renounces his share in that high fellowship. To this second phase of Parzival's life, a season of well-being and honour disastrously ended, belongs the second picture of Arthur's court, and this time it is a full and life-like picture of a great court renowned for its nobility.

[1] 285, 11—20.

It is thronged with personable figures : the impetuous young Segramors, who is always spoiling for a fight, the sardonic Kay, Gawan the flower of courtesy and kindness, in whom Parzival finds a new and steadfast friend, Beacurs, Gawan's devoted younger brother, who offers to do battle for him in his stead, the lovely and faithful Cunneware, whose affection for Parzival is so humbly and loyally true, Ekuba of Janfuse, the wise Indian queen. More especially, we may observe the firm and excellent portrayal of King Arthur himself, seen here in the round as a man of mature wisdom, with a strong sense of kingly duty and an ability to cope with the situation as it arises. At the beginning of Book VI, before Parzival re-enters, he and his court are encamped outside the forest encircling the hidden castle of Munsalvæsche. It is a perilous region. For the knights of the Graal who act as sentries have no mercy upon the intruder, whence to trespass on their domain is as good as death. Arthur knows his own knights and how eager they are for adventure, and he is not going to let his man-power be frittered away in unnecessary combats. So he orders his knights, let them like it or no, not to engage in combat without his consent ; and the simile he uses gives just the right tone to the sort of foolhardy courage he intends to check, and divests it of glamour. " If you want to rush one in front of the other like rude hounds which have been unleashed, that is not as I wish it."[1]

Subsequently, he does give leave, first to Segramors and then to Kay, to do combat with the stranger knight who all this time is Parzival, the very man they have set out to find. As with Chrestien, it is the courteous Gawan who discovers his identity and brings him back to the king's court, where he is warmly welcomed. And since the Table Round of which he is now made a member is not there in concrete reality (for how could they have carried it about with them?), a large piece of costly silk is cut out in the form of a disc to serve as symbol, and is spread on the blossoming field. They are not long seated here, when there comes riding into their midst 'trûrens urhap, freuden twinc'—a bringer of sorrow, a binder of joy—Cundrie, the ill-omened messenger of the Graal.

It is strange and paradoxical that the glory of Table Round seems to reach its height as Cundrie denounces it, denounces its lord King Arthur, and above all denounces Parzival, through whom, she declares, Table Round is disgraced beyond repair. In reality, her denunciation brings out both the splendour and the integrity of the Table Round. Its splendour, because in the wild rhetoric of her speech, and in the praise she mingles with her invective, we

[1] 281, 2—5.

catch the image of something great and glorious tottering to its fall. But this is illusion. The Table Round is unshaken by her speech and gives proof of its integrity. All are very sad because of the young man whom her words have stricken, but they do not feel themselves disgraced in him, and in this they judge rightly and sanely, just as he for his part does right in obeying the sterner voice of his own tortured soul. What the knights best remember of Cundrie's speech is the information she let fall that Parzival was the son of Gahmuret the Angevin, to her, the unworthy son of a noble father. But not to them. And some begin to say : Gahmuret the Angevin ! how well I remember him, the time he fought in the Tourney of Kanvoleis and won his bride. And now here is his son : he is welcome, both for his own and for his father's sake.

Then comes another denouncer, this time the proud knight of Ascalon who accuses Gawan of having murdered his lord by foul play, and challenges him to do combat. Before Gawan answers, the king takes up his nephew's cause, and in a speech of great dignity and power defends him. " Sir, he is my sister's son. Were Gawan dead, I would undertake that combat, sooner than let disgrace haunt his bones. If luck will, Gawan shall prove to you yet that he is blameless. Should any other man have likewise grieved you, blaze not his guilt abroad without due cause. For, if he prove his innocence and win your favour, what you have spoken against him will but weaken your own good name."[1]

The sixth book ends with the dispersal of the company. Parzival rides away to seek the Graal, Gawan to fight his combat, the guests of the Table Round go back to their own lands, and several of Arthur's knights set out for the Castle of Marvels (Schastel Marveil), of which Cundrie had told them before she left. Long afterwards in the story, Queen Guinevere laments the dispersal and loss of so many she had cared for.

The third picture of the Table Round follows on Gawan's great adventure of the Castle of Marvels, which in its turn is preceded by something far more momentous, and that is Parzival's stay with his uncle the hermit Trevrizent (Book IX). The pageant of Gawan's adventure shrinks in significance when compared with that finer adventure of the soul. In the hermit's cell, remote in its forest solitude from court or camp, we sound the depth of Parzival's spiritual experience, listen with him to Trevrizent's wise teaching as he expounds the mystery of man's life and the mystery of the Godhead ; and as the story is told of the race to which they both belong, we pass in imagination into a kingdom which is the seat of an

---

[1] 322, 15—30.

Order more austere and more magnificent than the Order of Table Round. It is in comparison with this grander Order that King Arthur's court appears from now on diminished in value. And when Parzival again takes his place in the fellowship of Table Round (in Book XIV), it is made abundantly clear that he no longer belongs to it, that it represents a sphere of life he has outgrown. Yet the picture is full of colour and action ; nor does it lack the aid of a congenial theme.

That theme, by which the third picture is pleasantly illumined, is, quite simply, the happiness of an unexpected family reunion. Chrestien breaks off with the coming of Gawan's messenger to King Arthur's court. Wolfram, continuing, describes the arrival of the king and queen and all their retinue at Schastel Marveil, where, after greeting with joy the long-missing Gawan, they discover, among the prisoners he has freed, four lost members of the family clan : Arthur's mother, the old queen Arnive, his sister Sangive, mother of Gawan, and Gawan's two young sisters, Itonje and Cundrie (second of that name). Arnive (Wolfram's substitute for Igerne, or its variant Iverne) is a spirited old lady ; but Sangive is colourless, and the girls, of whom Itonje alone has a definite part, are of somewhat tenuous charm. Bene, the ferryman's daughter, Itonje's friend, is more real than either, and Orgeluse, Gawan's proud lady, is the most real of all. So magnificently real that, beside her, the many conventional figures which fill that third picture are mere silhouettes.

King Arthur, it must be said, does hold his own. As before, we feel his benevolence, his avuncular goodness, not so much as in Book VI his kingly worth. He is especially charming in a scene with his young niece Itonje and her friend Bene. The two girls (Bene takes the lead) come to him in great distress, for Itonje's brother (Gawan) and her lover (Gramovlanz) are about to fight a mortal combat. King Arthur promises to intervene and stop it, and he is as good as his word. But what stays in one's memory is the perfectly charming way in which Arthur, " der wîse höfsche man ", the wise and courteous man, enters into his young niece's trouble, and asks her to tell him about her lover, saying : " Did he ever see your fair face and your sweet red mouth ?"[1] And Itonje says, No, but they have corresponded.

There is a lovable and laughable touch in the absurd extreme of King Arthur's kindness when, having duly accomplished Itonje's betrothal to Gramovlanz, he follows this up with the betrothal of her aunt and sister, for whom two more bridegrooms are somewhat quickly chosen. " Artus was frouwen milde "—Arthur was a

---

[1] 712, 18—20.

bountiful giver of ladies, is Wolfram's comment.[1] But, he adds, it was planned beforehand.

In this part of the epic, strictly speaking at the beginning of Book XII, allusion is made to King Arthur's dead son, Ilinot, who long ago had been slain in battle, fighting to win the prize of his lady's love. Only cursory details are given of a story which Wolfram assumes to have been already known. To us, it is tantalizingly aloof from all our knowledge. The name Ilinot must be derived in some way from Lohot ; but there is no other clue. We may console ourselves for the gap in our knowledge with the thought that King Arthur makes up nobly for the loss of his son in the affection he lavishes on his other young relatives. His son denied him, he remains a most excellent uncle. How fondly does he not speak of " mîn neve Gawân "— my nephew Gawan—then also, though in a more distant relationship, of " mîn neve Parzivâl ", and finally, when Parzival meets and introduces his half-brother Feirefîz, of " mîn neve Feirefîz "! That the word *neve* means both nephew and cousin is immaterial. For to all his young relatives Arthur is primarily uncle : that is his status.

In this and other ways, King Arthur remains true to himself, and the same can be said of his nephew Gawan, with his inbred courtesy and generosity of mind. Nothing in Gawan is more commendable than the readiness with which, after his own spectacular achievements he frankly recognizes that he has been excelled by Parzival. In Gawan, the brotherly spirit of Table Round is revealed incarnate, for, as Wolfram says elsewhere, " nieman nâch gegenstuole sprach "— no one laid claim to the best seat.

Queen Guinevere, in the little we see of her, remains true to type, as one to whom the court in which she moves is a circle of dear friends. As, formerly, she lamented the death of Ither, so now, looking back, she has poignant regrets for friends she had known and lost five years ago : Cunneware, who had been one of her ladies-in-waiting, and Jeschute, and Ekuba the Indian queen, who had been with them as guests.

Yet, in spite of all the charm and goodwill and generosity in the society of the Table Round, each time we are brought close to the mind of Parzival in its heroic solitude we realise, as in the first phase, but reversed, the disparity between two different planes of being. In the depth of his long inward suffering and in the strength of his unfaltering single purpose, Parzival stands out in strong relief against a world of ephemeral joys. The disparity reaches its climax in that wonderful scene where, in the night watches, Parzival lying awake and alone, thinking of his wife Condwiramurs, sees the

---

[1] 730, 11.

intolerable gulf between a sorrow bordering on despair and the light-hearted happiness around him, and resolves once more to break away from the Table Round, for " here in the midst of this joy I cannot stay. God give joy to all this company! I will depart and leave this joy behind." And in the grey light of dawn he rides away.[1] He returns, it is true, in a happier frame of mind, to introduce his new-found brother Feirefiz ; but a hint has been given that this last stay is only for an hour. For now, with sudden felicity, the Quest is ended ; and when, with Cundrie the messenger of the Graal as guide, Parzival and his brother Feirefiz ride away in the direction of Munsalvæsche, Table Round has played its last part. The company disperses. " I do not know," says Wolfram, " where they all went to," and indeed he does not care. And in the next line attention is riveted on the three figures who matter. " Cundrie and those two rode on." The scene then shifts immediately to Munsalvæsche, where Anfortas lives on in agony, kept alive against his will because the people now know that his deliverer is coming :

> Mîn hêr Hartmann von Ouwe,
> frou Ginovêr iuwer frouwe,
> und iuwer hêrre der künc Artûs,
> den kumt ein mîn gast ze hûs . . .

Harking back to the words in which Wolfram announces the arrival of his guest at King Arthur's court for the first time, we sense their significance in the light of all that has followed. For it is through the personality of this most individual guest that we get that threefold picture of Arthur's court, with its three grades of reality, which is Germany's chief contribution to the legend of the Table Round.

---

[1] 732, 1—733, 30.

# THE 'TITUREL' OF WOLFRAM VON ESCHENBACH: STRUCTURE AND CHARACTER

The *Titurel* of Wolfram von Eschenbach is a unique and daring experiment, to which in the rest of Mediæval German literature there is no near parallel. It is not (as the author of the *jüngere Titurel* mistakenly supposed) an unfinished epic, nor can its two separate parts be rightly designated as 'epische Fragmente', epic fragments. In form as in essence it is (for the most part) a lyrical reaction of epic material derived from *Parzival,* constructed therefore not as a straightforward tale but as a series of situations with threads of connecting narrative : situations impregnated with lyrical feeling and with an element of personal drama in the texture as well. For this kind of treatment, part lyrical and part dramatic, with narrative links of the utmost economy, Wolfram devised a four-line strophe of wonderful flexibility, capable of bringing out the highlights of the story and of investing its most striking moments with power and beauty. And while he no doubt took his cue from the example of the *Nibelungenlied* the difference outweighs the resemblance. For the four-line strophe of the *Nibelungenlied* is a good simple epic measure while on the other hand that of *Titurel,* with its more elaborate structure and greater amplitude, is the vehicle of a style too heightened and too embellished for pure story-telling. It demands from its substance a sustained emotional quality which excludes the soberer needs of the *raconteur.*

The metre has its own magical charm inherent in the elasticity of the rhythm, in the continuing melodious lilt of the feminine rhymes, in varying length of line, and in the ensuing variety of sentence-form.

The first line,[1] but for the feminine ending, has the same pattern as the basic line of the *Nibelungenlied,* and indeed tallies exactly with the slightly extended form which occurs at the beginning of Kriemhild's dream. Compare

> In disen hôhen êren     troumte Kriemhilde
> wie si züge einen valken     starc schœn und wilde

and

> Dô sich der starke Tyturel     mohte gerüeren,

or

> Kîôt ûz Katelangen     erwarp Schoysîânen.

---

[1] Quotations are from the text of Lachmann-Hartl (*Lieder, Parzival, Titurel*), Berlin : de Gruyter, 1952.

147

The second line has a longer sweep, and not infrequently conveys a heightening of emotional effect, as in

> er getorste wol sich selben     unt die sîne in sturme gevüeren :

Also in

> schœner maget wart nie gesehen     sît noch ê bî sunnen noch
> bî mânen.

The third line is short, and the fourth is of the same length as the second, but with its own characteristic function of giving emphasis and depth to the meaning or, if this is already complete, of adding a new thought or an arresting comment, for example :

> sît sprach er in alter 'ich lerne
> daz ich schaft muoz lâzen :     des pflac ich etwenne schône
> und gerne.

Each line has its proportionate length, and behind the diversity of structure there is a flexibly normal pattern.   It is important to note its flexibility.   The free and fluent rhythm allows for deviations from the norm, both in regard to length of line and, above all, to the position of the pause.   In the first line, for instance, this normally comes at the same point as in the *Nibelungenlied*, for example :

> Dô sich der starke Tyturel     mohte gerüeren,

or

> Got hât dich, sun, berâten     vünf werder kinde :

but falls differently in

> Du minnen ursprinc, [du] berndez     saf minnen blüete

and

> Dînes râtes, dînes     trôstes, dîner hulde
> bedarf ich mit ein ander, . . .

The amplitude of the strophe, to which is added the occasional use of *enjambement*, gives scope for larger sentence-units than could be gracefully and as effectively handled in the short rhyming couplet together with greater variety of sentence-form.   There is no need to illustrate what is so abundantly patent.   One particular point may be singled out : the opportunities the metre gives for a goodly display of names, for example :

> Kîôt ûz Katelangen     erwarp Schoysîânen.

Dô Tampunteire starp    und Kardeiz der clâre
in Brûbarz truoc die crône, . . .
In den selben zîten    was Kastis erstorben.
der hete ouch Herzeloüden    ze Muntsalvâtsche, die clâren,
erworben.
Kanovoleiz gap er der vrouwen schône,
und Kingrivâls : ze in beiden truoc sîn houbt vor vürsten die
crône.

As we know, the main theme is the earlier history of Sigune and
her lover Schionatulander.  This, in Part I, takes its starting-point
from *Parzival*, 141, 11—13.  Sigune, speaking to Parzival on the
occasion of their first meeting, tells him this :

Mir diende ân alle schande
dirre vürste von dîm lande :
dô zôch mich dîn muoter.

Thus determined, the first phase of the lovers' tale was when Sigune
was Herzeloyde's ward.  In *Titurel* this is matched with the happy
new idea of making Schionatulander a page in Gahmuret's train.
For the rest, but for this new factor, the narrative substance is fully
anticipated in *Parzival*, Book II.  It can, therefore, be handled with
dexterous concision, or enhanced by additional detail.
Similarly, Part II has its starting-point in what Sigune says of her
lover's death (*Parzival*, 141, 16) :

ein bracken seil gap im den pîn.

How this happened is never explained.  But from that one obscure
and arresting line a fascinating situation is developed, which, because
it is altogether new, is far more circumstantial than anything in Part
I.  It is also, with all its diversity, more unified in structure.
For Part I covers a good deal of family history and has in it four
main situations, with intervening distances of space or time.  The
first, from which the poem has its title, is complete in itself, while
serving also as prologue.  Apart from this, we can observe in the
general structure a distinction between (*a*) the relation of the action,
(*b*) the building-up of the situation, (*c*) the situation itself, dramatic
in form and at the same time lyrical in style and feeling.
The introduction to the lovers' dialogue, the second of the four
situations, is a superb rhapsody in which the verse rises to heights of
eloquence culminating in an impassioned contemplation of Love
as a mysterious and all-prevailing power.
The introduction to the dialogue between Gahmuret and his
lovelorn page consists both of description and of contemplation.

Its theme is the malady of love frustrated and hope deferred. The symptoms are fully dwelt on, but we also get, in passing, a lively glimpse of the normal activities of the other lads, for which the dejected lover has no heart or will :

> Swenn ander junchêrren    ûf velden unde in strâzen
> punierten unde rungen,    durch sende nôt sô muose er daz
>                                         lâzen.

The introduction to the parallel situation of Herzeloyde, in converse with her sorrowing niece is reduced to a minimum of a few lines only for, Sigune's case being similar to her lover's, to retail the same symptoms would have been to invite monotony. Instead, details of a more personal kind, concrete and moving, are woven into the girl's confession.

The first and longer part covers a considerable range, embracing four generations of the Graal-dynasty in the persons of (1) the old king Titurel, (2) his son Frimutel, who makes but a momentary appearance, (3) Frimutel's two eldest daughters, Schoysiane and Herzeloyde (his two sons and his youngest daughter have no part in the action), (4) Sigune, daughter of Schoysiane and Kiot. While Sigune's story has as its background the full relation of *Parzival*, Book II, curtailed in the retelling, the *Vorgeschichte* is based on events recorded in retrospect, incidentally and allusively. In *Titurel* these scattered statements, originally brief and bare, are co-ordinated, expanded, and embellished.

The poem opens with the old Titurel taking leave of his kingship and of his guardianship of the Graal, bequeathing both to his son Frimutel. The situation gives tangible substance to the frugal statement of *Parzival*, 251, 3—7 (Book v) :

> der bürge wirtes royâm,
> Terre de Salvæsche ist sîn nam.
> ez brâhte der alte Tyturel
> an sînen sun. rois Frimutel,
> sus hiez der werde wîgant :

Later on (at the end of Book IX) Trevrizent tells how Titurel had been the first keeper of the Graal until infirmity overtook him, since when, stricken though he was, he still gave counsel in time of need. Titurel is also twice introduced in person. Parzival, during his visit to Munsalvæsche, had caught a glimpse of him through an open door at the end of the hall, a beautiful old man " Noch grawer dan der tuft ". Afterwards, when he himself becomes king of the Graal, an occasion arises for Titurel to exercise his office as counsellor.

The opening situation of *Titurel*, which is the full development of these and other family details, is a small masterpiece, complete in itself, and it will repay to examine its structure. The theme which runs through it is the resignation, the deprivation of an old age seen in contrast with the glory which survives only in remembrance and the dawn of a new glory in the oncoming young generation. The old king's farewell speech is thus half elegiac and half prophetic. He recalls his bygone martial prowess in three strokes of brilliant hyperbole : if he could yet wield weapons, the air would be glorified in the crack of the bursting spear driven by his hand, the flying splinters would cast a shadow against the sun, and, with a change from the past subjunctive of what would be to the perfect indicative of positive remembrance of what was, many a crest on helm has caught fire from the edge of his sword. From manly prowess his thoughts now turn to the love that is also past, and again, his thought has a threefold structure. His love he remembers in three succeeding phases, first, as an aspiration and a hope, *ob ich von hôher minne ie trôst enpfienge*, then as an ecstasy invading his whole being, *und op der minnen süeze ie sælden craft an mir begienge*, finally, and with a change similar to that before, from the past subjunctive of the concrete personal relation to the past indicative, *wart mir ie gruoz von minneclîchem wîbe*. All that is past and over : *daz ist nu gar verwildet mînem seneden clagendem lîbe*.

From the past he turns to the future, speaking now of the spiritual legacy he leaves his heirs, to be kept by them untarnished : his blessed fortune, his purity of life, steadfastness of mind, and whatever honour his hand has won with bounteous giving or in the press of battle. In the last line the emphasis is on *wâre minne*, love sure and true, which is the crown of all the rest.

There follows, in four lines of simple eloquence, an exposition of what this means and of how two hearts united by it are separated by death alone.

Titurel next recalls that supreme moment of his life when from an angel messenger he received the Graal and became its first human guardian. In that splendid strophe Trevrizent's brief retrospects are renewed and magnified as an individual experience of memorable radiance and power.

Past and future are again met in the bequeathing of the Graal to Frimutel, the one surviving son : *nu enpfâch des grâles crône und den grâl, mîn sun der lieht gemâle*.

With this is reckoned all that spiritual heritage referred to before of which the Graal is both origin and symbol.

Frimutel's five children are named, with happy anticipation of the blessing and honour proclaimed by their ripening promise.

The old king ends as he began, with a backward glance at his bygone prowess and a facing of the renunciation which now must be. There was a time when he had come to his son's aid in battle duress, that is long past : *nu wer dich, sun, al eine :    mîn craft diu wil uns beiden enpfliehen.*

In a momentary glimpse of his audience is shown the sorrow of those whom in years past he had led forth to battle in the defence of the Graal.

The occasion and all its bearings are summed up with masterly completeness in the final lines of this momentous prologue :

Sus was der starke Titurel    worden der swache,
beidiu von grôzem alter    und von der siecheite ungemache.
Frimutel besaz dâ werdeclîche
den grâl ûf Muntsalvâtsche :    daz was der wunsch ob irdes-
chem rîche.

Next comes the story of Schoysiane's marriage with Kiot of Katelangen, of her death in childbirth and of the bereaved husband's unmitigable sorrow.    This last is directly linked with the situation of Kiot living in anchorite seclusion with his brother Manfilot, which is how he is first introduced in *Parzival*, Book IV.    Here it is made explicit what in *Parzival* is only implied, that he withdrew from the world because of his great sorrow.    A motive had then to be found for Manfilot's sharing of the same kind of life ; so it is said that out of sympathy for his brother he also parted from his sword and chose the religious life.

The entire episode is beautifully rounded and finished.    The basic facts of Trevrizent's brief record, combined with that of Kiot's relationship to his brother King Tampunteire, are filled out and presented anew as a sequence of clear and palpable impressions, so finely rendered and so fitly ordered as to give a complete unity of design.    Each strophe has its own definite content, its own perfect structure and individual tone.    The marriage, a union of kindred spirits, is shown as a dazzling high noon of fortune and honour and of unclouded bliss.    Then comes the sudden break ; and Schoysiane's death is linked with a forecast of her child's destiny, thus pointing forward to the main theme.    It is also shown in the context of a universal law, *sus nimet diu werlt ein ende :    unser aller süeze am orte ie muoz sûren*, and of Wolfram's own personal reaction.

A single strophe has sufficed to give a vivid picture of the marriage festival, here within the same compass is given a lovely and solemn picture of the funeral rites ; and between the two occasions there is one particular point in common.    Unnumbered guests came to the

wedding—*richer fursten ungezalt da waren.* So also, mourners from many lands came to pay their last homage to the dead : *vil künge unde vürsten litmon kom dar zer lîchlege an allen sîten.*
That is one contrast : here is another. In the time of his marriage, at the height of his fortune and honour, Kiot is praised for his outstanding prowess : and this is remembered later, Gahmuret referring to him with ardour as " *Kîôt der prîs bejagende in der scharflîchen herte* ". All the more striking, then, is the effect of his deep and inexorable sorrow, because of which he makes a clean break with the chivalrous life, renouncing of his free will, in the years of his prime, what the old Titurel had renounced at the bidding of age and infirmity.
Sigune now passes into the centre of the story. Her birth, her baptism, and the bestowal upon her of her father's ducal power, come first. That her uncle Tampunteire took her home to be the playmate of his own little daughter Condwiramurs is a minor episode for which there is small need, if any. It has its source in a late and somewhat hasty improvisation in *Parzival*, Book XVI. The essential factor is her upbringing by Herzeloyde, her mother's sister, and with this it becomes necessary to forge a link. So now it is said that when she was five years old, her uncle died, was succeeded by his son Kardeiz, and that Herzeloyde arranged for the child to be transferred to her guardianship ; and so *Kîôtes kint Sigûne alsus wuohs bî ir muomen.*
And if the next line was inspired by the obvious rhyme of *muomen* and *bluomen*, that in no way detracts from its beauty : *er kôs si vür des meien blic swer si sach, bî tounazzen bluomen.*
Herzeloyde's unfulfilled marriage with Castis, which left her queen of Waleis and Norgals, needed no such expansion in the retelling as her sister's marriage. In the two strophes allotted to it, the substance of Trevrizent's brief relation is restated without enlargement but with the enhancing effect of the more decorative and spacious style. Its focal-point is the anticipation of the second real marriage, vitally expressed in the long sweeping movement typical of the second line :

> Kastis Herzeloüden nie gewan ze wîbe,
> diu an Gahmurets arme lac mit ir magtuomlîchem lîbe:

With that marriage we pass from the scattered materials hitherto employed to the full relation of *Parzival*, Book II. Its events are admirably condensed, so as to make way with all speed for the main theme. The Tourney of Kanvoleiz is recalled in a single long sentence with a fine martial ring in its conclusion. And three lines suffice as reminder of how Gahmuret parted from Belacane, how he won Herzeloyde to wife, and how he broke with the French queen, Amphlise.

Schionatulander now comes into the story as Gahmuret's page, introduced in the first place simply as *ein kint*. The facts of his earlier history, unrecorded in *Parzival*, are a new invention. He had been a ward of the French queen Amphlise. When Gahmuret was knighted by her, she transferred the boy to his service. He accompanied his lord on his travels, and shared his return, so coming with him to Waleis. These facts are succinctly stated but the telling of them is retarded by interspersed reflections and comments. To say so is not meant as criticism ; and the comments include one particularly lovely line :

> dirre âventiure ein hêrre,    ich hân reht daz ich kint durch in grüeze.

The boy's pedigree comes next. Gurnemanz of Graharz was his grandfather, Gurzgri, son of Gurnemanz, his father, his mother was Mahaute, sister of Ehcunaht, and he himself was called Schionatulander. *Ein teil wil ich des kindes    art iu benennen*, says Wolfram, and he does more than " benennen ". The strophic measure gives him an opportunity to embellish what in a plainer metre would have been a plain register of names. Of the descriptive touches the most arresting is that attached to the name of Gurzgri : *der lac tôt durch Schoy de la curte*, a summary allusion to that tragic death, details of which had been given by Gurnemanz. That Mahaute did not long survive her husband may be inferred though never expressly stated, seeing that Amphlise became the boy's guardian.

Of his family not all has been told, and the expression *ein teil* indicates something left in reserve. A later occasion brings to light that Gahmuret is closely related, and this is through the boy's mother Mahaute, who was the sister of Schoette, Gahmuret's mother. So the page is Gahmuret's young cousin.

Further, and this also at a later stage, Schionatulander is given the title of *talfîn ûz Grâswaldân* (Dauphin de Graisivaudan), inherited from his father.

The scene is now set for the story of the two young lovers. This, in its earliest phase, is sheer lyrical drama, so sublimated as to be almost lacking in realistic detail. There is a mystical rapture in the mention of Sigune's lineage, because of which she has been given precedence over her lover, she being an offspring of the dedicated race chosen to serve the Graal. Wherever that seed was sown, it bore good fruit. So from Munsalvæsche a blessing spread to Kanvoleiz, the environment in which those two children met, idealised as " der triuwen houbetstat " by their pure and steadfast love.

One circumstance only brings us down to earth, namely that

Der stolze Gahmuret     disiu kint mit ein ander
in sîner kemenâten     zôch.

There are no other details as factual as this.     The rest is a treading on air.

Praise of the Graal's elect and praise of Kanvoleiz as a home of true love are succeeded by a lament for the plight of those two innocent victims of Love's unsparing tyranny—*owê des, si sint noch     ze tump ze solher angest*—widening into a reverie on its mysterious and manifold power.     Then back again to the individual case of those two poor children, and so, thought by thought, to the conversation between them, when at last they break silence and come to a mutual understanding.     The dialogue is prefaced by an appeal to all true lovers to attend and listen.

There is, on the surface at least, an affinity here with a particular genre of the medieval love-lyric, a debate between a lady and her lover on the nature and doctrine of courtly love.     It is a conventional pose for the lady to profess herself more ignorant than she is and ask her friend to instruct her, which he readily does.

Here the conventional pose becomes a reality.     Schionatulander, having in former days carried messages between his mistress Amphlise and her lover Gahmuret, is well versed in the language of courtly love and so far qualified to act as instructor.     Sigune, on the other hand, is quite unsophisticated : she is as yet a simple child whose mind has not learned how to interpret the feelings of her heart. And so, Schionatulander, as the more self-conscious and the more articulate, is the first to speak.

He begins tentatively and humbly, using in succession three keywords, first *helfe*, then *genâde*, and lastly *minne*.     And each time Sigune misunderstands him.     When he pleads with her for help, she asks him to be more explicit, what kind of help does he mean— " *Bêâs âmîs, nu sprich,     schœner vriunt, waz du meinest.*"     When he dwells on the word *genâde* she thinks of material favour and tells him he should ask that of someone more powerful than she ; for she is herself an exile, far from her own people and land.     And finally, when he comes to *minne* as the source of his heart's trouble, she, like Lavinia in Veldeke's *Eneide* (from which Wolfram undoubtedly took the hint) does not know what the word means :

Minne, ist daz ein er ?     maht du minne mir diuten ?
ist daz ein si ?

Then he launches into a description of the being whose name is *Minne*, beginning with the traditional image of the well-aimed darts no living soul can parry, then speaking of what he knows himself, how like a thief she steals joy from our hearts before we are aware. And now Sigune speaks of her own feelings, and he tells her she needs no more teaching from him; she herself knows what love means.

They can now exchange thoughts with each other, but when Schionatulander pleads for a speedy fulfilment of their love, Sigune draws back : it is, she says, too soon for her to yield her free body to his keeping, he must first win her with the service of the shield. To this he readily consents, at the same time asking her to promise him the hope of guerdon.

The dialogue takes place without any definite and immediate background, and with no preliminary action.

The action which follows, however, is drastically real. Once again, the events of *Parzival*, Book II come into play. First, the news that the *baruc von Baldac* (or Caliph of Bagdad) is hard pressed by his enemies. Then, Gahmuret's response to the urgency of the call. The relation is swift and forceful. Nowhere, indeed, is the art of condensation more brilliantly shown than in the summary account of Gahmuret's last enterprise and death, packed as it is within the limits of the four-line strophe, with a singling out of the most significant details. First, that he set out secretly ; then, that he went as a simple knight-at-arms and with no shield but his own, and yet, in contrast with this, he had great royal power, all of which he forsook ; and the impelling reason was the love which drove him to his death (not love for his wife nor for any other woman but for his old master). The factual point, that it was Ipomedon who slew him, alone is new, and is an effective final touch of realism.

> Gahmuret . . . sich huop des endes tougen,
> et mit sîn eines schilde.     er hete ouch grôze craft âne lougen :
> wan er pflac wol drîer lande crône.
> sus jaget in diu minne an den rê :     den enpieng er von
> Ipomidône.

From the end of that enterprise the story turns back to its beginning, now showing its impact upon the destiny of the young lovers. What was Gahmuret's glory means for those two the sorrow of separation. It is as though Love had become a hostile being ; she is pictured as riding down upon their hidden shelter : *in zwein reit diu minne ûf die lâge.* The parting between them is short, and very poignant.

The figure of Gahmuret again dominates the foreground. Once more it is emphasized that he set out secretly and with no shield but his own. Details are added of his small yet splendid equipage : twenty young pages of noble rank, eighty squires well armed but for the shield, five fine horses, much gold and precious stones of Azagouc.

An indication of his route—*Uz Norgâls gein Spâne* (*unze*) *hin ze Sibilje*—is outweighed by the elegiac allusion to the hero's death. It must be inferred that he spent the winter in Seville, waiting for a favourable passage. For, as we turn to Schionatulander, to be immersed at some length in the description of his melancholy plight, we are told that he pined for Sigune month after month, winter as well as summer : *er qual et al die mânen,     swie sich diu zît huop,* (*den*) *winter und den sumer.*

The conversation which ensues between Gahmuret and his young cousin brings more especially into play the personality of the former, quick to sympathise and to understand, ready to help, instinct with kindly humour and with a delightful buoyancy. The lad, for his part, is restrained and troubled, yielding only by degrees to the cheering optimism of Gahmuret's counsel, which is to persevere in knightly service and so surmount the social obstacle of which they are both aware. In this lies a dramatic problem, implicit throughout but never so clearly envisaged as it is here. Its urgency is heightened by the lyrical vitality of the style. Gahmuret's exhortation is lit by an unclouded hope and winged with words of loveliest praise for her who is the desired goal :

> si liuhtec bluome ûf heide, in walde, ûf velde !
> hât dich mîn müemel betwungen,     ôwol dich der lieplîchen melde !

The scene of the conversation is indicated by a tactful gesture on the part of Gahmuret :

> er nam in sunder ûf daz velt von strâze :

And this is his first inquiry :

> " wie vert nu Anpflîsen     knabe ? sîn trûren kumt mir niht ze mâze."

Beside the bond of kinship, there is another noteworthy tie between these two, a mutual affection for the French queen Amphlise, to whom they refer naturally and freely.

The parallel conversation between Herzeloyde and her love-stricken niece, which has a similar purpose, is more leisurely and more complex. Whereas Gahmuret is impetuously frank and straightforward, Herzeloyde is more tentative in her approach, wistfully anxious in her more intimate realization of a heartache so akin to her own. Both express concern for the wasting effects of the hidden passion and in words also almost the same. Gahmuret says : " *ôwê durch waz hât sich geloubet     dîn antlütze lûterlîcher blicke ?* " and Herzeloude says : " *war kom dîn sunneclîcher blic ?*

157

*wê wer hât denn verstolen dînen wangen?*" But then Gahmuret comes directly to the point : "*Ich spüre an dir die minne*". Herzeloyde evades the main issue in suggesting that her niece may be pining for her own land and people : "*An land unde an liuten sprich waz dir werre.*"

Signune in response pays tribute to one who has been to her a second mother and reveals her trouble. Her confession has but one mark of diffidence, that while speaking freely of her absent friend, she keeps his name for the end. Otherwise, in her moving self-revelation her thoughts lie open to the listener. She describes with tangible and touching detail in three successive pictures, how and in what extremity of longing she goes on waiting for her friend's return. First, how many an evening she looks out from windows over fields up the road and towards the shining meadows and all in vain. Then how she climbs the battlements and looks out over the land, now east, now west. Lastly, how she goes faring a while on the wild wave, gazing out to sea over more than thirty miles in the hope that some news is coming. The three pictures, united by the one mood of desperate longing, form a crescendo : Signune first looking out over the nearer landscape, then over the whole wide land, and lastly into the distance beyond the sea . . . "*ich var ûf einem wilden wâge eine wîle*" : it sounds improbable but there is nothing in syntax or in style to indicate that this experience was not as concrete as the other two. Perhaps all we can say is that the lyrical intensity of the mood and the picturesque beauty of the changing details outweigh any regard for strict realism.

Herzeloyde's reaction to the girl's confession is of so complex a nature that it takes more than a few explanatory words to disentangle its contradictory trends. Her first feeling is one of dismay. From Schionatulander her mind leaps to his former mistress Amphlise, once her rival for Gahmuret's love. Had she devised this subtle vengeance to train young Schionatulander in deceiving arts and counsel him to use them on Signune that the child might suffer and that through her she (Herzeloyde) might suffer too. It is a strange thought and the language in which she gives it utterance is strangely involved and incomplete and obscure for almost in the same moment she checks a suspicion which, she is well aware, does the boy wrong. With his noble lineage, his own gallant and stainless breeding, he should be found a worthy and a faithful lover. If, then, they love one another truly, her advice to her niece is " Do not spoil your lovely looks, for his sake call back the colour to your cheeks " Unlike Gahmuret, she sees no disparity of rank between them ; rather, she tells Signune she need not hestitate to bestow her reward on one so well-born, and of such noble promise. Yet even while she seeks to inspire Sigune with hope and courage, the thought still troubles her that the girl has come all too soon to a knowledge of the love which, as she understands it herself, brings sorrow in its train. " *Ich klage daz du bist alse fruo sin amie.*" Then rising to the occasion, she heartens her niece with a glowing eulogy of her lover's grace and prowess.

And so both of them, both Schionatulander and Sigune, have received the encouragement and help they need from their understanding elders. The first part of *Titurel* ends thus on a note of joyful expectation.

Aldâ was minne erloubet mit minne beslozzen. . . .

The first part of *Titurel* is an organised series, with an impressive opening and an exhilarating conclusion. The second part is structurally different. It consists of a single vivid and rich situation of crucial importance, in which a sense of crisis is quickened and reinforced by the dynamic urgency of the style and movement. The action that courses through it is in no way retarded and indeed gains momentum from the audacious brilliance of the descriptive details and from the pregnancy of the interspersed reflections. Dramatic instancy blends here in absolute fusion with the beauty of enriching circumstance and with high-pitched lyrical tension. A concentrated and splendidly strong piece of creative work, this inspired second part is, nevertheless, with its abrupt beginning and suspended ending, more justly to be called a fragment than the first part, which, with all its discursiveness, has a definite beginning and ends on a satisfying pause.

The scene is a tent in the forest where the two lovers are discovered resting together, with no explanation of how they came to be there. The adventure begins with an exciting leap *in medias res*. Very effective here is the use made of *enjambement*. The first half-line is a complete short sentence of four words :

Sus lâgen si unlange :

Then the sense runs on from the end of the line right through the long sweep of the second line and rises to a climax in the third :

do gehôrten si schiere,
in heller süezer stimme    ûf rôtvarwer verte nâch wundem
tiere
ein bracke kom hôchlûtes zuo ze in jagende.

The fourth line brings a forecast of the final tragedy :

der wart ein wîle gehalden ûf :    des bin ich durch vriunde
noch der clagende.

What follows is an elucidation at long last of that cryptic phrase : *ein bracken seil gap im den pîn*. This in *Parzival* comes from Sigune's lips as an isolated and unexplained statement, with nothing in Chrestien's *Conte del Graal* to serve as clue. The question arises whether the idea was virtually Wolfram's own or came to him from an unknown literary source. In the latter case, one would wish also to know how far the situation developed from it in *Titurel* II was his invention. We can at least content ourselves with the thought that what was told matters less to us now than its unsurpassable telling.

Here, as briefly as possible (for it is difficult to curtail such wealth of detail), is the content of this enthralling new episode.

As the lovers lay resting in their tent, there broke suddenly upon their hearing the baying of a hound in full chase, the forest echoes replying to its din. Schionatulander, springing up, ran out, waylaid and captured the questing brach, took it in his arms and carried it back to Sigune. The dog, early that morning, had escaped from its master dragging with it the leash attached to its collar. The young man had gained a rich prize : collar and leash were of fantastic cost, of rich texture studded from beginning to end with precious stones, emerald, ruby, diamond, chrysolite and garnet, and these were ingeniously arranged in the form of letters, with further construction of words and sentences. Sigune, left alone with her new possession, began reading the words inscribed on collar and leash. First, the inscription on the collar : the dog's name *Gardeviaz* and its interpretation *Hüete der verte* to which is added this comment, that while it is a dog's name, it is also a rule of life for all true men and women. Sigune continued reading and now came to the inscription on the leash. Here she found recorded an actual story telling about the young queen Clauditte of Kanadie, who had sent the dog with its collar and leash as a gift to her friend. Her name and his come first, the story follows. Clauditte, urged by her nobles to wed and give her land a ruler, chose out of all her suitors one she loved already, *duc Ehkunahten de Salvâsch flôrien* (interpreted by Wolfram as *der herzoge Ehcunaber von Bluome diu wilde*). The two had been lovers before she thus openly chose him, except that they had never lain together, *wan bî ligender minne*. And now, to match his name, she had sent him this wild missive, *disen wiltlîchen brief*, this brach which, as his nature bade him, traced and followed all paths of field and forest. On the leash this also was inscribed, *daz si selp wîplîcher verte hüeten wolte*.

Wolfram does not say, but one is tempted to say it for him, that Sigune saw in the tale of Clauditte's betrothal an analogy with her own, and that it was this living link and not mere romantic interest which made it so compelling. Wolfram may have meant in this way to refer indirectly to a critical event of Sigune's life, left unrecorded.

I do not think this is altogether too fanciful. Sigune we know to have remained with Herzeloyde until after Parzival was born. But she did not share the flight to the forest, and in that case must have returned to her own land. It is legitimate to assume that, on coming of age, she was approached by a number of high-born suitors, none of whom she would consent to wed, for the sake of her absent friend. Schionatulander was not there to press his claim ; as we know, he was engaged in defensive warfare against the invader of Parzival's lands. To have reached the forest of Brizljân, the scene of their encounter, Sigune must have left her own land with a small retinue in order to seek out her lover. And now, after long separation, they met again. And the opening sentence of *Titurel* II indicates how near they came to *bî ligende minne*.

From this dangerously tempting field of speculation we return to the safety of the written word.

Following the words on the leash, Sigune came to where it was knotted to the tent-pole to keep the dog under control. She undid the knot in order to read to the end and that was fatal. Two of her maids came hurrying to bring the dog his food, but that did not stay him. Tugging wildly, he broke loose from Sigune's hold, bounded out into the open, and was soon heard pursuing his quarry as before. Then Schionatulander, standing bare-legged in the clear woodland stream with his fishing rod in his hand, heard the dog's baying, knew that he had escaped, and tried to recapture him. Not succeeding, he returned to the tent, running at full speed, his legs torn with briars. He bade them be washed ere he came into the tent. There he found Sigune in sorry plight, her hands scarred grey as with hoarfrost " like a jouster's hand ", for, while she was struggling to keep a grip on the leash as the dog tugged it from her, the hard gems, cutting into her skin, left cruel marks on her poor hands. But what distressed her most was that she had not read to the end of the story.

> Si sprach " dâ stuont âventiure geschriben an der strangen :
> sol ich die niht ze ende ûz lesen, mir ist unmære min lant ze
> Katelangen.

Then, her whole mind obsessed by an insistent longing for this one thing, she begged Schionatulander to sally forth again, recapture the dog and restore the leash to her, that she might finish reading what was on it. If, said she, he would do her this one service, she would reward him with the fulfilment of her love. To this, while pleading that he had already waited long, he gave his unwavering consent, and is seen for the last time alive, setting out, fleet of foot and fearless of heart, on that gallant and useless adventure which led to his death. The poem ends in a mingled strain of foreboding and of triumphant expectation.

> . . . anevanc vil kumbers, wie wart der geletzet !
> daz vreischet wol der tumbe und ouch der grîse
> von dem unverzageten sicherboten,      obe der swebe oder sinke an dem prîse.

It is futile to speculate how Wolfram would have continued or in what way he could have bridged the gap between the two parts of this apparently unfinished poem. We say " apparently " because it is doubtful whether in the last resort Wolfram intended more. Or, at least, much more. He would probably have meant to carry the situation sufficiently far back to give it a rounded and complete beginning. He must certainly have had in mind both the intervening and the subsequent events of the tale ; but these alone would not have served his poetic purpose. The strophic measure he had created imposed its own limitations. The strength of the poem lies in the lyrically toned dramatic situations, in the concentrated flash of the swiftly recorded action, in the interwoven deeply personal reflections, and in the vividly picturesque descriptive phrases, also in sheer feats of originality and daring in the use of words. For all these, the strophic measure gives admirable scope ; it can also all too readily obey the temptation to wordy rhetoric, more especially in the filling out of the last line. That it could not with impunity be overworked may be judged by its far too extensive use in the hands of Wolfram's imitators. For Wolfram, who had created the metre and understood its laws, it is fair to assume that his achievement was commensurate with his ultimate aim, and that he avoided subjecting his medium to an inordinate strain. In fact, that he himself knew what he could and could not do with this enchanting measure. In that case, the two parts of *Titurel* should not be regarded as fragments of an undefined whole but rather as two separate preludes, composed as antecedents to the story of Sigune's life-in-death, as related episodically in *Parzival*. In these four episodes there is no more approach to epic continuity than in the two separate parts of *Titurel*. An unexplained blank lies between Parzival's first meeting with Sigune in the forest of Brizljân and the second in the neighbourhood of Munsalvæsche, and also (though the transition here is more easily imagined) between the second meeting and the third. It is thus artistically consistent that a gap should be left between *Titurel* I and II. What binds the whole series together is the lyrical unity of a love revealing itself in successive phases ; in the beauty of its ripening promise ; in the blindness of its unguided impulse ; in its tragic frustration through death ; in its aftermath of unmitigable sorrow ; and, finally, in the dawn of a new fulfilment in the life that is eternal.

In *Titurel* the lyrical theme is enlarged and embraces more lives than those of the two central figures. Furthermore, in the appeal to *Al die minne pflâgen und minne an sich leiten* is included a host of unseen witnesses, and in Schionatulander's ardent description of Love's dominion her power is shown extending over all that runs or creeps or flies or swims.

In the procession of kindred fates the aged Titurel comes first, with his elegiac lament for the love that has passed into the grave before him and with his clear and steadfast vision of the essence of true love, of *wâre minne*. Schoysiane next, then Kiot, renouncing in the prime of life sword, helmet and shield for the sake of a love transformed by death into the likeness of sorrow.

Of Gahmuret we know that love drove him to his death : *sus jaget in diu minne an den rê*. It is in keeping with his own impetuous temper that Love in his case is credited with this accelerating and impelling power. Her effect is similar on those two young lives involved in that swift decision : *in zwein reit diu minne ûf die lâge*. The words, though probably without intention, sound wellnigh prophetic of the final crisis which begins so suddenly with *sus lâgen si unlange*.

For Herzeloyde, on the contrary, love, even in its earliest phase, takes on the semblance of a slow persistent sorrow. Its joy, no less real, has by comparison the intensity of a short-lived rapture. With the tragedy of Gahmuret's death still to come, she is already well aware of the hardships that love entails. Equally so in her own ordeal, that of separation from her absent husband and in what she recalls of Mahaute's more strenuous lot when, wedded to Gurzgri, she became the sharer of her husband's adventurous journeys. And in Sigune's love for Schionatulander she sees first the image of her own heart's longing, then a forecast of the lot she will have inherited from Mahaute, lastly a vision of ecstasy so thrilling that, for the time being, the shadows are dispersed in light. But the ultimate end confirms the initial affinity. For them both, with differing prelude, the final issue is the same, a farewell to the world's joy.

There is a similar affinity between Gahmuret and Schionatulander. Of the latter it may be truly said that love drove him to his death : *sus jaget in diu minne an den rê*.

Lastly, from the tale within the tale inscribed on the hound's leash emerge the figures of two young queens, Clauditte and her sister Florie. The story of the one, up to the point where Signe loses the dog and it together, is bright with promise. That of Florie, reported previously in *Parzival*, Book XII, is complete in tragical fulfilment. For Ilinot, her lover, was killed in combat, whence, as told in a single eloquent line, she died of the same spear-joust though her body was untouched by point of spear : *Flôrîe starp ouch der selben tjost, doch ir lîp nie spers orte genâhte.*

The *Tristan* of Gottfried von Strassburg has been entitled *ein Hohelied der Minne*. The *Titurel* of Wolfram von Eschenbach may also lay claim to a share in that title ; it would seem as though here, for once, would the two rival poets meet on the same ground. Even so, they remain, as always, incommensurable, differing from one another in quality, not in degree. As the *Tristan* of Gottfried is, of its kind, the most exquisite thing in all mediæval German poetry, so the *Titurel* of Wolfram is the most magnificent. The difference is fundamental. Wolfram can never compete with Gottfried in pure lyricism. As a Minnesinger in the *tageliet* or dawn-song, he had shown himself a master of the dramatic lyric ; and in *Titurel* that early gift of his reappears triumphant upon a larger scale. The style is both dramatic and lyrical, neither wholly dramatic as in the *Nibelungenlied* at its best, nor wholly lyrical, as in the finest passages of *Tristan*. To the difference in style between the two rivals corresponds a difference of attitude towards their central theme, that of *wâre minne*. Gottfried sees this predominantly under the aspect of its eternal and absolute value as a mystical union of two kindred souls. Wolfram sees it thus also, but only in fugitive glimpses ; his predominant trend is towards the conception of love in close relation to the changing pageantry of the chivalrous life with its liberality, its prowess, its transitory glory. Each of these interacting factors is raised to a high pitch of lyrical fervour in the daring beauty of language and rhythm, while in the interaction itself can be seen the mainspring of the dramatic, recurrent and in-sistent, touched from time to time with a sense of fatality, and finally quickening to its last degree of intensity in the culminating crisis.

That *Titurel* was Wolfram's last work cannot be categorically proved, but the reasons in favour of this are so convincing, that, in the absence of any real counter-evidence, they must be allowed to stand. The reasons alleged for placing it between the last two books of *Willehalm* have been based on gratuitous assumptions which cannot be accepted as valid. Personally, I incline to a view expressed to me in conversation by a veteran scholar of a past generation whom it was my privilege to meet : that *Titurel* was begun in the interval between *Parzival* and *Willehalm*, begun but not publicized, and then set aside for the sake of *Willehalm*, just as, later on, *Willehalm* was set aside incomplete for the sake of *Titurel*.

## Appendix IV

# 'DIE EDELN ARMEN':
# A STUDY OF HARTMANN VON AUE

> Swen dise edeln armen
> niht wolte erbarmen,
> der was herter danne ein stein.

That is Hartmann von Aue's comment upon the straitened means of the courteous and hospitable family with which Erec finds lodging for the night ; and the words have a value beyond their context, since they contain the key to all that is best in the poet's art, to his innate sympathy with nobility sans wealth and his love of quiet decency.

In his understanding for *die edeln armen* we strike the fullest chord of Hartmann's nature. Characters of this type give tangible form to the ideal principle of *mâze* by which he attempted a reconciliation of two opposite lives, that of this world and that facing the world to come. From the subject-matter of his four narrative poems stand out in harmonious succession pictures, which form the most durable part of his work. *Erec* leads the way with its freshly told idyl of the lord Coralus and his wife and daughter, living serenely among the ruins of their former state ; and with the later story of Enite married, deprived of her rights of ladyhood and forced to do service as her lord's groom. While the tale is not Hartmann's creation, the personal element can be recognized in the way it is told, even admitting that the deviations from Chrestien have less weight than formerly. For these, as Zenker has shown, reveal points of contact with the version of the Welsh *Mabinogion* sufficient to prove the use of a second source, about which we would like to know more.[1]

We may at least discard Sparnaay's theory of an alternating use of the sources for different sections, by which Hartmann's work is reduced to the level of a mere compilation.[2] Methods typical of the fourteenth century cannot be assumed without precedent for the twelfth. It is far more likely that Hartmann used Chrestien's *Erec* as main source, but knowing another version of the tale drew on this where it pleased him better. As for Sparnaay's theory of a third source, the thread of coincidence on which this hangs is no real proof.

Hartmann's aim in the first part of *Erec* is abundantly clear. He knows what to do with that picture of dignified poverty, so attractive

---

[1] *Zeitschrift für frz. Sprache und Lit.* xlv. 47 ff.
[2] H. Sparnaay, *Hartmann von Aue : Studien zu einer Biographie* (1933), 69 ff.

in its purity and calm ; and he strengthens the effect by representing Iders fil Niut as an insolent braggart, the congenial Erec as a modest and well-bred youth, who with his thoughtfulness and tact is the right guest for that impoverished household, the right wooer for a girl so simply reared as Enite. With Chrestien, the two champions are equally matched in outward fashion, in prowess, and in noble fieriness of speech. Hartmann gives us instead a sharply defined contrast so characteristic that, whatever details he took from his other source, we must regard the conception as his own. The arrogance of Iders, flinging ill-bred contempt on Enite's shabbiness, —" ez ensol iu niht sô wol ergân, ir dürftiginne ! "—and boastfully warning his young opponent to leave well alone—" jüngelin, ob iu wære der lîp ze ihte mære, sô liezet ir enzît iuwer kintlîchen strît "— is the foil to Erec's quiet self-control. The difference in their manners is stressed by the difference in their equipment also, the one so splendid and the other so dingy ; and the combat as it proceeds is full of interesting touches. There is not, of course, the excitement and dash of Chrestien's more vivid spectacle. Hartmann cannot compete with the French poet's brilliance ; but he has his own line, and is quick to discover moments which give the affair its dramatic, as compared with its scenic value. He records the friendliness of the crowd looking on. " ' Got gebe iu heil hiute ', sprach ein gemeiner munt " and when, at the sixth encounter, Iders is hurled to the ground by the younger man's onset, there is great joy over that. " Erec in von dem rosse schiet, ze spotte aller der diet." The fight is renewed on foot ; for Erec spares his foe and fair-mindedly gives him another chance. He also forsees the gain to his reputation : " er wolte bezzer wort bejagen." (O excellent young man !)

The gradual conversion of Iders is well shown. First, he undergoes wholesome surprise on finding himself hard pressed by one who had seemed to him a mere sprig of a boy (763—781). Later on, he proposes a rest, and his mild and apologetic tone proves that he has now learned to respect his peer (897—909) ;

> " Enthalt dich, edel ritter guot . . .
> ob ez iuwer muot niht vervât
> für zageheit, sô ist min rât
> daz wir ditz blœde vehten lân
> und eine wîle ruowen gân."

He touches bottom at last in his plea for mercy (956—963). This is the final stage. Nothing remains but to stress the moral ; and Hartmann is not the man to omit that epilogue : the moral is laid on with a trowel.

This Erec, whose temperate nature contrasts so favourably with the rude ways of Iders, and of his low-bred dwarf, is perfectly planned, and fits happily into the opening chapters. We see him there as a young untried soldier of fortune, whose unadorned valour triumphs admirably over the ostentatious pride of his rival. The poet pursues that same line in his account of the tourney fought between Tarebron and Prurin. There is no great need why Erec should appear this time also as a soldier of fortune, but it pleases Hartmann to depict him as such and to find reasons for it. So we hear that Erec, being far from his own land, lacked means to support a show of royalty ; had he accepted King Arthur's bounty, he could have had all he needed, but he preferred to abuse this as little as possible and rely mainly on what he had himself (2247—2284). This is certainly very nice conduct ! So far, Erec has played the part given him consistently and well.

But Hartmann, unlike his hero, does not look ahead, and the story punishes him for his want of forethought. The main plot finds him unready. Consider it : the case of a man who passes from one extreme to another, first neglecting his knightly duties for the pleasures of love, then, in sudden annoyance at the wife who is the innocent cause, hauling her with him on a course of wild adventure without rhyme or reason. For this Chrestien's Erec, frank, debonair, impetuous and headstrong, is a happier choice than Hartmann's. The Erec whom Hartmann prematurely conceived as an embodiment of his ideal of *mâze* is now saddled with a theme requiring the opposite character, and for this embarrassing turn no excuse is ready. " Sîn site er wandeln began." Hartmann leaves it at that ; and perhaps it is just as well.

But the change does not last. The first heat over, Erec resumes his former settled character which, in these new circumstances, becomes obnoxious. We cannot excuse him on the ground that he does not think. On the contrary, he does, and with the set purpose of making his wife's lot harder. Further, the dry, unfriendly tone in which he speaks to her, his churlishness where she is concerned, is displeasing in contrast to the different standard of courtesy he observes towards others. Then, though he undergoes the same hardships and suffers as many wounds as Chrestien's Erec, we cannot feel that his adventures take it out of him as much : his self-possessed manner reveals no trace of tension. In fact, even his good qualities turn the scale against him, and leave nothing in his favour.

But Enite suits the story at every point. She also fits Hartmann's ideal of womanhood, which is a thing nearer his heart and expressed with far greater spontaneity than his carefully reasoned study of well-bred manhood. Enite he loves and instinctively understands.

There is the freshness of spring in his description of her first appearance, of the girl's young beauty shining out from her workaday clothes like a lily among thorns. And how delightfully he brings out the full impression of Enite, the white-handed groom, tending Erec's horse for him because they are too poor in that house to afford a man (352—356).

> daz pfärt begienc ze vlîze
> ir hende vil wîze :
> und wær daz got hein erde rite,
> ich wæn in gnuogte dâ mite,
> ob er solhen marstallære hæte,
> swie si schein in swacher wæte,
> sô weiz ich daz wîp noch man
> süezern schiltkneht nie gewan
> dann Erec fil de roi Lac . . .

That impression of her is renewed and deepened when, under circumstances far harder, she again has to act the part of Erec's squire. The task allotted her now is that of keeping together the eight captured horses, in the first place, no work for a woman, then, at best, not even the work of one squire but of four. She could not have done it, the poet says, but that kind Fortune watched over her, and the courtesy of God, and then, that the horses liked her for herself and did as she bade them (3460—3471). Here we notice the personal touch, " ob mîner frouwen ", and the beautifully inspired phrase, " diu gotes hövescheit ", so appropriate where the courtesy of man has been found wanting.

These two occasions, taken together, yield the same picture and show the essential quality of Enite, whom we must not treat as a mere patient Griselda, even though the circumstances suggest that type. It would be unfair to do so. Behind her submission, and in spite of her fits of timidity, there is the stength of a loyal and steadfast soul. She is a true child of that uncomplaining, quiet household in which she learned to bear adversity humbly and without repining. Her constancy impresses us the more as it is thrown into relief by the change in Erec. How different this tone is now from that of the courteous guest who intervened with her father on her account, saying he would sooner attend to his horse himself and spare her the trouble !

One is glad that the poet instinctively gave the first place to Enite. From the time they set out on their wanderings it is she, not Erec, on whom the attention is focussed. Hartmann enters into her feelings, gauges the extent of her physical sufferings, shows the sympathy evoked by her beauty and patience. The squire whom they meet, and with whom Enite exchanges greetings before Erec comes up, is especially troubled to see her so overworked with the horses. He offers, vainly, of course, to lead them for her—" der dienst ist mir süeze "— and his first words when he sees his lord again are of Enite's beauty, not as with Chrestien, of Erec's good looks and prowess. She, again, is more vividly present than Erec during their stay with King Arthur. What stands out here is the charming and intimate scene where Queen Ginover takes Enite away to her own room " al besunder von ir manne ", and there makes much of her, caring for her needs and with warm enquiries drawing her story from her (5100—5115).

In his portrait of Enite Hartmann shows himself true poet. Here is evidence of a creative trend which never fails him, so long as he can discern among his characters the type he loves.

From Enite we pass to Gregorius, whom we learn to know in two different states of poverty. First, as the nobly-born wait tossed ashore and reared as a fisherman's child, who longs secretly for the life of chivalry which is his birthright. A proud, warm, sensitive nature, grateful for kindness, stung to the quick by insult, courageously conscious, as the truth comes home to him, of his status as *ellender kneht*.

Afterwards, as *der rîche dürftige* who, having put off wealth and honour of his own free will, goes out into the wilderness to suffer the last extremity of human need, in atonement for sin.

Other figures succeed. " Der arme Heinrich ", struck down at the height of his fortune with plague-driven body and bruised spirits. Iwein fallen from his lady's grace and from the high estate of knighthood, wandering witless in the forest, then struggling back to daylight through that strange twilight of the mind in which the past glory of his life appears a dream. " Ist mir getroumet mîn leben ? " Lunete, wrongfully accused and sentenced to death for her faithfulness, and humbly thankful to her rescuer. Iwein, clothed and in his right mind, but self-banished and self-condemned. " Ich bin Iwein der arme."

Of all these Gregorius is the most arresting. More especially, the boy Gregorius, who as *ellender kneht* is realised with an intensity worthy of Wolfram von Eschenbach. In this fine creation Hartmann reaches his highest level ; and little as we know of the poet's life, we can hardly resist the conclusion that Gregorius, cloister-bred, book-weary, lured by the magic of knighthood and striving to justify it on moral grounds, is the poetic embodiment of Hartmann's youth, when he too stood at the parting of the ways and made his choice.

This would explain the unusual depth of the achievement. In addition, we may note the life-like adequacy of two other figures in the drama : the fisherman's wife with her ungovernable mother's instinct leaping out in defence of her own child against the foundling they have housed so long, and the abbot who cares for the boy as his own son, and with more than a father's wisdom.

In *Gregorius*, as in *Erec*, finer and baser natures are set over against one another in realistic interplay. There is nothing clearer in Hartmann's mind than the difference between good breeding and bad, and he knows how to make this plain, striking the authentic note of courtesy and expressing in rude speech the workings of a coarse or distempered mind. He distinguishes, too, between the churl of high and the churl of low degree, both graceless, but in a different style. In *Erec*, with Iders as the main but not the only example, the first type is shown, marked by showy arrogance and a bullying kind of violence. In *Gregorius* the second type, its form of baseness a resentful hatred of all that transcends its narrow sphere. The fisherman's wife is a case in point, with her spite at the child who is none of theirs, and at the favours shown him (1321—1324) :

> " Ich sage ez al der werlde wol
> daz er ein funtkint ist
> (sô helfe mir der heilege Krist),
> swie hôhe er nu ist gesezzen."

She is coarser than her husband, for whose mistaken kindness she has words of scorn. The same crude bitterness, but uglier and more prolonged, is expressed in the sneering abuse of the *übele vischære* to whom Gregorius comes on the eve of his first day of exile. Here it is the wife who compensates, as in the former case the husband. These fisher folk are not Hartmann's creation, they are found in his source ; but his graphic interpretation, the felicity with which he catches the very accents of low life, point to personal contact with a social sphere which Wolfram, with all his variety, seems scarcely to have known.

Poverty, less of means than of the niggardly mind which fears to spend, is depicted in Gawein's satirical sketch of another type, the country landlord who has lost touch with courtesy (*Iwein* 2808—2858). Such a one, with his boorish appearance, barelegged and uncombed, his grudging hospitality and limited range of topics,— the crops and the weather and the difficulty of making ends meet— is the very antithesis of Enite's father, with his smoothly combed white hair and perfect manners (*Erec* 274—291).

But Hartmann shows further how, in a humbler rank of society also, in the class of the free-born peasant, true breeding, homelier than that of the nobly-born but no less sterling, has its natural place. The farmer in whose plain, comfortable household " der arme

Heinrich " finds a refuge when his rich friends desert him, is an illustration of this. Faithful kindliness, harmony and content—in other words, *triuwe* and *mâze*—are the attributes of that family circle (*Der arme Heinrich* 295—300) :

> Got hete dem meier gegeben
> nâch sîner ahte ein reinez leben.
> er hete ein wol erbeiten lîp
> und ein wol werbendez wîp.
> dar zuo het er schœniu kint
> die gar des mannes fröude sint.

From this idyllic picture emerges the tenderest, most youthfully appealing of Hartmann's creations, the girl who desires so fervently to sacrifice her life for Heinrich's. Akin to Enite, but raised above her through the exaltation of her dream of martyrdom, and with a lovably childish grace and boldness which is her own. She is certainly one of the *edeln armen*, this girl who comes of the stock of Nature's gentlefolk and is fair as a king's daughter (309—312) :

> si was ouch sô genæme
> daz si wol gezæme
> ze kinde dem rîche
> an ir wætlîche.

That story ends with Hartmann's one perfect marriage : the only one, in which nothing at all goes wrong. Heinrich's union for life with his friend in need, his *trûtgemahel*, is the natural fulfilment of a comradeship which has stood the test. These two have trodden a hard path together and have proved severally their inborn nobleness, she by her staunch devotion, and he by that sudden and clear awakening in which all at once his will starts up and conquers hers. In this supreme crisis Heinrich proves himself all he had failed to be, strong in fortitude, in patience, and in true lowliness of heart. " Do erzeicte der heilic Krist wie liep im triuwe und bärmde ist ", and all is well.

Of Iwein, that " very parfit gentle knight ", there is less to say, because the story to which he belongs is not sufficiently real to quicken any permanent sense of character. There is great poetic charm in the figure of the lonely knight-errant accompanied by his faithful lion, and Hartmann certainly brings out the feeling of the remote and solitary life his hero leads in the passage from one adventure to another better than Chrestien ; but he is still not able to energize this conception beyond the point where romantic convention begins to shade off into reality. The strength of the poem lies less in the hero's actions than in his melancholy musings on the reverse of fortune for which, with self-accusing candour, he blames himself, not Fate (*Iwein* 4250—4254) :

> " Ich hete êren genuoc :
> waz half mich daz ich golt vant ?
> ez ist et vil unbewant
> ze dem tôren des goldes vunt :
> er wirfet ez doch hin zestunt."

One general criticism must be made. There is no denying that Hartmann utterly forsakes his ideal of *mâze* once his love of rhetoric gets the upper hand. Then even his best creations suffer. A glaring example of this is Enite's long lamentation (*Erec* 5774—6109), so out of keeping with her quiet true self. Another, the midnight sermon of Heinrich's *trûtgemahel*, which her parents, amazed at their child's preternatural wisdom, ascribe to the working of the Holy Ghost. Alas, not so ! We know well enough that this is Hartmann speaking.

There is compensation, however. We know other passages too, where the poet's rhetoric, tempered to lyrical purity, falls movingly on our ears. In the best of Iwein's monologues this is so. And in the description of Heinrich's fall from high to low estate (*Der arme Heinrich* 153—156) :

> ein swinde vinster donerslac
> zebrach im sînen mitten tac,
> ein trüebez wolken unde dic
> bedahte im sîner sunnen blic.

*Die edeln armen* who appeal so intimately to Hartmann have an equal hold on the feelings of his successor and rival, Wolfram von Eschenbach. Naturally so, since both belonged to a class in which indigence and precarious fortune were the frequent corollary of knightly birth and training. And of Wolfram we know for certain that he was a poor man. Of Hartmann we may guess the same ; but it is Wolfram who tells us explicitly of his needy household. To his description of the starved garrison of Pelrapeire he joins a personal comment on the scarcity of food in his own home. " Dâ heime in mîn selbes hûs, dâ wirt gefreut vil selten mûs." There are other passages which bear this out ; and a penetrating allusion to the added hardship of those who are poor yet noble occurs in the exhortations of Gurnemanz, when he bids young Parzival care especially for such (*Parzival* $170^{29}-171^2$) :

> " Der kumberhafte werde man
> wol mit schame ringen kan

(daz ist ein unsüez arbeit) :
dem sult ir helfe sîn bereit."

Both poets, then, know what poverty means, and are all the more
ready to distinguish the essence of chivalry from its adjuncts. It is
quality that matters, not wealth, not even high rank, since the service
of the shield is a link between all men of gentle blood. Thus
Gahmuret, when Schionatulander tells him of his love for Sigune
who is of nobler rank than he, encourages the young man to go on
and win her ; the brave man blest in himself has a stronger chance in
the winning of a high-born lady than the wealthy laggard. " Werdiu
minne ist teilhaft ordenlîche. si hât der sælige ellenhaft erworben ê
der zagehafte rîche " (*Titurel* 102). And Guivrez, as he offers his
surrender to Erec, says : " I care not who your father may be :
your own valour so ennobles you that I am glad to acknowledge you
as my lord " (*Erec* 4456—4459).

There is a difference, however, in the way the two poets envisage
their common ground.

In Hartmann we sense a man of temperate and frugal habits, who
in his heart prefers the restraint of the poor man's lot to the burden
of riches. He does not share Wolfram's love for the splendour of
life, and is happiest in describing a lot cast modestly midway between
high fortune and sheer misery. So in his account of Enite's peaceful
home, or of the simple farmstead where " der arme Heinrich "
finds a welcome shelter. But he can transcend the idyllic tran-
quillity of scenes like these. A sterner content, pure as the heart
of winter, reveals itself in his attitude to the ascetic life of bodily
need cheered only by the light within. It is this stronger Hart-
mann who speaks to us in the picture of Gregorius turning his face
towards the wilderness in quest of martyrdom—*spilnde bestuont er
dise nôt*. Or again, in the austere joy of his Crusading lyrics :
" Dem kriuze zimt wol reiner muot und kiusche site . . ." (*Minnesangs
Frühling* 209[25]).

Wolfram differs from Hartmann in the exuberance and breadth
of his outlook on knighthood. Deeply aware of its ethical value and
able, when he chooses, to dispense with the pageantry of circumstance,
he delights none the less in the outward glory which is the symbol of
an inward strength and grace. A man of aristocratic temper, he
confronts his own poverty with racy independence and humour,
and his sympathy with those in need flows in a wider channel than
Hartmann's, in proportion as he cares more for the brilliance of the
great world, and sees that it is good. Different, too, is his attitude
towards the ascetic life. He does not despise the world as Hartmann
does in his intenser moods, but he knows that there are times in the

life of man when the world loses its value, and poverty becomes a sacred thing. So with Herzeloyde, Sigune, Trevrizent.

The main result is that, in Wolfram's interpretation, *die edeln armen* stand out in bolder relief and awaken a stronger emotion than in Hartmann's more limited approach to his characters. This is evident if we compare Enite's case with Jeschute's. The circumstances are similar, but that Erec's pique is a weaker motive than Orilus' jealousy. Leaving this aside, here are two innocent and helpless wives, each the victim of her husband's rancour. The same kind of sympathy is felt for both, yet, though we know Enite better, we are made to feel that Jeschute's sufferings are more poignant. And this is largely because we have a clearer impression of the luxury her lord heaped upon her while she was his pampered darling. It may be objected, that Chrestien's *Perceval* already contained the substance of her story ; yes, but as a mere conventional sketch to which Wolfram gave life. And it is worthy of note that nothing in Chrestien's picture suggests the culminating stroke in Wolfram's when, with a sudden furious gesture Orilus pulls down the costly canopy under which he had left his wife sleeping, tears her palfrey's saddle to pieces and fastens it together again with hempen cords.

We notice further how the poverty of Trevrizent stands out sharply against the memory of his magnificent young days of knighthood, and gains in austerity and nobleness from that contrast. Whereas Gregorius discards the world's honour as though it had never been.

Again, the barren loneliness of Parzival's quest is accentuated by the realisation, more vividly concrete than in the case of Iwein, of all he had lost or left behind. Then, coming to Trevrizent, he finds in the midst of that anchorite poverty a wealth of storied wisdom and a glory of kindness which gladden him more than all material riches ever could. Hartmann, lover of the simple life, must here yield place to Wolfram. As we see those two, the hermit and his guest, gathering herbs for their dinner and lying down at night on a bed of leaves, the severe beauty of a life stripped of all luxury comes home to us with a thrill of adoration and wonder (*Parzival* 501[7ff.]) :

> Wênc wart in bette und kulter brâht :
> si giengen et ligen ûf ein bâht.
> daz leger was ir hôhen art
> gelîche ninder dâ bewart.

Of Parzival we hear that he had taken fine care of his body's pride, but that this brave show did not mean warmth and comfort : his armour was very cold. Hartmann draws a distinction between *gemach* and *êre* (*Gregorius* 1677—1688). Wolfram realises this in the concrete.

He realises, too, the misery which can exist at the centre of riches. Anfortas, living on in the midst of his court, surrounded by fabulous wealth which, in his agony, he cannot enjoy, is a sadder figure by far than " der arme Heinrich," who casts off wealth and power. But this is touching on differences which depend too much on different degrees of poetic imagination to be scrutinised further. There are depths of pity and awe in the greater poet, such as Hartmann, with all his seriousness and tender feeling, had never sounded.

# INDEX OF PROPER NAMES

Werner, Bruder, 10.
Wernher von Tegernsee, 20.
Wolfram von Eschenbach, 4,
6–7, 20, 57, 65, 88 *et seq.*, 102.

Walther von Hausen, 33.
Wenceslaus I, King of Bohemia,
10.
Wolfger, Bishop of Passau, 10,
53.

*Lords and Patrons—*

Charles IV, the Emperor, 9.

Dietrich, Margrave von Meissen,
10, 39, 40.

Eleanor, Duchess of Aquitaine
(and Queen of England), 19.

Frederick I, the Emperor, 33.
Frederick II, the Emperor, 4, 9.
Frederick I, Duke of Austria, 4.
Frederick II, Duke of Austria, 9,
103–4.

Henry VI, the Emperor (Kaiser
Heinrich), 9, 11, 26, 33.
Henry VII, King, 10.
Hermann, Landgrave of Thur-
ingia, 10.

Katzenellenbogen, Graf von, 10.

Leopold V, Duke of Austria, 64.
Leopold VI, Duke of Austria, 9.
Lewis, Duke of Bavaria, 103.

Otto IV, the Emperor, 9, 74.
Otto, Duke of Bavaria, 103.
Ottokar II, King of Bohemia, 10.

Philip (of Suabia), King, 9.
Philip Augustus of France, King,
33.

Rüdiger Manesse, 10.

*Poetic figures—*

Adelber, 106.

Belacane, 98.
Berewin, 102.
Berewolf, 102.
Berhtel, 109.

Condwiramurs, 94, 98.
Cunneware, 98.

Eberhard, 106.
Elle, 106.
Engelber, 102.
Engelbolt, 102.
Engelher, 102.
Engelmar, 102, 106–7.
Engelram, 102, 107.
Engelwan, 102.
Eppe, 104, 106.

Frideliep, 106.
Friderun, 107.

Gawan, 94.
Geppe, 106, 109.
Ginover, 98.
Gisel, 106, 109.
Giselbolt, 107.
Gotelind, 106.
Gumpe, 104, 106.
Gundrat, 109.

Hadewig, 106.
Herzeloyde, 98.